0   250   500   750   1000 km

Map produced by ZOI Environment Network, January 2012

This report is part of a series undertaken by the Europe and Central Asia Region of the World Bank.
Earlier reports have investigated poverty, jobs, trade, migration, demography, and productivity growth.
The series covers the following countries:

Albania	Latvia
Armenia	Lithuania
Azerbaijan	Moldova
Belarus	Montenegro
Bosnia and Herzegovina	Poland
Bulgaria	Romania
Croatia	Russian Federation
Czech Republic	Serbia
Estonia	Slovak Republic
FYR Macedonia	Slovenia
Georgia	Tajikistan
Hungary	Turkey
Kazakhstan	Turkmenistan
Kosovo	Ukraine
Kyrgyz Republic	Uzbekistan

EURASIAN CITIES

EURASIAN CITIES

New Realities along the Silk Road

Souleymane Coulibaly
Uwe Deichmann
William R. Dillinger
Marcel Ionescu-Heroiu
Ioannis N. Kessides
Charles Kunaka
Daniel Saslavsky

THE WORLD BANK
Washington, D.C.

ISBN (paper): 978-0-8213-9581-3
ISBN (electronic): 978-0-8213-9582-0
DOI: 10.1596/978-0-8213-9581-3

Cover design: Naylor Design, Inc.

Library of Congress Cataloging-in-Publication Data
  Eurasian cities : new realities along the Silk Road / Souleymane Coulibaly ... [et al.].
    p. cm.
  Includes bibliographical references.
  ISBN 978-0-8213-9581-3 (alk. paper) — ISBN 978-0-8213-9582-0
  1. Cities and towns—Eurasia. 2. City planning—Eurasia. I. Coulibaly, Souleymane.
  HT119.E9697 2012
  307.76095—dc23   2012020577

Contents

Foreword   xiii
About the Authors   xvii
Acknowledgments   xxi
Abbreviations   xxiii
Overview   xxv
Chapter Summaries   xxxvii

1. Rethinking Cities   1

The Effect of the Breakup of an Empire on
    the Region's Cities   5
Back to the Market: New Realities for Cities
    since the Breakup   12
Going Forward: Rethinking Eurasian Cities   20
Notes   32
References   32

2. Planning Cities   35

The Soviet Past: The Era of Soviet Planning   37
The Transitional Present: Planning's
    Fall from Grace   45
A Sustainable Future: The Rebirth of Planning   60
Annex 2A   76
Notes   79
References   80

3. Connecting Cities   **83**

The Soviet Past: Connecting to a
  Preeminent Center   86
The Transitional Present: Living in a Multihub
  World   90
A Sustainable Future: Moving toward
  Better Integration   105
Annex 3A   122
Notes   128
References   133

4. Greening Cities   **137**

The Soviet Past: Institutions without Markets   140
The Transitional Present: Weak Institutions and
  Weak Markets   152
A Sustainable Future: Strong Institutions and
  Strong Markets   169
Annex 4A   183
Notes   184
References   185
Statistical Websites   186

5. Financing Cities   **189**

Intergovernmental Financing in the Soviet Union   191
Intergovernmental Financing during the Transition   194
Intergovernmental Financing Today   197
Conclusion   230
Annex 5A: Financing Connectivity   231
Notes   238
References   242

Boxes

1.1   Local Institution Development in Kazan   24
2.1   Housing Swap Scheme in Georgia   70
3.1   Declining Road Safety   94
4.1   What Is the Best Way to Reduce Emissions
       from a Taxi Fleet?   172
5.1   The Communist Party and the Soviet Political
       Structure   193
5.2   Territorial Reform in Georgia   200
5.3   Norms, Inefficiencies, and Unfunded
       Mandates in Ukraine   208

5.4   Choosing among Local Benefit Taxes   216
5.5   Subnational Finance in China   222
5.6   Resistance to Homeowner Associations in
      the Former Soviet Union   224
5.7   Technical Constraints on Water Metering   227
5A.1 Financing Highways with Toll Roads   235
5A.2 Is Earmarking Road Taxes a Good Idea?   235

Exhibits

O.1   Size Distribution of Cities in the Soviet
      Union, 1939, 1959, 1974, and 1989   xxvi
O.2   Population Trends in Eurasian Cities,
      1992–2011   xxx
1.1   Population Trends in Eurasian
      Cities, 1992–2011   4
1.2   Mean Surface Temperature in the
      Soviet Union, January 1990   8
1.3   Size Distribution of Cities in the Soviet Union,
      1939, 1959, 1974, and 1989   10
1.4   Development of Baku, 1918, 1940, 1960,
      and 1980   22
1.5   Pollution in Former Soviet Union Cities,
      1992 and 2004   25
2.1   Floor Area of Food and Consumer Goods
      Stores in Moscow, 1989   45
2.2   Industrial and Similar Uses in Selected
      Cities in the Former Soviet Union, 2009   50
2.3   Distribution of Males in the Soviet
      Union, 1989   60
3.1   The Trans-Asia–Europe Optical Fiber
      Cable Network   118
4.1   Air Pollution from Transport in the Soviet
      Union, 1988   148
4.2   Moscow Green Areas   152
4.3   Air Pollution from Stationary Sources in Cities
      in the Russian Federation, 1992 and 2009   158
4.4   Developments in Public Transport in
      Selected Eurasian Cities   161

Figures

O.1   Population Shares Living in Cities of 1 Million
      People or More, 1990–2010   xxix

1.1   Destination of Nonnatural Resource–Intensive
      Exports from the Central Asian Countries, 2003
      and 2008   18
2.1   GDP per Capita in Selected Countries,
      1990–2008   46
2.2   Density in Selected Cities and Their
      Peripheries, 1990   48
2.3   Industrial Area as Percentage of Built-Up
      Area in Selected Cities, 2010   49
2.4   New Construction in Armenia and
      Georgia and Their Capitals   51
2.5   Young and Old People, by Country,
      1991 and 2008   60
3.1   Railway Traffic Volumes in the Soviet Union
      and Successor Countries, 1985–2007   93
3.2   Time, Cost, and Distance of Transport along
      the Almaty-Berlin Trade Route, circa 2003   109
3.3   Internet Penetration Rates in Selected
      Countries, 2010   113
3.4   Share of Broadband Subscribers per
      Capita in Selected Countries, 2009   113
3.5   Number of Fixed Broadband Connections in the
      Former Soviet Union and the
      World, 2000–08   114
4.1   Electricity Production in Western Europe
      and the Soviet Union, 1950–80   145
4.2   Production of Primary Energy in the
      Soviet Union and Elsewhere, 1950s–80s   146
4.3   Carbon Dioxide Emissions in Selected
      Countries, 1989–2007   154
4.4   Carbon Dioxide Emissions in Selected
      Countries, 1990 and 2007   155
4.5   Electric Power Consumption in Selected
      Countries, 1990–2007   156
4.6   Composition of Energy Sources in
      Selected Countries, 1990 and 2007   157
4.7   Motor Gasoline Consumption in
      Selected Countries, 2000 and 2008   160
4.8   Household Consumption per Capita in
      the Former Soviet Union, by Country,
      1991–2008   164
4.9   Water Use in Selected Countries, by
      Sector and Year   167

4.10 Municipal Water Withdrawal in
Selected Countries, 2002   167

4.11 Respiratory Diseases per 1,000
People in Selected Countries, 2004   169

4.12 Indexes of Exposure to Climate Change
and Adaptive Capacity to Climate Change
in the Former Soviet Union, by Country   170

4.13 Net Energy Imports in the Former Soviet
Union, by Country, 2007   175

4.14 Real Prices of Coal, Gas, and Oil on
World Market, 1991–2008   175

4.15 Proposed Clean Energy Mix for California   177

4.16 Retail Prices for Gasoline in Selected
Countries, 2008   178

5.1 GDP in the Russian Federation, 1989–2009   202

5.2 Revenue Composition in St. Petersburg,
2005–09   211

5.3 Expenditure Composition in
St. Petersburg, 2010   211

5.4 Revenue Composition in Kiev, 2007–09   212

5.5 Municipal Expenditure Composition
in Kiev, 2009   213

5.6 Municipal Expenditure Composition
in Tbilisi, 2009   214

5.7 Aggregate Tax Burden in the Former
Soviet Union, by Country, 2009   215

5.8 Personal Income Tax as Percentage of
GDP in Selected Countries, 2009 or Most
Recent Available   219

5.9 Property Tax as Percentage of GDP in
Selected Countries, 2009 or Most
Recent Available   220

5.10 Household Payments for Communal Services
in the Russian Federation, 1994–2005   225

5.11 Cost-Recovery Levels in Public Transit in the
Russian Federation, by Mode, 1995–2003   228

5A.1 Number of Telephones per 100 People in
Selected Countries, 2009   238

Tables

O.1 Issues That Cities Face in the Former Soviet
Union and Ways Forward   xxxiii

1.1   Industrial Production in the Former
      Soviet Union, by Ownership Type, 1928,
      1937, 1950, and 1960   6
1.2   Ethnic Composition of Net Migration
      from Eurasia (Excluding the Russian
      Federation) and the Baltics to the Russian
      Federation, 1990–94   15
1.3   Percentage of Total Exports, Unless
      Otherwise Indicated   19
1.4   Issues That Cities Face in the Former
      Soviet Union and Ways Forward   29
2.1   Housing Conditions in Selected Cities in
      the Former Soviet Union, 1988   42
2.2   Homeownership Rates in
      Selected Countries, 2005   52
2.3   Number of Passenger Cars, by Country,
      1993 and 2007   57
2.4   Average Daily Hours of Operation of
      Water Services, by Country   59
2.5   Reported Numbers of Homeowner
      Associations in the Former Soviet Union,
      by Country, 2010   69
2.6   Water Tariffs and Cross-Subsidy Rates
      in Regions' Capital Cities, 2010   73
2A.1 Car Registration in the Former
      Soviet Union, by Country   76
2A.2 Length and Capacity of Metro Systems in
      the Former Soviet Union, by City, 2010   78
3.1   Maritime Port Volumes in the Former
      Soviet Union, 2009   96
3.2   Centrality Indicators for Capital Cities in
      Eurasian Aviation Network   98
3.3   Number of Weekly Direct Services and
      Indirect Connections at Main Hubs   101
3.4   Selected Bilateral Agreements with
      the Russian Federation   111
3A.1 Air Carriers' Networks, 2000–11   122
3A.2 Peripheralization of Eurasian Cities   124
3A.3 Onward Connectivity: Number of
      Available Indirectly Connected City Pairs,
      by Origin City, Hub, and Destination   125
3A.4 Hub Connectivity: Number of Connected
      City-Pairs via Selected Airports   126

3A.5 Total Turnaround Costs for Selected Cities   127

4.1 Atmospheric Pollution Emissions in
Selected Cities, 1987   142

4.2 Vehicle Production in the Soviet Union
and Selected Countries, 1960–86   147

4.3 Generation and Disposal of Toxic Waste
in the Soviet Union, by Sector, 1990   149

4.4 Performance of Water and Wastewater
Sector in the Former Soviet Union, 1989   150

4.5 Commuter Statistics in Selected Cities, 1998   162

4.6 Waste Disposal Methods in Selected
Cities, 1998   165

4.7 Market, Mixed, and Government
Solutions to Increasing Energy Efficiency   173

4A.1 The 25 Coldest Cities in the Russian
Federation and North America with
about 500,000 People, 2001   183

5.1 Structure of Subnational Government in
the Soviet Union   192

5.2 Distribution of Tax Instruments across
Subnational Tiers of Government in
the Russian Federation, 2009   203

5.3 Distribution of Shared Taxes in
Tajikistan, 2009   206

5.4 Distribution of Shared Taxes in
Ukraine, 2009   207

5.5 Personal Income Tax Rates in the Former
Soviet Union, by Country, 2010   218

Foreword

Eurasian cities, unique in the global spatial landscape, were part of the world's largest experiment in urban development. The challenges they now face because of their history offer valuable lessons to urban planners and policy makers across the world—from places that are still urbanizing to those already urbanized.

More than three-quarters of the built environment in Eurasian cities was developed after 1945 in a centralized fashion. Central planners could implement whatever they considered good practice planning solutions, and Eurasia's cities became their drawing boards. The central planners got a lot right—easy access to public transportation, district heating networks, almost universal access to water systems, and socially integrated neighborhoods. At the same time, they failed to acknowledge the importance of markets and individual choice in shaping sustainable and congenial places for people to live in.

From a spatial point of view, it became clear that many Eurasian cities were developed in places where they should not have been. To populate sparsely inhabited territory, Soviet planners pushed urban development toward the heart of Siberia. Many of the resulting cities had no rural hinterland to rely on for daily food needs and had to depend on subsidized goods and services.

To be viable in a market economy, Eurasia's urban structures have to be rethought. This book builds on the insights in the *World*

Development Report 2009: Reshaping Economic Geography to inform this rethinking.

From a planner's perspective, land and housing markets were frequently mismanaged in the former Soviet Union. Although Eurasian cities were largely spared the negative side effects of organic urban growth such as sprawl, central planners were not the best judges of how and where land should be developed. Indeed, large industrial areas still occupy prime land in Eurasian cities, even when they should be used for other purposes. Flat-panel concrete apartment blocks, built quickly and cheaply to accommodate rapid urban expansion, often had a short life—sometimes as few as 25 years—but continue to be inhabited. In many cases, these apartment blocks have not been upgraded since the end of communism.

The collapse of the Soviet economy weakened the connectivity between Eurasian cities. Without subsidies for transporting goods and services cheaply from one city to another, the more remote cities are isolated from global markets and increasingly uncompetitive. Rail networks are hard to run efficiently, even with the lowest electricity prices in Europe. Road networks are expensive to maintain and upgrade. And air infrastructure is becoming more and more important for connecting a landmass that spans nine time zones.

Many Eurasian cities face an overdeveloped public service infrastructure that is hard to maintain and upgrade. Facing an economic downturn in the 1990s and lacking experience in decentralized urban management, many local authorities struggled to run these services. Public transport ridership fell in most cities, with more people commuting in private vehicles. Recycling networks disappeared, and soaring consumption overwhelmed solid waste management systems. District heating systems became large energy sieves—hard to run and maintain without subsidies. Plaguing water systems are large shares of nonrevenue water, and low tariffs do not ensure the cost recovery needed for upgrades and repairs.

Finally, many Eurasian cities do not have the capacity to be self-sufficient financially. These cities depend largely on central government transfers, and progress in creating tools for generating more local revenue (for example, strategically using municipal land) has been slow. Moreover, a reluctance to charge market prices for public services has led to the continuing deterioration of existing systems. For example, heating tariffs, kept artificially low, not only encourage people to squander energy, but also make it hard for district heating systems to cover operating costs.

Eurasian cities have to find the right balance between markets and institutions to become sustainable. Before the 1990s, institutions were strong, but markets were nonexistent. In the 1990s, many institutions crumbled, and markets did not develop as fast as has been hoped. The 2000s were a decade of readjustment, with incipient market principles making more headway in Eurasian cities and with local institutions becoming stronger and more self-reliant. The future should see Eurasian cities continually straddling a fine balance between markets and institutions—a balance key to their sustainable development.

This book discusses all five of these issues—*rethinking, planning, connecting, greening,* and *financing*—in more detail. It seeks to analyze the key challenges created by central planning, outline how these challenges were addressed in the transition years, and identify some steps Eurasian cities should take to chart a sustainable development path for themselves. The book also shows how some of the most progressive cities in the region have been tackling these problems and, in doing so, shedding the last vestiges of the socialist economy.

Philippe Le Houérou   Indermit Gill
Vice President   Chief Economist
Europe and Central Asia   Europe and Central Asia

About the Authors

Souleymane Coulibaly is the lead author of this book. He is currently the World Bank Senior Country Economist for Armenia and the Europe and Central Asia regional trade coordinator. He was one of the principal authors of the *World Development Report 2009: Reshaping Economic Geography.* His publications and ongoing research focus on the impact of geography on firms' location, trade flows, and regional integration. Prior to joining the World Bank, he was a lecturer at the Ecole Nationale Superieure de Statistiques et d'Economie Appliquée (ENSEA) of Abidjan, a teaching assistant at the University of Lausanne, and an economist at the Economic and International Relations department of NESTLE in Vevey, Switzerland. He holds a dual Ph.D. degree in International Trade and Economic Geography from the University of Paris 1 Pantheon-Sorbonne and the University of Lausanne.

Uwe Deichmann is a researcher in the Environment and Energy Team of the World Bank's Development Research Group, where he works primarily on spatial economic and environmental issues. He was one of the principal authors of the *World Development Report 2009: Reshaping Economic Geography.* Prior to joining the World Bank, he worked for the UN (United Nations) Environment Program and the

UN Statistics Division. He holds a Ph.D. in Economic Geography and Regional Science from the University of California.

William R. Dillinger has a B.A. from the University of California at Berkeley and a master's degree from Harvard University. He joined the World Bank in 1978 and has devoted most of his career to public finance, regional development, and human resource management issues. He has worked in 35 developing and transitional countries in all six of the World Bank regions. His recent publications include "Poverty and Regional Development in Eastern Europe and Central Asia" (World Bank Working Paper 118, 2007) and "Intergovernmental Fiscal Relations in the New EU Member States: Consolidating Reforms" (World Bank Working Paper 111, 2007).

Marcel Ionescu-Heroiu joined the World Bank in April 2008, and since then has worked on a range of issues, such as brownfields redevelopment, cultural heritage development, solid waste management, energy efficiency in cities, one-company towns, interjurisdictional spillovers, and more general urban planning and urban economics areas. Prior to joining the Bank, he was a project manager for a small software company in Cluj-Napoca (Romania) and was lead editor for the *Worldmark Encyclopedia of Nations*. He also worked as a teaching assistant and lecturer at Cornell University. He has a Ph.D. in Regional and Urban Development from Cornell University.

Ioannis N. Kessides is a Lead Economist in the World Bank's Development Research Group. His areas of specialization are competition, regulatory, and privatization policies in network utilities; market structure and firm conduct; determinants of entry and exit; and contestability analysis. Prior to joining the World Bank in 1990, he taught at the University of Maryland and was an economist in the Line of Business Program of the U.S. Federal Trade Commission. More recently he taught at Princeton University. He received B.S. and M.A. degrees in Physics and Plasma Physics from Caltech and Princeton, and a Ph.D. in Economics from Princeton.

Charles Kunaka is a Senior Trade Specialist in the International Trade Department of the World Bank. He works on trade facilitation and logistics with a particular focus on trade and transport facilitation projects and trade corridor diagnostics. He has published on logistics for small-scale producers in lagging regions and on the regulation of international road freight transport services. He has a Ph.D. in Transport Economics and Policy from University College London. Before joining the International Trade Department, he was with the Sub-Saharan Africa Transport Policy Program in the Africa Region, and prior to that, he was a senior officer with the Southern African Development Community.

Daniel Saslavsky joined the World Bank in 2009 to work as a trade facilitation and logistics consultant for the International Trade Department. Prior to this post, he was Deputy Director of the International Trade Program of the Center for Implementation of Public Policies for Growth (CIPPEC), the leading public policy think tank in Argentina. He has also worked for the Inter-American Development Bank and other multilateral institutions. He completed his graduate studies in International Affairs at SAIS-Johns Hopkins University and Universidad Torcuato Di Tella. His main areas of expertise are trade facilitation and logistics.

Acknowledgments

This book was prepared by a core team led by Souleymane Coulibaly and including Uwe Deichmann, William Dillinger, Marcel Ionescu-Heroiu, Ioannis Kessides, Charles Kunaka, and Daniel Saslavsky. Austin Kilroy prepared the spotlights, chapter summaries, and key issues. Chorching Goh and Christine Kessides co-led the team that started this study, with support from Igor Burakovsky (Institute for Economic Research and Policy Consulting, Kiev), Mikhail Dmitriev (Center of Strategic Research, Moscow), Vladimir Dubrovskiy (Center for Social and Economic Research, Kiev), Vernon Henderson (Brown University), Obid Khakimov (Westminster International University, Tashkent), Leonid Limonov (Leontief Center, St. Petersburg), Aleksander Puzanov (Institute of Urban Economics, Moscow), and Joseph Salukvadze (Tbilisi State University). Otto Simonett, Viktor Novikov, and Zurab Jincharadze from Zoinet provided useful comments and produced most of the maps included in the book.

The book benefited from thoughtful comments by peer reviewers Ellen Hamilton, Somik Lall, and Yan Zhang, as well as from Elena Karaban, Andrew Kircher, Larisa Leshchenko, and Tamar Sulukhia. Elena Kantarovich and Rhodora Mendoza Paynor provided timely support to the team. Asad Alam, Pedro Alba, Ivailo Izvorski, Stephen Karam, Motoo Konishi, Laszlo Lovei, Martin Raiser, and Yvonne Tsikata provided managerial support, guidance, and oversight. Bruce

Ross-Larson edited the book, and Zakia Nekaien-Nowrouz and Sarah Nankya Babirye formatted it. The team especially thanks Indermit Gill for his time, advice, suggestions, and ideas about the book's structure and contents.

Background notes were prepared by Evgeny Vinokurov and a team in the Strategy and Research Department of the Eurasian Development Bank: Jennet Hojanazarova (Turkmenistan), Farhod Jurahonov (Uzbekistan), Vahram Avanesyan (Armenia), Lado Vardosanidze (Georgia), Volodymyr Vakhitov (Ukraine), Dymitro Lyapin (Ukraine), Victor Moroz (Moldova), Valeriu Prohnitchi (Moldova), Sergey Belanovsky (the Russian Federation), Denis Kadochnikov (Russia), Arthur Batchev (Russia), Nikita Mkrtchyan (Russia), Vyacheslav Baburin (Russia), and Ilya Voznyuk (Russia). Barbara Lipman, Richard Podolske, and Irina Novikova (World Bank consultants) also provided useful background notes.

Abbreviations

ASA	air service agreements
BSFOCS	Black Sea Fiber Optic Cable System
Btu	British thermal unit
CEE	Central and Eastern European
CIS	Commonwealth of Independent States
COMECON	Council for Mutual Economic Assistance
EPA	Environmental Protection Agency
ESCAP	United Nations Economic and Social Commission for Asia and the Pacific
EU	European Union
EU15	European Union-15
FDI	foreign direct investment
FFFSR	Federal Fund for the Financial Support of Regions
GDP	gross domestic product
GFS	Government Finance Statistics
IATA	International Air Transport Association
ICAO	International Civil Aviation Organization
ICT	information and communications technology
KAFOS	Karadeniz Fiber Optik Sistemi
kbps	kilobits per second
Mbps	megabits per second

MMBtu	million British thermal unit
OECD	Organisation for Economic Co-operation and Development
RCC	Regional Commonwealth in the field of Communications
SAR	special administrative region
STM	Synchronous Transport Module
SZD	Sovetskie Zheleznye Dorogi
TAE	Trans-Asia–Europe
TASIM	Trans-Eurasian Information Superhighway
TIR	Transit International Routier
TRACECA	Transport Corridor Europe-Caucasus-Asia
VAT	value-added tax
WTO	World Trade Organization

Note: All dollar amounts are U.S. dollars unless otherwise indicated.

Overview

The *World Development Report 2009: Reshaping Economic Geography* shows that agglomeration, migration, and specialization cause cities to become the main driver of growth through the structural transformation from agriculture to industry to services (World Bank 2009). This is true even in regions where the location of economic activities is a political decision engineered and imposed from the top. Consider the former Soviet Union, excluding the Baltic countries (Eurasia). Before the breakup of the Soviet Union, the population was increasing, and cities were expanding (exhibit O.1). Estimated at 280 million in 1990, the population reached 283 million in 1993. By then, the Soviet Union had disintegrated, inducing movements of people across and beyond the newly established borders. The population began to fall steadily and stabilized at below 277 million by 2007, before climbing back to 280 million in 2011.

These population dynamics reflect tremendous changes in Eurasia: the breakup of the Soviet Union; the return of the market as the driving force in society; and the emergence of regional powers such as the European Union (EU), China, and India competing with the Russian Federation over its former satellites. For centuries, burgeoning cities along the Silk Road traded goods between east and west, including jewels, spices, glassware, medicines, musk and other

EXHIBIT 0.1

Size Distribution of Cities in the Soviet Union, 1939, 1959, 1974, and 1989

a. 1939

b. 1959

continued

EXHIBIT 0.1
Continued

c. 1974

d. 1989

● > 1,000,000   ● 300,000–1,000,000   ● 50,000–300,000

Source: Authors, based on data from Lewytzkyj (1979).

perfumes, and silk, satin, and other fine fabrics. During the Romanov Dynasty and the Soviet era, a north-south trade axis overlay Eurasia, with Moscow as the main hub. To face the postbreakup changes, Eurasia needs to rethink its cities along the Silk Road.

First, urbanization has regained momentum in Eurasia, if at a slower pace than in the rest of the world. The share of the people in cities of more than 1 million rose from a plateau of 14 percent over 1990–94 to 15 percent in 2011, compared with a rise from 17 to 20 percent in the rest of the world. The share of Eurasians of working age fell from 65 to 64 percent over 1990–94 before rising to 70 percent in 2011—fewer than half of them men. And the share of elderly rose from 9 to 12 percent over 1990–2007 before falling to 11 percent in 2011, with more than 90 percent of them women.

These population dynamics suggest that the function and form of Eurasian cities have to change. Urban planning in a country with a shrinking urban population is not the same as that in a country with growing cities. Connecting cities in a country specializing in services is not the same as that in a country strengthening its manufacturing or agriculture. The livability of cities in an aging country implies a different design from that in a country striving to attract young families.

Looking ahead, policy makers need to promote changes that will make Eurasian cities the main drivers of growth. For this, they need to identify the changes to be promoted or combated—and to explore all the financing available to afford these changes. This book proposes some ideas for rethinking Eurasian cities.

Eurasian Cities Are Reorganizing

Based on the population share of cities with more than 1 million people in a country's total population, Armenia, Azerbaijan, and Georgia are urbanized, and the nine remaining Eurasian countries are urbanizing (figure O.1). After the breakup of the Soviet Union, the share of the people in the capital city stabilized at 35 percent in Armenia and 25 percent in Georgia, while it has consistently declined in Azerbaijan, if still above the world trend. The growth of urban primacy in Belarus, the Kyrgyz Republic, and Russia has been close to the world trend, while Kazakhstan, Tajikistan, Turkmenistan, and Ukraine trended 5 to 10 percent below it.

Due to agglomeration, some cities expanded while others shrank (exhibit O.2). A diverse portfolio of places is emerging in Russia and Ukraine, while the rest of Eurasia faces a simple consolidation of

FIGURE 0.1

Population Shares Living in Cities of 1 Million People or More, 1990–2010

percent

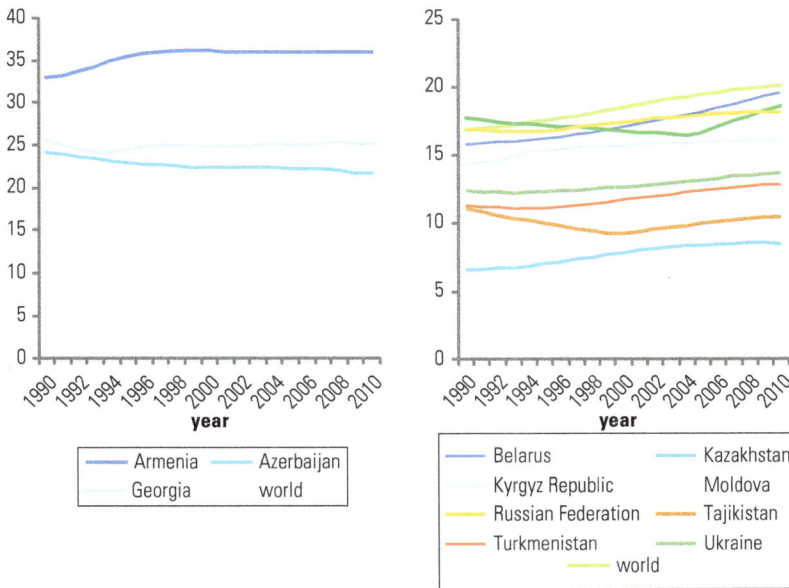

Source: World Bank 2011.
Note: Number of people living in the largest city is used for the Kyrgyz Republic, Moldova, Tajikistan, and Turkmenistan.

core-periphery differences between the capital city and the rest of the country. Some regional hubs—Almaty, Astana, Kiev, Minsk, St. Petersburg, and Tashkent—are also emerging, while Moscow remains the only Eurasian city with the potential to become a global city like London, New York, Paris, or Tokyo.[1]

This spatial reorganization is driven by renewed mobility in Eurasia. The early years of transition, with high cross-border migration after the removal of Soviet restrictions on mobility, were followed by the eruption of civil and transborder conflicts among the region's newly emergent countries. As conflict abated and economic reform took root, economic motivations became the key driver of migratory flows in former communist countries. People in the rest of Eurasia migrated to their capital cities and to Russia and Ukraine, while those in Russia and Ukraine migrated to Europe.

Accompanying these labor movements were changes in the direction and composition of trade that reinforced labor mobility and agglomeration in leading Eurasian cities. For instance, the rapid diversification of the export products and trading partners of Russia and Ukraine favored the emergence of secondary cities to

EXHIBIT 0.2

Population Trends in Eurasian Cities, 1992–2011

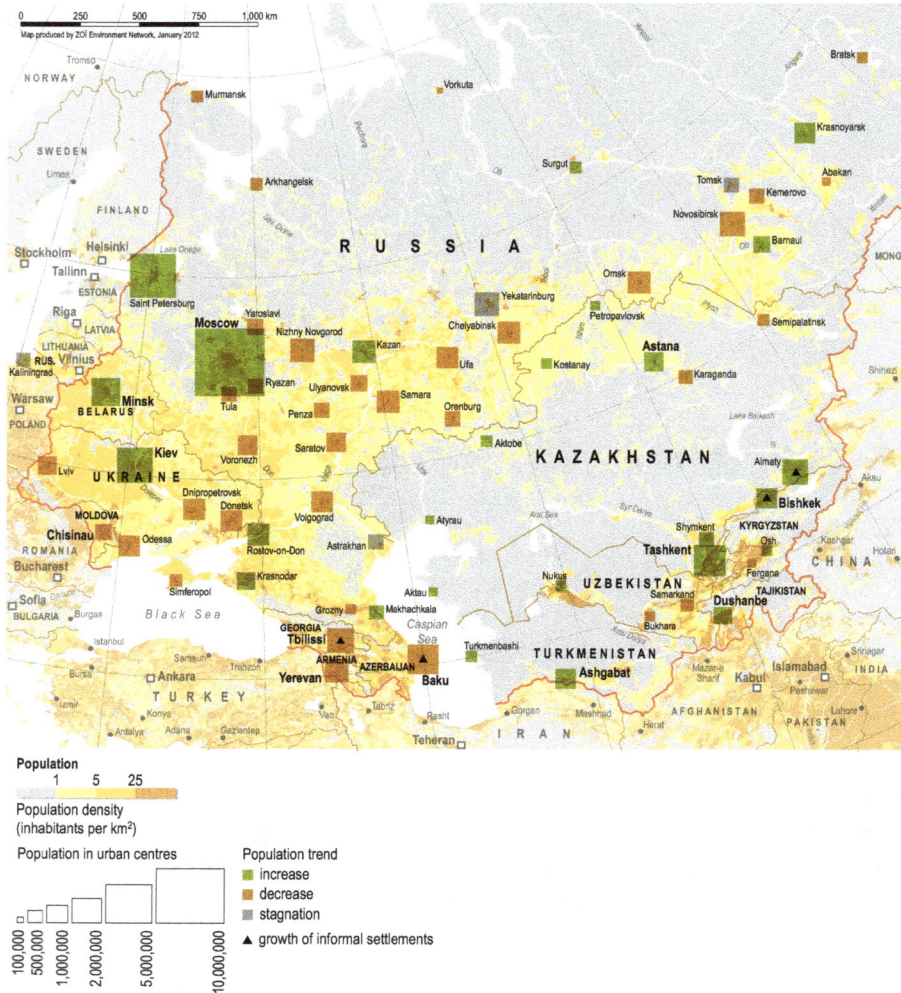

Source: World Bank data.

complement Moscow—St. Petersburg and Kiev—while exports of
the rest of Eurasia remained concentrated on traditional products
and trading partners, reinforcing the largest cities' role as production and transportation hubs.

Eurasian Cities Need Better Planning, Better Connectivity, and Better Greening

In the post-Soviet era, the proximity to the EU market and the deeper
integration shaped the internal geography of Central and Eastern

European countries, favoring the emergence of urban centers closer to Western Europe while reinforcing economic diversification in their capital cities. Agglomeration dynamics in Eurasia were attenuated due to the long distances to leading world markets, which favored the consolidation of capital cities and a few other leading cities such as Almaty, Kazan, and Yekaterinburg. This is not a handicap.

Around the world, leading cities play a key role in production and export by delivering a range of services, sustaining economic activities, and driving the urbanization dynamics in the rest of the country. Leading cities tend to be well connected domestically and externally—and to offer the most diversified production. Leading Eurasian cities in the former Soviet countries are no exception, and they can drive the integration of the region into world markets. But for this to happen, policy makers need to plan their cities better, connect them better internally and with key external hubs, and green them to make them more attractive to young and talented workers.

Planning cities better means promoting policies to develop land and housing markets and improve public service delivery. Policy makers need to modernize and enforce land use regulations and building codes, lower the costs of land transactions, use public infrastructure development to guide land development strategically and sustainably, and build the institutional capacity to redevelop brownfields. In housing, policy makers need to unlock rental markets, revitalize homeowner associations, create and enforce rules for using public spaces, and lower the costs of property transactions, such as buying an apartment block. For public service infrastructure, policy makers need to continually upgrade and maintain utility networks, adjust tariffs to ensure system sustainability, encourage and enable interjurisdictional cooperation to provide such services as regional sewage and water management systems, and maintain and extend public transit networks.

Connecting cities—with transport and telecommunications to facilitate the movement of goods, people, and information across cities and countries—requires new policies, institutions, and infrastructure. To foster interurban connectivity, policy makers need to upgrade the transit system in large cities, improve the energy efficiency of private vehicles by introducing market prices for gasoline, introduce or adjust gasoline taxes where needed, and encourage walking and biking through the redesign of city centers. In addition to leveraging the hub function of Moscow on air and rail connectivity, they need to devise and implement airline policies that increase competition in air service and adopt open sky policies with other strategic partners to substantially reduce the cost of transporting goods and people across and beyond Eurasia. And they need to reinforce the connectivity of emerging regional hubs by developing the institutional framework to support road transport and ensure smooth cross-country connections. In addition, Eurasian cities need to be anchored in the digital era by participating in regional and global information and communications technology (ICT) initiatives.

Greening Eurasian cities means ensuring their sustainable development through strong markets and institutions that encourage the efficient use of resources and deliver growth. To use resources efficiently, policy makers need to put in place adaptation and mitigation measures. Policy makers need to scale up interventions to address immediate pollution problems. They need to promote the planning of greener cities in new developments and brownfield redevelopments, which will help Eurasian cities in the global competition for investments and skilled labor. Indeed, cities offering a high quality of life—through better air and water quality, less congestion, more green space, and other amenities—will be better positioned to attract skilled workers and innovative firms.

Eurasian Cities Need New Financing Mechanisms

The system for financing cities—and the infrastructure connections among them—have transformed substantially since the breakup of the Soviet Union. On subnational finance, policy makers first need to improve the technical and economic efficiency of public utilities. Only then will it make sense to explore ways of making people who benefit from public service infrastructure pay by increasing taxes. This could include increasing personal income tax rates in big cities; taxing agglomeration rents; improving the administration of property tax; and increasing tariffs and fees through enforcing the payment of housing maintenance fees, raising water tariffs, expanding metering, and raising public transport tariffs to at least cost-recovery levels.

Several Eurasian countries have been encouraging more private sector investment in transport and other infrastructure investments, reflecting the global trend that started in the 1990s. But private sector investments have been limited because the financing of cross-country infrastructure is affected by externalities and coordination failures. Depending on the public good, policy makers could consider different means of financing: purely private (some telecom infrastructure is commercially viable); public-private partnerships using, say, tolls to partly recover costs; richer or leading countries' subsidies of infrastructure for poorer countries if this reinforces network externalities

TABLE O.1

Issues That Cities Face in the Former Soviet Union and Ways Forward

Period	Planning	Connecting	Greening	Financing
Soviet past	Master plans instead of zoning and central planners instead of urban planners; cities built around industrial areas and land misallocated	Hierarchical structure oriented toward Moscow, with limited horizontal links among lower order centers	Cost of externalities not considered in public policies; broad access to public transport; high rates of access to water and sanitation; recycling programs	System based on plan targets and intraparty negotiations; tariffs highly subsidized
Transitional present	High ownership rates and weak rental markets, with misallocated housing stock and missing or poorly enforced city planning regulations	Institutions established to manage connectivity infrastructure and develop sector plans, but progress moving at different pace across the region	Reduced pollution as firms went bankrupt; collapse of recycling systems; deterioration of public transit	Move to modern subnational finance with transparent systems of revenue sharing and equalization transfers, with some countries moving faster than others
Market future	Collaboration between local and central government to solve property issues, modernize land use regulations, and use public infrastructure development strategically	Promotion of a few cities well connected to world markets by road, rail, air, and telecommunication links; development of regional institutions for corridor management and interstate cooperation on connectivity issues	Preservation of positive features of the former Soviet Union; enforcement of existing regulations; improvement of livability by building cities for people and taking care of the environment	Increase in personal income tax rates; enforcement of payment of housing maintenance fees; increase in water tariffs; expanding of metering and raising of public transport tariffs; for big cities, exploration of public-private partnerships for large connectivity projects

in their own country; contributions from a reputable regional development bank, leveraged with funds raised on international markets.

Planning, greening, and connecting Eurasian cities will require scaling subnational finance as well as adopting instruments to facilitate cross-country finance and help these cities prepare for a sustainable future (table O.1).

Structure of the Book

This book responds to pressing questions for policy makers in Eurasian cities and national governments. Faced with changing economic circumstances and a reorientation of trade toward Europe and Asia, will Eurasia's cities be able to adjust? Will some cities be granted the flexible regulations and supportive policies necessary for growth? And will some be permitted to shrink and their people assisted in finding prosperity elsewhere in the region?

According to the evidence in this book, some Eurasian cities and countries have adjusted better than others. Economic activity is becoming concentrated in specific cities, reflecting the economic advantages those places offer and a trend toward decentralization and autonomy in setting regulations to exploit the advantages. But even as Eurasian cities diverge, they face shared challenges. Policy makers have a key role in assisting spatial restructuring, particularly in addressing imperfect information and coordination failures.

The book has five chapters: Rethinking Cities; Planning Cities; Connecting Cities; Greening Cities; and Financing Cities.

- "Rethinking Cities," an overview from a regional vantage, traces the historical origins of Eurasia's urban structure, which evolved as a function of the "Silk Road" linking Asia and Europe, and later as a product of Soviet planning. Since the end of the Soviet Union, Eurasia's economy has been reoriented spatially toward Europe in one direction and Asia in the other. But Eurasia's urban structure has not yet fully responded to reflect these new economic realities, and national policies have tended to be preoccupied with spatial equity.

- "Planning Cities" focuses on the structural changes in Eurasian cities, together with the regulatory and planning constraints they face. Special attention is given to weak rental markets, misallocated housing stocks, and missing or poorly enforced city planning regulations. These bottlenecks on efficient cities could be alleviated through collaboration between local and central government to resolve property issues, modernize land use regulations, and implement strategic public infrastructure. Cities must be able to respond flexibly and dynamically to changing economic circumstances. Land use planning should protect cultural heritage buildings and provide social services and parkland—but where there is no clear reason for government intervention, decisions on land use should be left to land purchasers, without overly prescriptive zoning and attempts to second-guess what is best for a city.

- "Connecting Cities" reviews the progressive changes in Eurasia's physical and ICT infrastructure, from a hierarchical structure oriented toward Moscow and to a more multipolar structure that reflects the emergent economic importance of Europe and Asia in Eurasia. It highlights the economic gains from better interstate cooperation on transport corridor management, since borders and bottlenecks hamper trade. Cities could better connect by introducing less restrictive international aviation policies, encouraging competition in air transport markets, and promoting ICT connectivity.

- "Greening Cities" shows how Eurasian cities have many of the ingredients for sustainable urban development: extensive public transport systems, dense residential areas, and district power and heating systems that carry economies of scale. But recycling systems have collapsed since the end of the Soviet Union, and public transit has deteriorated amid rapidly increasing car ownership. Despite some successes (in reducing greenhouse gas emissions even while Eurasia's economies have been growing), Eurasia is still the world's least energy-efficient region. Quality urban environments are integral to a city's economic success because they contribute to competitiveness and facilitate economic activity.

- "Financing Cities" surveys how Eurasia is moving toward modern subnational finance, with equalization transfers and transparent systems of revenue sharing, and notes how some countries are moving faster than others. It explores the room for local revenue enhancement through increasing personal income tax rates, enforcing the payment of housing maintenance fees, raising water tariffs, expanding metering, and raising public transport tariffs. It closes with an annex that looks at options to finance cross-country connectivity infrastructure.

Note

1. Sassen (1991) identifies four new ways that global cities function: as highly concentrated command points in the organization of the world economy; as key locations for finance and specialized service firms, which have replaced manufacturing as the leading economic sectors; as sites of production, including the production of innovation, in these leading sectors; and as markets for the products and innovations produced.

References

Lewytzkyj, Borys. 1979. *The Soviet Union: Figures-Facts-Data*. Munich: K. G. Sauer.

Sassen, Saskia. 1991. *The Global City*. Princeton, NJ: Princeton University Press.

World Bank. 2008. *World Development Report 2009: Reshaping Economic Geography*. Washington, DC: World Bank.

———. 2011. *World Development Indicators*. Washington, DC: World Bank.

Chapter Summaries

Chapter 1

Rethinking Cities

For centuries, the Silk Road joined Asia and Europe through an extensive network of overland and maritime trade routes, with cities emerging at key locations. Later, during the Soviet era, central planners determined a city's location based on transport efficiency, interregional equity, and defensive capacity. Some cities were created to colonize empty territory. Today, this urban network does not fit Eurasia's emerging economic profile. Eurasian cities must respond to three big changes: the breakup of the Soviet Union, the return of the market as the driving force of society, and the emergence of regional powers such as the European Union, China, and India that are competing with the Russian Federation for markets and influence in its former satellites.

Several methods of analysis indicate an imbalance across Eurasia, implying a need to readjust Eurasia's urban structure. For example, Russia has fewer midsize cities than do Brazil or the United States. Its population is still scattered, even though economic activity is concentrated in a few regions. Compared with similarly remote regions of Canada, Siberia and the Far East may have about 18 million too many people. Between 1989 and 2004, almost all new firms chose to locate near Moscow and St. Petersburg. Policy makers may need to help Russia's population to move to economic density as firms are doing.

National policies in Eurasia are still preoccupied with spatial equity. But the concentration of economic activity in large cities is fundamental to national competitive advantage: they foster innovation through their diversity of industries—and reduce production costs through their economies of scale.

Chapter 2

Planning Cities

Following the demise of communism in the early 1990s, many countries reversed course, adapting systems in which the market reigned supreme and planning played little or no role. With almost complete laissez-faire approaches, dwindling budgets, and minimal experience of decentralized city management, many Eurasian urban centers struggled during the transition to a market economy.

Good planning is part of the basic toolkit of public interventions for enhancing market efficiencies (business competition, access to information) while mitigating market inefficiencies (pollution, congestion). This does not mean choosing one urban design that optimizes a city forever—impossible, since the configuration of economic activity will change over time. Rather it means putting regulations and institutions in place that allow a city to respond flexibly and dynamically to economic circumstances. Land pricing and land regulations are important components of this system. Land pricing ensures that not all people and businesses locate in just one city, since people must pay more to be in the most successful cities. Individuals and firms that do not need to be there will locate elsewhere. Within a city, the same rationale applies. Land should be permitted to be traded freely and transparently to respond to changing circumstances. Property rights should be guaranteed. And transaction costs in land markets (say, the cost of finding the owner of a parcel of land) should be reduced.

Eurasian cities are undergoing profound changes: population densities in Moscow's central city are rising, while densities at its periphery are falling. But many cities still lack responsiveness to new circumstances. Some cities have an acute shortage of rental housing, leading to disproportionately high rents. An apartment in Almaty, Kiev, Moscow, or St. Petersburg is more expensive than a similar apartment in Amsterdam; Berlin; Stockholm; or Washington, DC. Bishkek and Dushanbe have housing shortages measured in hundreds of thousands of units. Eurasian cities are still underserved for retail space—in 2007, the Russian Federation had 39 square meters of gross leasable shopping center space per 1,000 inhabitants, and Ukraine had 19, compared with 448 in the Netherlands, 408 in Sweden, 266 in the United Kingdom, and 245 in France.

Policy makers must be willing to facilitate adjustments using land and property regulations. This is already happening in some places—of the 10 Russian cities sampled by the World Bank's subnational Doing Business Indicators, Kazan is far more competitive than Moscow, thanks to reforms to its construction and property regulations. But Armenia, Georgia, and the Kyrgyz Republic beat even Russia's most progressive cities: obtaining a construction permit in these countries requires 10–20 procedures, compared with more than 20 in Kazan. Indeed, Georgia ranks first in the world in the ease of registering property, and fourth in the ease of dealing with construction permits. But Moldova, Russia, Tajikistan, Ukraine, and Uzbekistan have some way to go to meet these high standards. For example, St. Petersburg's land use regulations include 54 different land use categories.

Some public interventions may be required, too. "Brownfield" (formerly industrial) land is often in prime areas in central cities, but it may require public funds to catalyze its redevelopment for residential or commercial uses, especially by helping to remove site contamination. Roads and parking spaces are underprovided and require public investment.

Policy makers facing these recommendations may ask: Where should the balance of government intervention lie? And when should city planners intervene and when should they let land markets decide? Good planning helps ensure that socially valued outcomes take place and that individuals' pursuit of well-being does not unduly affect the well-being of others. Land use planning should seek to protect cultural heritage buildings and provide social services and parkland—but where government intervention lacks a clear rationale, decisions on land use should be left to land purchasers, without overly prescriptive zoning and attempts to second-guess what is best for a city.

Chapter 3

Connecting Cities

Potential trade between the former Soviet Union and the European Union has been estimated at more than four times higher than the actual volume of trade between the two regions at the time of the Soviet Union's collapse. Trade with Asia, which has been growing over the past two decades, also has a large potential.

In recognition of this potential, there have been considerable efforts to define and develop a network of land trade routes across Eurasia, including through regional agreements and through programs and development projects—like the Central Asia Regional Economic Cooperation corridors, the Transport Corridor Europe-Caucasus-Asia (TRACECA), and the Eurasian Economic Community. New roads, railways, ports, and other transport are being built along such corridors. Overall, more than 40 trade route initiatives link more than 130 major cities across Eurasia.

But the sheer number of initiatives means there has been some duplication and waste; more important, there have been problems, such as border delays, an onerous bureaucracy, and informal payments, in harnessing these initiatives. Transit fees should be harmonized, taking into account the interests of both the transit country and the landlocked country, along the lines of work ongoing under TRACECA. Border procedures for road and rail should be harmonized across the former Soviet Union, and the Transit International Routier (TIR) Convention should be adhered to, including abolishing customs escorts for normal, nonsuspicious cargo. Another impetus for these improvements would be if participant countries were to systematically monitor and assess the performance of transport corridors.

Commercial air networks have also changed considerably since the Soviet era. Bottoming out a few years after the breakup of the Soviet Union, air traffic rebounded impressively in the past 10 years. Eurasian capital cities and other regional centers (especially Moscow) have expanded the number of available nonstop destinations, while smaller cities have become less connected and increasingly reliant on connecting flights through hubs (most notably Moscow). Even so, connectivity varies greatly among Eurasian cities, depending on—among others—the extent of liberalization and competition in air transport markets. In general, the sustainability and accessibility to air services could benefit from improving regulations and strengthening the capacity of institutions governing this sector.

Increased knowledge can enhance the role of Eurasian cities in the global urban system.

A complete understanding of "connectivity" should also include information and communications technology (ICT) infrastructure and links. Several recent studies suggest that the economic impacts of broadband are substantial and robust, improving an economy's global integration and competitiveness. Indeed, a 10 percentage point increase in broadband household penetration has been associated with a 1.3 percentage point increase in economic growth. Broadband penetration remains fairly low in Eurasia (around a quarter or less of the rates in the United States or Europe). Improving this situation will require new investment and regional cooperation—as with the Trans-Asia–Europe fiber-optic cable system and the Black Sea Fiber Optic Cable System. Additional improvements could include constructing parallel emergency lines, a prerequisite for successful competition in international data transit markets.

Eurasia has thus seen a reorientation of land transport links and emphasized concentration of air transport links on the old center of Moscow and a few other large cities. ICT connectivity is more flexible, and Eurasian cities and countries have several evolving options for regional and global connectivity.

Chapter 4

Greening Cities

The core challenge for city administrators is to enhance and encourage the positive aspects of urban development (for example, the connections between related industries), while mitigating the negative side effects (such as pollution and congestion). This chapter focuses on policies to mitigate these negative side effects. Such policies include direct interventions, such as enforcing pollution regulations, but they also involve longer term goals, such as developing urban areas around transportation hubs to increase the efficiency of a city's public transport network and thus reduce people's incentives to travel by car and create congestion.

The first section of this chapter argues that the Soviet Union failed to tackle environmental challenges adequately because, despite having strong government institutions, it had no market signals to ensure that resources were used efficiently and no nonstate institutions to promote environmental causes.

The second section reviews the environmental performance of cities in the former Soviet Union during the transition. It argues that the first half of the transition—from 1991 to the late 1990s—was plagued by weak state and nonstate institutions, and by a lack of well-functioning, formal markets. The transition provided some environmental dividends, as the most inefficient industries went out of business, but it also led to the widespread disintegration of the infrastructure for environmental management. The second half of the transition (until 2010) saw markets for goods and services emerge and initial institutional support for environmental policies develop. With diverging growth paths of countries in the former Soviet Union came growing differences in the managerial and financial capacities of cities.

The third section discusses why cities in the former Soviet Union should improve environmental management—and how. It argues that, for these cities to develop sustainably, they need both strong markets that deliver growth and encourage resource efficiency and strong institutions that ensure inclusive and sustainable growth.

Eurasian cities have inherited a number of problems from the Soviet era—but also a number of benefits:

- Industrial concentration in some cities generated *pollution* on an unprecedented scale. The Russian city of Norilsk, for example, emitted more sulfur dioxide in 1989 than all of Italy. But this same industrial concentration may make it easier to mitigate pollution, and countries in the former Soviet Union have been among a select group that have reduced their greenhouse gas emissions in the 1990s and 2000s while increasing economic growth.

- *District heating plants* were built with poorly insulated, low-quality piping, leading to losses of heat and water. Heat is not always delivered when needed—such as on cold autumn days—and residents cannot adjust the temperature to their needs, leading to phenomena like Siberian housing blocks with their windows flung wide open in winter. But if these problems can be fixed, these plants are potentially a cost-effective and environmentally friendly way of delivering heat—as shown by their adoption in forward-looking cities, like Copenhagen and Stockholm.

- *Public transport networks* in Eurasian cities are extensive but have been allowed to deteriorate in recent years. Since 1993, car ownership rates have tripled in Belarus and Russia; have more than doubled in Azerbaijan, Kazakhstan, and Moldova; and have almost doubled in Turkmenistan and Ukraine. Traffic gridlocks, already a daily happening in Moscow, are considered one of the city's most pressing problems.

- *Residential housing* was similarly designed, with thin walls and large windows, regardless of local climate conditions—in Ashgabat in the Central Asian desert or in Norilsk above the Arctic Circle.

- *Recycling networks* in most cities in the former Soviet Union disappeared during the 1990s. The networks had no funding, no adequate pricing, and no institutional oversight or proper management.

Creative, cost-efficient solutions include charging people who drive cars in the city for congestion, reserving parking spaces for environmentally friendly cars, upgrading district heating networks, and providing public information on the benefits of housing insulation. This chapter reviews a number of these problems and their potential solutions.

Chapter 5

Financing Cities

Subnational governments in the former Soviet Union are responsible for a wide range of urban infrastructure services, such as constructing and maintaining streets and operating the water supply, sewerage, district heating, and public transport systems. These services are financed in large part through central government transfers. Over the past 20 years, such transfers have become increasingly transparent, objective, and predictable. Even so, cities find themselves unable to raise additional revenues from the most appropriate source: the consumers of urban services themselves. This chapter reviews the subnational financing in several Eurasian countries—and discusses the merits of alternative sources of tax revenues and urban service charges. This chapter closes with an annex that looks at options to finance cross-country connectivity infrastructure.

CHAPTER 1

Rethinking Cities

Spotlight—Rethinking Kramatorsk, Ukraine

Like many Eurasian cities, Kramatorsk in Ukraine has lost many inhabitants in the past two decades. Its population shrank 15 percent between 1989 and 2010, from 198,000 to 167,850. Its main employer—a heavy machinery plant—was one of the largest in the Soviet Union, but its workforce has diminished from 40,000 to 14,000.

How is Kramatorsk responding to changed circumstances? First, it is capitalizing on its location: it is about 1.5 hours from the regional capital, Donetsk, and not too far from the of the Russian Federation border. Kramatorsk's heavy machinery plant exports 40 percent of its production to the European Union, Japan, Brazil, and elsewhere. Second, the city is modernizing its infrastructure. The machinery plant has made its production line more competitive, and the city is upgrading its urban infrastructure, such as district heating networks, though expensive financing is hindering this process greatly. Third, Kramatorsk is reorienting its economic profile. Some jobs lost from manufacturing have been taken up by an emergent jewelry industry, which now produces about 10 percent of Ukraine's jewelry output and aims to reach 20 percent. The industry began with a family business repairing earrings and necklaces, which then evolved into a workshop to craft them from raw materials. Now, it has large office buildings with jewelry exhibition rooms, and the industry continues to grow.

Key Issues

- Eurasian cities evolved as a function of the Silk Road linking Asia and Europe, and later as a product of Soviet planning.

- Since the end of the Soviet Union, Eurasia's economy has been reoriented spatially toward its edges—Europe in one direction and Asia in the other.

- Policy makers need to accept the growth of some cities and the shrinkage of others. Remote regions of Siberia and the Far East may now have about 18 million too many people.

For centuries the Silk Road connected the Far East, the Middle East, and Europe through an extensive network of overland and maritime trade routes. Transport costs were high, but long-distance trade was an integrating dynamic in developing the great civilizations of Arabia, China, Egypt, India, Persia, and Rome. Goods, transported on an east-west axis, included jewels; glassware; spices; medicines; musk and other perfumes; and silk, satin, and other fine fabrics, which, because of high transport costs, were luxuries. In modern times, trade in the former Soviet Union was mainly on a north-south axis, with Moscow serving as the main hub.

Through most of the 20th century, Soviet planning controlled the economies of many nations once located along the Silk Road. Since the fall of the Soviet Union, transport costs have fallen. The transport network for the 21st century aims to carry more diverse trade in goods, services, capital, labor, and ideas and information. It encompasses air, rail, and road transportation and telecommunications. When a new "Silk Road" emerges, it will have to be biaxial, in response to opportunities presented by the three most important development stories in the past several decades:

- *The fall of the Soviet Union.* The failure of the Soviet economic model opened the former Soviet Union to market-oriented reforms that stimulated growth and integrated the region into the global economy. Within the region, production and intraregional trade can expand in line with comparative advantage.

- *The rise of the European Union (EU).* Western Europe has risen in prominence, purchasing power, and ease of access. Further, the EU has adopted an explicit policy to deepen its economic ties with Eastern European countries through the European Neighborhood policy.

- *The rise of Asia.* China, Japan, and the Republic of Korea have been the most dynamic growth stories of the past 50 years. They will offer new trade opportunities as they continue to integrate with the world economy. India joined them two decades ago and is also reaping the growth benefits of reforms and new investments.

This book focuses on the former Soviet Union (Eurasia), excluding the Baltic countries, and addresses two questions: How is the spatial structure of economic activity being reorganized in the face of these changes? How will Eurasia's economic landscape evolve as its cities are reshaped by migration and trade with the EU and Asia (exhibit 1.1)? These questions are fundamental, since cities are engines of growth. Policy makers can influence the economic landscape over the next 20 years if they carefully rethink the form, function, and connectivity of cities.

The book provides a framework for rethinking Eurasian cities in a way that supplements today's main economic centers—Moscow and St. Petersburg—with other vibrant cities along a 21st-century "Silk Road." It looks at how Eurasian cities can diversify by promoting trade, mobility, and scale economies. As a country moves from low to medium to high income, it undergoes a structural transformation from agriculture to industry to services. Traditional agriculture tends to be replaced slowly as agriculture-related activities emerge in response to more demand from urban areas within and outside the country (World Bank 2007a). In these activities—such as storing, sorting, conditioning, packaging, transporting, processing, distributing, and risk management services—internal and external economies of scale drive productivity and the ability to export.

EXHIBIT 1.1

Population Trends in Eurasian Cities, 1992–2011

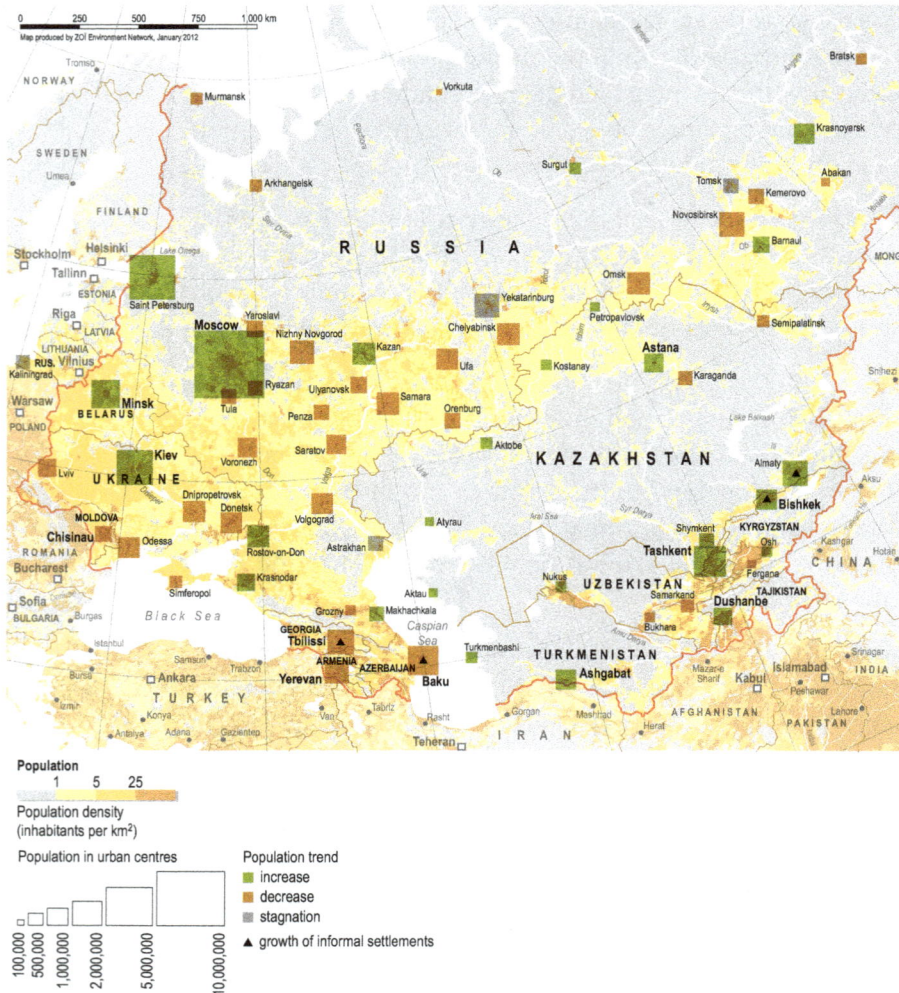

Map produced by ZOI Environment Network, January 2012

Population

1   5   25

Population density
(inhabitants per km²)

Population in urban centres

100,000
500,000
1,000,000
2,000,000
5,000,000
10,000,000

Population trend
- increase
- decrease
- stagnation
- ▲ growth of informal settlements

Source: World Bank data.
Note: Km² = square kilometer.

Urbanization results from the spatial transformations accompanying this process (World Bank 2008). Enabling cities to support this process is challenging, because cities have inertia built in by their inherited geography and infrastructure. Mobility should increase urbanization, and a more urbanized region will be a more integrated region, trading domestically and externally. As this structural transformation occurs, cities tend to play an increasing role in production and trade. Agriculture modernizes and requires fewer workers, freeing the surplus labor to migrate to cities and participate in the advanced division of labor that is the essence of any city. Cities allow the sharing of private and public production factors, the pooling of labor markets, and the sharing of information.

This process has a cumulative effect, making some cities global players that shape the world economy. Global cities function in four new ways (Sassen 1991):

- As highly concentrated command points in the organization of the world economy

- As key locations for finance and specialized service firms, which have replaced manufacturing as the leading economic sectors

- As sites of production, including the production of innovation, in these leading industries

- As markets for the products and innovations.

Although not all cities can become global cities, the diversity of Eurasian cities suggests that some may become lively nodes of a more integrated region in a globalized world.

This chapter examines three key periods: the Soviet past, the transitional present, and the market future. During the Soviet era, the location and size of cities were centrally planned in Moscow to fulfill the objectives of successive five-year plans. During the transition, market forces within former Soviet republics reinforced the role of cities as drivers of productivity and diversification within the newly established independent countries. While continuing to promote this internal dynamic, policy makers now need to connect these cities through regional and global integration policies to strengthen market forces and complete the transformation of Eurasian cities sustained by a new biaxial Silk Road (north-south and east-west).

The Effect of the Breakup of an Empire on the Region's Cities

Cities have always been the driving forces of world civilizations. Niniveh was at the heart of the Assyrian civilization, and Babylon was the symbol of the Babylonian civilization. When Peter the Great, third in the Romanov Dynasty, became Russia's ruler in 1696, the influence of Moscow began to expand. Peter strengthened the rule of the tsar and westernized Russia while at the same time making it a power in Europe and greatly expanding its borders. By 1918, the year that saw the end of the Romanov Dynasty, the Russian empire covered a vast territory from Western Europe to China.

As Peter the Great and his successors strove to consolidate their reign over this empire, major social, economic, cultural, and political changes were in the making in the urban centers. Moscow led these changes, followed by St. Petersburg, which was built as a gateway to

filter and channel western civilization through the empire. By fostering diversification through connectivity, specialization, and scale
economies, these cities started the structural transformation of the
Russian empire away from depending on commodities and limited
markets in a way that more effectively served local demand (World
Bank 2008). Some of its city-based activities, such as literature and
art, became prominent, with the production of such literary master-
pieces as *Crime and Punishment* and *War and Peace* and the painting
"Ivan the Terrible and the Death of his Son" by Ilya Repin. The Soviet
era altered this dynamic.

Framework of Spatial Location during the Soviet Era

Although market forces were inherently present during the Soviet
era, the state apparatus altered them through each five-year plan
(known as Gosplan), with the ownership structure biased toward an
almighty state. Three forms of ownership operated (table 1.1):

- Public ownership was vested in the government.

- Cooperative ownership was vested in cooperative associations,
  whose members were either workers engaged in or consumers
  patronizing the organization.

- Private ownership was also present.

In the early days of the Soviet Union, private producers contributed
nearly 20 percent of total production, mainly reflecting farmers' contribution to the economy. The ownership of land, including mineral
deposits and forest reserves, became vested exclusively in the government, while individual farmers became inconsequential when the
government decided to collectivize wholesale activities in January
1930. This shift became irreversible as the five-year plans became the
major policy-making tool of the Soviet Union by 1957 (Bergson 1964).

TABLE 1.1

**Industrial Production in the Former Soviet Union, by Ownership Type,
1928, 1937, 1950, and 1960**

percentage of total industrial production

Ownership type	1928	1937	1950	1960
Public	69.4	90.3	91.8	97.0
Cooperative	13.0	9.5	8.2	3.0
Private	17.6	0.2	0	0

Source: Bergson 1964.

Production was also organized spatially to consolidate the Soviet Union. The underlying driver of this spatial organization was the attempt to address the mismatch of factors of production in the Soviet Union, in which raw material wealth was most plentiful in Siberia, natural population growth was highest in Central Asia, and industrial plant and skilled labor were most abundant in European Russia. Schiffer (1989) describes Soviet decisions on spatial resource allocation as based on efficiency, equity, and geopolitics.

The efficiency factor suggested that production should be close to raw material and energy sources, that production of manufacturing goods and services (intermediate and final) should be close to urban centers, and that economic regions and administrative units should specialize in producing goods in which they had a competitive advantage, while ensuring that local demand for basic consumer goods was satisfied locally. The equity factor implied that economic activities should be evenly distributed throughout the country to maximize labor, infrastructure, and natural resources. The goal was to equalize industrial development across republics and regions, providing the population with comparable standards of living. Production was supposedly located in such a way as to eliminate the social and economic differences between urban and rural areas. The geopolitics factor suggested that the choice of location for production units had to be consistent with the need to strengthen the defensive capacities of the Soviet Union. In the mid-1960s, Soviet policy makers also adopted the notion that economic activities should no longer be concentrated in large cities. Later, territorial specialization was defined to include the entire Council for Mutual Economic Assistance (COMECON).

But no planner can ensure that a city will be a successful place to live and work—only the people who live there can do so. What is within the planners' purview is to make it easier for residents and firms to choose among good alternatives, such as moving to a different city or building strong roots locally. Good planning helps ensure that certain socially valued outcomes take place and that individuals' pursuit of well-being does not adversely affect the well-being of others. Good planning is a fundamental tool of efficient local governance—a means of expressing and carrying out public choices about the community's growth and development.

During the Soviet era, almost all decisions were made centrally, with almost no powers or major responsibilities devolved to local authorities. Few levers or incentives promoted efficient local governance. Urban officials could not receive signals from the market, so they used planning in a directive rather than corrective manner. The physical development of cities was based not on zoning plans (which would guide development and indicate only what was not accept-able), but on master plans that dictated what was permitted. Land markets were nonexistent (all land was publicly owned). Housing markets were weak and inflexible (governed by the *Propiska* city per-mits system, a residence permit and migration recording tool whose use was documented in local police registers—and designed and developed by central authorities). Rental markets were mainly infor-mal. And services and infrastructure were subsidized heavily and coordinated from the center, primarily to serve production processes and citizens as workers in the system.

Impact of the Plan on the Structure of Soviet Cities

The plan affected the spatial allocation of people and activities—at the country level, by incentivizing people to places where markets would not have led them, and at the city level, by neglecting the externalities of urban growth. One of the defining features of the Soviet city was that it was built around a factory. In most cases, cities were developed as centers of production. Some cities were run by the industrial enterprises around which they were built. After World War II, Soviet planners pushed urban growth toward the colder areas, in an effort to populate the country's vast territory (exhibit 1.2). Markets

EXHIBIT 1.2

Mean Surface Temperature in the Soviet Union, January 1990
degree Celsius

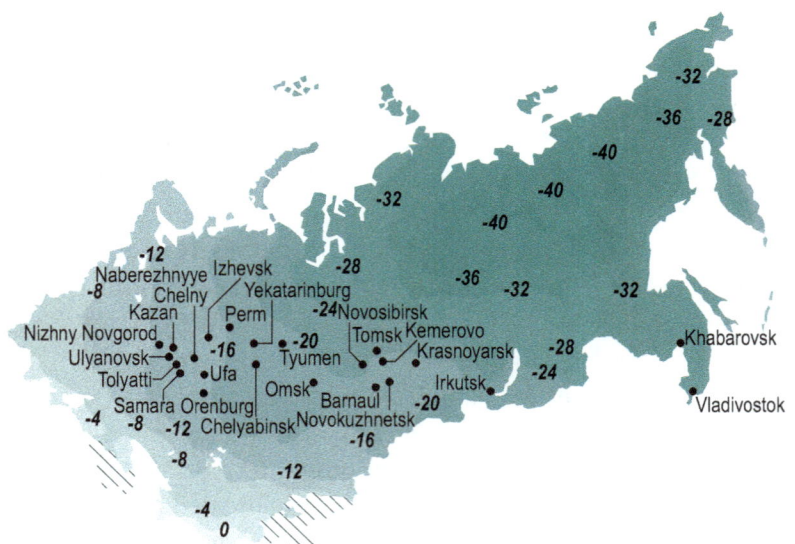

Source: Lydolph 1990.

certainly would have favored the growth of already established cities. Several smaller cities in the heartland grew to more than 30 times their original size (Hill and Gaddy 2003).

Within 50 years, many Soviet oblasts (second-tier administrative subdivisions in the former Soviet Union) went from being mainly rural to being at least 70 percent urban (Lewytzkyj 1979). Cities' growth in these oblasts did not happen organically. Some people were forcibly moved to cities, but most were induced to move by various incentives. The transfers helped colonize empty territory, guard the vast empire's borders, and exploit rich mineral deposits. The "booming" cities in Siberia often had no rural hinterland and were poorly connected to other urban centers. Food and service delivery were heavily subsidized, and many cities were completely cut off from the outside world in the harsh winter months. The pattern of city development and growth was the opposite of what the market would have dictated—moving inward and away from density (exhibit 1.3).

In a market economy, market forces dictate the size and distribution of cities (World Bank 2008). People generally follow jobs and other people. Quality of life issues (clement weather, good local services and infrastructure, affordable housing) also motivate people to locate in one place or another. Successful cities (those able to deliver productive employment and a good quality of life for residents) tend to breed more success through circular and cumulative causation; unsuccessful cities endure slow or even negative growth. In successful cities, the concentration of people creates a large market, which will attract more businesses, more jobs, and more people.

The great differentiator in this equation (what ensures that not all people and businesses end up in one city) is the price of land, which tends to rise in successful cities as more people and firms move there.[1] As the price goes up, it tends to reach a threshold that blocks entry for some people and firms, who relocate to cities that can meet their needs at lower cost. But the falling values of land and property in less successful cities deter potential developers who avoid Eurasian cities. These price signals profoundly influence both the distribution and the size of cities in a country. In a market-driven country like the United States, the largest cities are trade outposts situated along the Atlantic and Pacific coasts or on major lakes and rivers, while the interior of the country is less populated.

Although Russia has a population less than half that of the United States, it has about the same number of cities with populations of 500,000 or fewer (Hill and Gaddy 2003). But it has a much smaller number of mid-size cities. Just 15.5 percent of the Russian population lives in cities of more than 1 million. By contrast, 51.9 percent of

EXHIBIT 1.3

EXHIBIT 1.3

Size Distribution of Cities in the Soviet Union, 1939, 1959, 1974, and 1989

a. 1939

b. 1959

continued

EXHIBIT 1.3
Continued

c. 1974

d. 1989

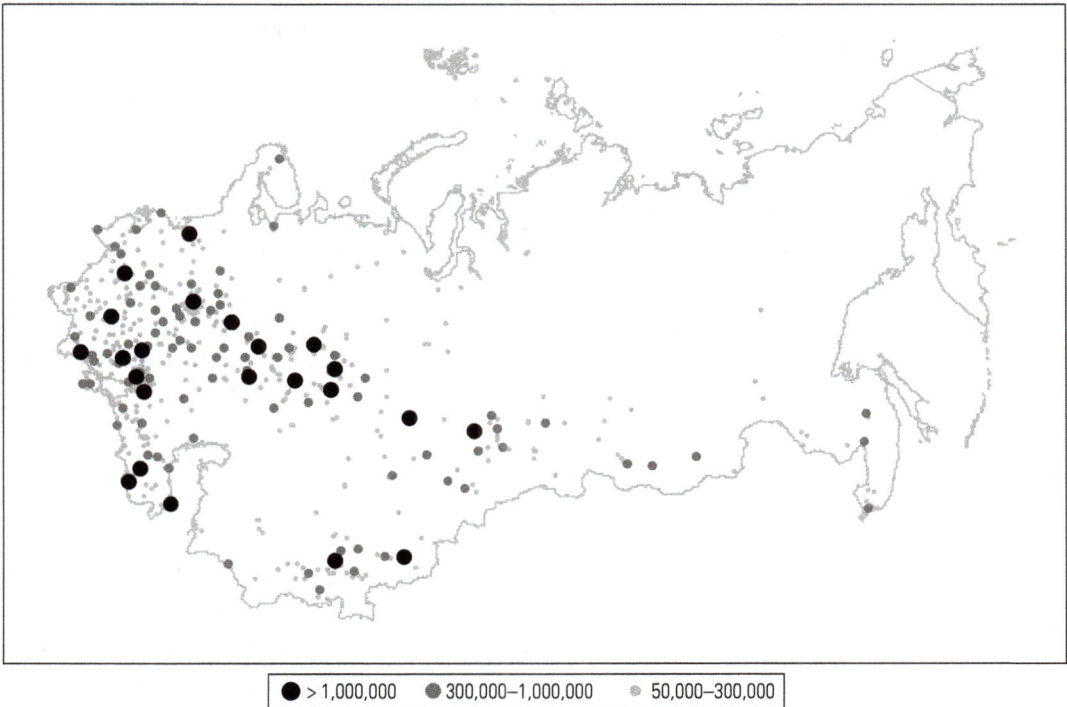

● > 1,000,000   ● 300,000–1,000,000   ● 50,000–300,000

Source: Authors, based on data from Lewytzkyj 1979.

the U.S. population lives in such cities. Comparisons with Brazil, a country closer in population size and development level to Russia, are also revealing. Both countries boast two large metropolises: Moscow (10.1 million people) and St. Petersburg (4.7 million) in Russia and São Paolo (10.3 million) and Rio de Janeiro (6.2 million) in Brazil. But while Brazil has four cities with populations of about 2.5 million, Russia has none in this middle range—St. Petersburg is followed, at some distance, by cities of about 1 million people.

Back to the Market: New Realities for Cities since the Breakup

After 1991 many of the industrial enterprises of the Soviet era found themselves with overinflated rosters of workers. As people in industry started losing their jobs, many moved back to the rural areas they originally had come from, eking out an existence by subsistence farming. Capital cities were also preferred destinations for internal migrants looking for job opportunities. But the most important flow was across borders, with workers from Central Asia and the South Caucasus choosing in large numbers to migrate to cities like Moscow and St. Petersburg, and workers from these cities trying to reach Western European cities. For former communist countries as a whole, the share of world value added in manufacturing decreased from 19.3 percent in 1980 to 8.9 percent in 1990 and 2.7 percent in 2001 (Teignier-Baqué 2010). Trade among them also collapsed due to the drop in economic output; the erection of border controls and trade barriers, including export controls; and complications arising from the methods used to resolve payments as new currencies were introduced. The Commonwealth of Independent States (CIS) countries lost their preferential access to their former allies in Eastern Europe, who reoriented their trade toward Western Europe. The loss of these "captive" markets rendered many of the low-quality manufacturing goods produced in the former Soviet Union uncompetitive and unmarketable on world markets.

The dissolution of the Soviet Union was followed by the integration of the former communist countries into the world trading system. In 1998, the EU accepted applications from 13 of these countries; on May 1, 2004, 8 joined the EU (the Czech Republic, Estonia, Hungary, Latvia, Lithuania, Poland, the Slovak Republic, and Slovenia). Two more, Bulgaria and Romania, joined on January 1, 2007. At the same time, Russia remained the largest country in the world in area and the largest natural gas producer, the second-most-powerful country in nuclear capabilities, and the world's second-largest producer of crude oil. Because of its dominance, it pulled Eurasian countries back into its sphere of economic and political influence, though Georgia has been demarcating itself. These two anchors, the EU and Russia, have been driving the economic and spatial restructuring of Eurasia.

In the end, the dismantling of central planning made it possible for the market to become the force driving the relocation of production and people. As the new economic geography and new trade theory suggest, the competitive advantage of leading markets depends largely on how efficient urban centers are (Fujita, Krugman, and Venables 2001). Given increasing returns to scale in production, transport costs, and trade, large urban centers better connected to domestic, regional, and global markets enjoy a self-sustaining agglomeration of economic activities, making it easier to diversify and expand production and exports.

New Realities of Agglomeration Economies

The new economic geography establishes that the internal geography of a country is shaped by the "home market effect" according to which leading production locales are more productive and thus attract more economic activities, reinforcing the divergence between leading and lagging areas (Fujita, Krugman, and Venables 2001). Openness to trade reinforces this effect, though the impact on the internal geography depends greatly on where the leading market is located. For instance, integration with the United States has led to a relocation of Mexican industry away from Mexico City and toward states along the U.S. border with good access to the U.S. market (Hanson 1996, 1997, 1998). Further, employment has grown more in regions that have larger agglomerations of industries with buyer-supplier relationships, suggesting that integration has made demand and cost link important determinants of industrial location.

Closeness to the EU explains the difference in the agglomeration dynamics observed between Central and Eastern European (CEE) countries and the Eurasian countries. After the overthrow of their socialist regimes in 1989–90, most CEE countries rapidly adopted market-based economic systems and redirected their political and economic relations toward the EU. One of the main benefits of the EU enlargement has been the boost in economic activity in both accession countries and member states. Eurasian countries, at the other end of the former communist empire, were exposed to weaker global trade flows. Russia remained the major trading partner for Central Asia, the South Caucasus, and other CIS countries, confining their exposure to the market forces of agglomeration, migration, and specialization to a Russia-centric bloc (Broadman 2005; World Bank 2008).

All capitals and leading cities of Eurasia attracted labor-intensive economic activities, but countries closer to the EU experienced the emergence of specialized urban centers along the border region. Cieślik (2004), looking at the difference in the attractiveness for foreign direct investment (FDI) of various Polish regions, found that regions bordering Belarus, Russia, and Ukraine were less attractive than regions along the European Union-15 (EU15) border of Poland. And Traistaru, Nijkamp, and Longhi (2003) found similar results for the geographic concentration of manufacturing in Bulgaria, Estonia, Hungary, Romania, and Slovenia. They found that all things being equal, industries with large economies of scale tended to locate close to large urban centers while research-oriented industries were attracted by regions closer to the EU15. Using regional data for 1996–2000, Brülhart and Koenig-Soubeyran (2006) also found similar results in their analysis of the structures of wage and employment within the Czech Republic, Hungary, Poland, the Slovak Republic, and Slovenia.

Entrepreneurs prefer to concentrate production when their activities generate increasing returns to scale. By contrast, public policy in Eurasia is still concerned with spatial equity, even after the breakup of the Soviet Union (World Bank 2009). The same concern is expressed in Kazakhstan, as reflected in the country's territorial development strategy. Most Eurasian countries have designed or are thinking about designing national strategies to facilitate the adoption and coordination of policies for regional and spatial development. Looking ahead, policy makers need to promote the changes that will make Eurasian cities the main drivers of growth in their countries. For this, they need to promote the policies that can unleash the positive externalities of agglomeration economies while containing negative externalities such as congestion and pollution.

New Realities of Migration

The early years of transition saw high levels of cross-border migration, as populations previously unable to move because of Soviet restrictions relocated to their ethnic or cultural homelands (Mansoor and Quillin 2006). These flows emerged simultaneously with refugee movements resulting from erupting civil and transborder conflicts among the region's newly emergent countries. As conflicts abated and economic reforms took root, economic motivations became the main driver of migration in Eurasia. The result of these trends has

been a broad biaxial pattern of migration among the transition economies, with one axis from the western part of the region to the EU
and another from the southern to the northern countries of Eurasia.
Although most migrants from the poorer Eurasian countries traveled
to middle-income Eurasian countries, many also moved west, toward
the EU and Turkey, seeking higher earnings. A number of Eurasian
migrants spent time in CEE countries or Turkey, hoping to move to
Western Europe.

The collapse of the Soviet Union provoked a large-scale repatria-
tion, the most massive of which was that of Russians (table 1.2).
Between 1990 and 1994, 1.7 million Russians residing in non-Slavic
republics—14 percent of the total Russian population in those
areas—moved to Russia. The numbers moving from areas of armed
conflicts were substantially higher: 42 percent of Russian residents
left Tajikistan, and 37 percent left the Trans-Caucasian countries.

TABLE 1.2

**Ethnic Composition of Net Migration from Eurasia (Excluding the
Russian Federation) and the Baltics to the Russian Federation, 1990–94**

thousands of people

Ethnic group	1990	1991	1992	1993	1994
Armenians	16.1	10.5	23.6	42.7	60.7
Azerbaijanis	−3.9	−3.8	−2.9	4.7	13.1
Belarussians	19.4	−0.9	−10.6	−5.9	10.1
Estonians	0	−0.1	0.2	0.3	0.3
Georgians	−2.8	−3.1	0.4	6.1	12.5
Kazakhstanis	−2.9	−6.6	−10.8	−6.8	1.1
Kyrgyz	−1.5	−2.1	−2.1	−1.0	0.1
Latvians	−0.4	−0.3	—	0.3	0.3
Lithuanians	−0.8	−0.8	−0.1	0.2	0.4
Moldovans	−2.1	−2.0	−3.0	—	3.2
Russians	199.9	117.7	360.1	419.4	612.4
Tajiks	−0.4	−0.6	0.5	2.9	3.9
Turkmens	−0.5	−1.6	−2.1	−1.2	—
Ukrainians	22.0	−25.9	−64.3	11.0	79.2
Uzbeks	−3.2	−4.5	−2.9	0.3	3.7
Others	49.3	29.0	69.7	80.8	113.4
Total	288.3	104.9	355.7	553.8	914.6

Source: Zaionchkovskaya 1996.
Note: Net migration is the difference between the number of migrants leaving and entering the region. — = not available.

Repatriations became the norm in the former Soviet Union and were not limited to Russians. In the early 1990s, all titular nationalities began to leave Russia for their homelands, though this pattern shifted again in 1993 and 1994.

Labor migration to thriving cities is now the most dynamic and large-scale migration flow in Eurasia. The interstate labor migration in the region is estimated at about 6.5–7.0 million, with about 1.5–2.0 million leaving Russia for jobs outside Eurasia, about 3 million entering Russia from the other Eurasian countries, and about 2 million (not including Russians) migrating to other Eurasian countries or outside Eurasia (Teignier-Baqué 2010). Nearly 1 of 3 families in Armenia, Azerbaijan, the Kyrgyz Republic, and Moldova and 1 of 10 in Kazakhstan, Russia, and Ukraine depend on migration-related earnings and remittances by relatives (Teignier-Baqué 2010). In 2007, these remittances amounted to 46 percent of gross domestic product (GDP) in Tajikistan, 34 percent in Moldova, 19 percent in the Kyrgyz Republic, 9 percent in Armenia, and 4 percent in Azerbaijan (Canagarajah and Kholmatov 2010).

Migration dynamics in Eurasian countries reinforced their connection with Russia's booming regions and with a few other Eurasian leading urban centers, mainly the capital cities. In the world's most dynamic economies, people move to maximize the returns to their education and skills (World Bank 2008). But with their legacy of centrally planned factory-cities and their inefficient facilities, Eurasian countries entered the post-Soviet era with an economic geography that sapped growth (Kontorovich 2000). The location of human and capital resources across regions and throughout the urban hierarchy differed from the patterns in advanced market economies. The movement out of lagging regions has been small relative to the total Eurasian population. The estimated surplus population of Siberia and the Far East remains high, at 17.6 million.[2] Eurasia has considerable scope for further internal migration to rebalance the location of economic activity and thus increase economic growth and improve social welfare. The leading urban centers of the region are the ideal candidates to attract these new workers.

New Realities of Trade Specialization

Trade among the former Soviet republics declined sharply after the dissolution of the Soviet Union, largely reflecting the disruption in production that the transition to a market mechanism caused, which required changes in supply patterns and a shift in output to goods demanded by the market (Havrylyshyn 1994). Another reason was the unnaturally high inward orientation of trade among the former Soviet republics, which caused trade flows with regions outside the COMECON to be much lower than they otherwise would have been. With independence and market reforms, a reorientation of trade to the rest of the world was to be expected. Indeed, seven years after the start of the transition, trade statistics showed that countries in Central Europe and the Baltics had trade-to-GDP ratios similar to those of market economies with comparable size and development levels (Havrylyshyn and Al-Atrash 1998). By contrast, many Eurasian countries appeared to be far less open and were unable to increase the degree of geographical diversification of their exports—a dichotomy confirmed by Broadman (2005).

Recent trade data show that the Russian-centric bloc identified by Broadman (2005) seems to be slowly changing in Central Asia. Indeed, in 2003 the top export destinations for nonnatural resource–intensive products from the Central Asian countries were Europe and Central Asia, including Russia and Turkey (32 percent); the EU15 (27 percent); and China (20 percent; figure 1.1). By 2008, the EU15 had taken the top spot (35 percent), followed by Europe and Central Asia (34 percent) and China (13 percent). While overall exports to Europe and Central Asia remained stable, exports to countries other than Russia and Turkey decreased from 15 percent to 9 percent. Exports within Central Asia remained low, at 1 percent.

The trade structure of Eurasian countries reveals much about their ongoing structural changes. The top three groups of exports from Central Asia countries during 2003–08 were mineral fuels, manufactured goods, and crude inedible materials (table 1.3). In 2008, mineral fuels represented 62 percent of exports from Central Asia, up from 47 percent in 2003. This trade structure differs greatly from that of Southeast Europe, where the top three exports were machinery and transport equipment (25 percent), manufactured goods (24 percent), and textile products (19 percent).

Eurasian countries' market potential was assessed by identifying their neighbors' access to the broader trade network through the import and export of intermediate goods. For this estimation, the neighbors of countries in Central Asia and the South Caucasus were ranked according to a market potential proxy measured as the neighbor's total trade in intermediate goods, using average trade data for 2003–07 from the United Nations Commodity Trade Statistics Database (COMTRADE). The difference in trade structure and trade direction between CEE countries and Eurasian countries was explained largely by the market potential of their respective neighborhoods.

FIGURE 1.1

Destination of Nonnatural Resource–Intensive Exports from the Central Asian Countries, 2003 and 2008

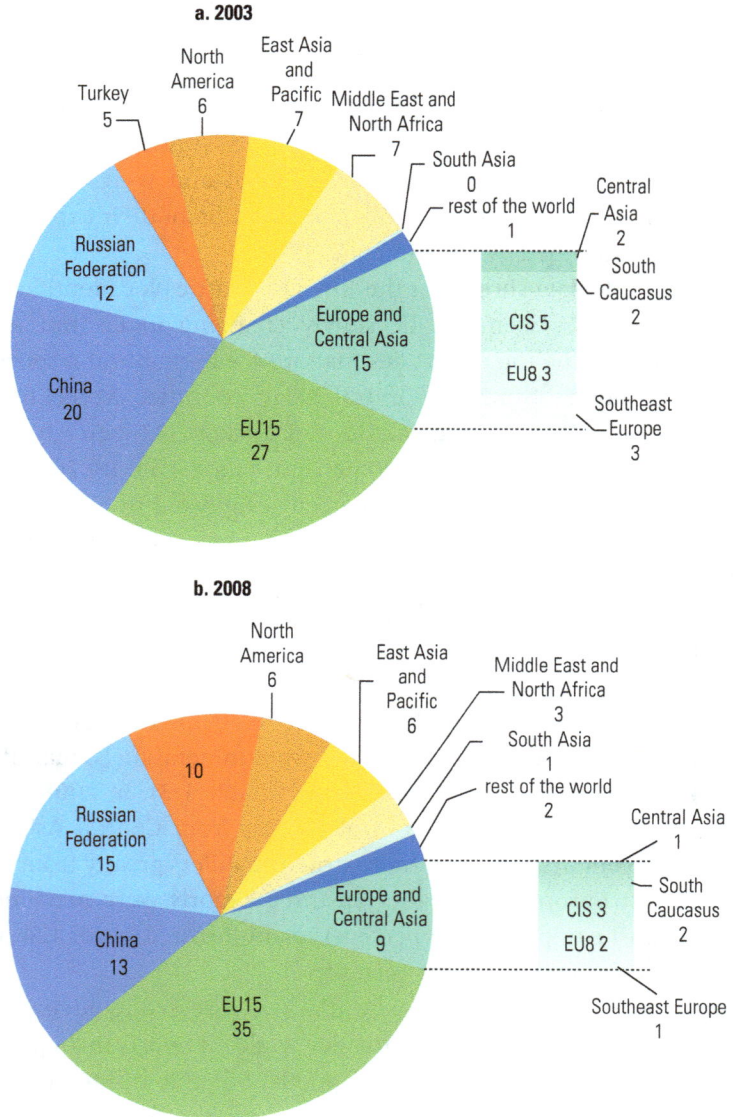

percent

a. 2003

b. 2008

Source: International Monetary Fund Direction of Trade Statistics database.
Note: CIS = Commonwealth of Independent States; EU8 = European Union-8; EU15 = European Union-15.

Many Eurasian countries are landlocked, and their production structure is skewed toward natural resource–intensive goods, making them less likely to attract substantial FDI outside these rent sectors. Diversification could start at the regional level if investors (domestic or foreign) find it profitable to establish production and

TABLE 1.3

Percentage of Total Exports, Unless Otherwise Indicated

trade structure, Central Asia and Southeast Europe, 2003 and 2008

Region	Food and live animals	Beverages and tobacco	Crude inedible materials except fuels	Mineral fuels, lubricants, and related materials	Animal and vegetable oils, fats, and waxes	Chemicals and related products	Manufactured goods	Machinery and transport equipment	Textile products	Commodities not classified elsewhere	Total trade, US$ millions
2003											
Central Asia	6.47	0.32	14.38	47.41	0.03	3.02	23.31	1.75	1.23	2.08	16,730
Southeast Europe	5.58	1.19	6.75	4.71	0.18	6.25	21.54	16.95	35.92	0.94	35,946
Europe and Central Asia	5.19	0.63	5.23	20.39	0.27	6.49	21.79	24.92	12.63	2.48	455,874
2008											
Central Asia	4.36	0.13	8.42	61.70	0.02	3.16	16.69	1.99	0.51	3.03	70,187
Southeast Europe	6.08	1.59	6.88	8.11	0.45	7.50	24.35	24.53	18.56	1.96	94,668
Europe and Central Asia	4.66	0.63	4.54	29.09	0.32	6.80	18.95	23.69	7.10	4.22	1,343,808

Source: United Nations Commodity Trade Statistics Database.

Note: Column headings reflect Standard International Trade Classification categories, revision 3.

distribution networks through the import and export of goods and services based on each country's competitive advantage. The *World Development Report 2009: Reshaping Economic Geography* proposes a policy framework for unleashing these forces, recommending institutions that unite places, infrastructure that connects places, and incentives that target places (World Bank 2008). Needed institutional reforms involve measures behind the border (macroeconomic stability, business environment, and standards and conformity issues), at the border (goods, services, people, and capital mobility across borders), and between borders (trade and transport facilitation initiatives). And needed infrastructure investments include productivity-enhancing infrastructure (information and communications technology, and research and development–related facilities), mobility-enhancing infrastructure (education/training and research centers), and connectivity-enhancing infrastructure (transportation infrastructure, transport, and logistics facilities). Such improvements can be made if urban centers are better connected to surrounding markets.

Going Forward: Rethinking Eurasian Cities

Eurasian countries have been through three major changes: the breakup of an empire, which transformed regions of the former Soviet Union into independent countries with sometimes competing interests and cumbersome border-crossing operations; the unleashing of market forces of agglomeration, migration, and specialization, which affected the form and function of settlements within these new countries; and the emergence of regional powers such as China, the EU, India, and Russia, which affected the structure and direction of trade of the new countries.

Looking ahead, the form and function of these cities need to be rethought to take advantage of market forces. The main issues are enhancing their connectivity to domestic and external markets to take advantage of the new biaxial Silk Road—and changing how they are financed to allow other Eurasian cities to complement Moscow, St. Petersburg, and Kiev as the anchors of this region in world markets.

Rethinking the Form and Function of Cities

After years of central planning, one of the main characteristics of Eurasian cities is the misallocation of land. Land in and around Soviet cities had two major idiosyncratic characteristics: it was centrally owned, thus preventing local stakeholders from responding flexibly to local dynamics, and its value was not factored into city development decisions. Cities other than Moscow could not adjust to a sudden influx of migrants by building new housing, by virtue of the *Propiska* system. Yet, people in the Soviet Union found their way to regional centers, altering the equilibrium between urban infrastructure and city dwellers. As economic prospects in only a few Eurasian cities continue to attract an increasing number of workers, it will be important to rethink the form of cities by revisiting their planning.

Most Eurasian cities did not have suburbs—not necessarily a bad thing, as compact development has benefits that far outweigh sprawl. But older urban centers, with traditions of growing organically, developed beyond the municipality itself. They tended to be surrounded by villages that provided some of the food needs of urban dwellers. As cities grew, so did these satellite developments.

In contrast to most Eurasian cities, Baku followed an organic growth pattern. In 1918, the city was fairly compact, with a population of 312,700 (exhibit 1.4). As it grew, satellite villages and towns started to develop around it. Some of Baku's rural communities have been swallowed by the expansion of the city, and new ones have formed farther out. This is how most cities, especially large ones, develop. For most cities, there exists a close relationship and interdependence with adjacent rural areas that often goes beyond simple trade. For example, rural land is often converted to allow city expansion, and the labor force in rural areas fills the demand in the city's growing economic base.

The planning of Eurasian cities should reflect this organic growth, allowing land and housing markets and urban infrastructures to adequately respond to the migration of workers to economic densities as countries move along the structural transformation from agriculture to industry to services. For this to happen, strong local institutions and supporting national institutions are needed, as Kazan, Russia, illustrates (box 1.1).

Modern planning suggests that where no clear reason for government intervention exists, decisions on land use should be left to land purchasers, with the government protecting some key locations, such as parkland, cultural heritage buildings, and social service provision centers. Local authorities should work with the central government to solve all property issues in order to reduce the costs of land transactions as much as possible. Land use regulations and building codes also need to be modernized and enforced. Using public infrastructure strategically will guide land development in

EXHIBIT 1.4
Development of Baku, 1918, 1940, 1960, and 1980

a. 1918

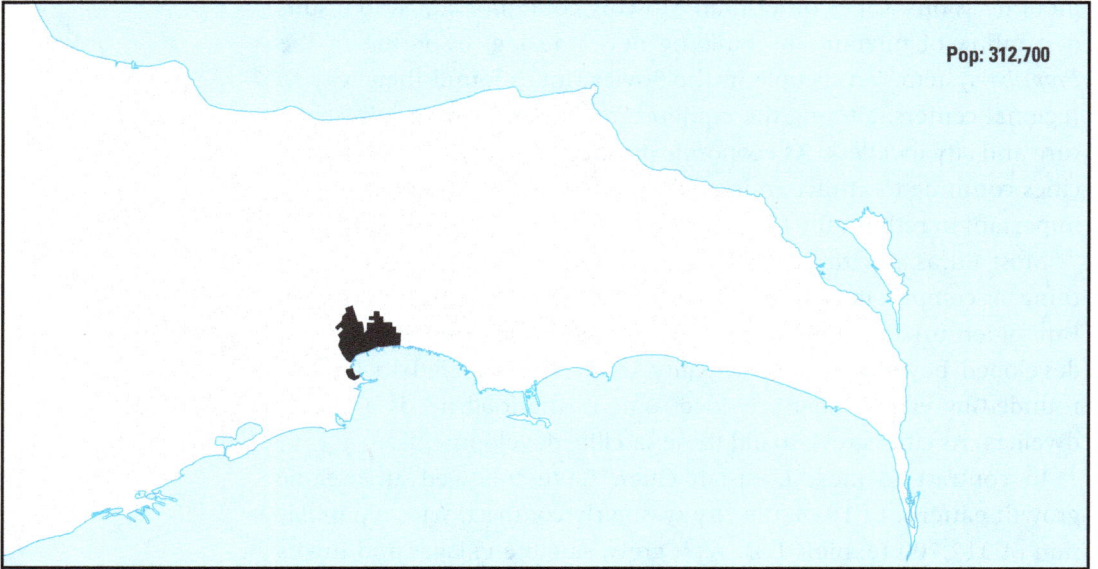

Pop: 312,700

b. 1940

Pop: 791,200

continued

EXHIBIT 1.4
Continued

c. 1960

Pop: 967,700

d. 1980

Pop: 1,595,000

Source: Baku master plans.
Note: Black areas represent built-up urban areas.

BOX 1.1

Local Institution Development in Kazan

Kazan scores best of the 10 Russian cities sampled by the World Bank's subnational Doing Business Indicators. Construction permits involve 54 different procedures in Moscow but only 23 in Kazan. Transferring property costs 0.35 percent of its value in Rostov-on-Don and only 0.15 percent in Kazan. These reforms were possible thanks to major governance changes, such as the election of city officials instead of their appointment by the president of the Republic of Tatarstan as before. The city administration now has greater incentive to serve the people with efficient and transparent regulations.

But more can be done. Armenia, Georgia, and the Kyrgyz Republic easily beat even Russia's most progressive cities. Obtaining a construction permit in these countries requires only 10–20 procedures (though the cost of permits and property registration may sometimes be expensive relative to per capita income). In Kazan, obtaining a construction permit still takes about 350 days, and the permit may be refused if the construction proposal is inconsistent with the city's master plan, which dictates what types of land use should take place where. These planning decisions have been made with opinion polls of public and private organizations across the city, thus they partly reflect the wishes of land users, not just the wishes of planners. But changing a zoning decision is still convoluted and time-consuming: a proposal must be made to the city's department of architecture, then to the city's land commission, and finally to the city parliament.

response to market needs. To revitalize the housing market in booming Eurasian cities, it will be important to develop rental housing markets, support homeowners associations, create and enforce rules for the use of public spaces, and offer incentives for façade improvement and maintenance.

The functions of Eurasian cities also need to be rethought. The rural settlements, towns, and cities of a country coexist, delivering different services to firms and people. Rural settlements tend to engage in agricultural activities. Towns engage in the nonfarm activities that increase the marketability of agricultural products in urban areas and outside the country. Cities permit the sharing of private and public factors of production, the pooling of labor markets, and the sharing of information. The diversity of cities favors an advanced division of labor allowing specialization in various activities.

The greening of cities is now an integral component of their competitive advantage. As such, the authorities of Eurasian cities as well as national authorities need to address city pollution appropriately (exhibit 1.5). Green spaces help cool air during summer, reduce

EXHIBIT 1.5

Pollution in Former Soviet Union Cities, 1992 and 2004

Map produced by ZOÏ Environment Network, January 2012

Pollution

~~~ river pollution   //// sea pollution   ■ most polluted cities

Air emissions from stationary sources (thousand tones/year)

○ 1992 (no data available for Astana, Luhansk, Makeevka, and Shymkent)

● 2004

500
200
100
50
20
10

Source: World Bank data.

greenhouse gas emissions and air pollution (they are one of the most effective carbon sinks), conserve energy and reduce storm water runoff, and add to quality of life. Safe, efficient, and environment-friendly public transportation is also important for a city's competitiveness. To compete with cities worldwide in attracting skilled workers—which cities must do as urban economies become the driving force of production and trade—policy makers need to improve the livability of Eurasian cities, at least the leading ones. Protecting the stock of urban green space; reducing industrial pollution; making public services infrastructure more efficient; and reducing, reusing, and recycling waste are key investments for Eurasian cities that can help the cities attract more sophisticated workers and firms. This in turn will facilitate the structural transformation of Eurasia from an inward-looking region to one connected to global value chains in key industry and service sectors.

Rethinking the Connectivity of Cities

By expanding to what was then called Turkestan (covering what are now the five Central Asian countries) in the 19th century, the Russian empire's main goal was to solidify its positions in the south to stop British expansion. Later the economic significance of the region started to rise, with Turkestan becoming an important producer of cotton when the American Civil War started driving up the price of cotton. The empire also implemented cotton industrial projects in the region, including improvements in hard infrastructure. One of the key improvements was the launch of the Trans-Caspian Railway in 1880, from Krasnovodsk to Samarkand, which it reached in 1888, and on to Tashkent. In 1906 another railway—the Trans-Aral Railway—started to operate on the route from Orenburg to Tashkent.

Russia understood the strategic importance of linking an east-west rail axis to the north-south connection. In March 1891, the future Czar Nicholas II inaugurated the construction of the Far East segment of the Trans-Siberian Railway, completed in 1916. Its main route originated in St. Petersburg at Moskovsky Vokzal and ran through Moscow, Chelyabinsk, Omsk, Novosibirsk, Irkutsk, Ulan-Ude, Chita, and Khabarovsk to Vladivostok through southern Siberia. The Chinese Eastern Railway was constructed as the Russo-Chinese part of the Trans-Siberian Railway. It connected Russia with China and provided a shorter route to Vladivostok.

The evolution of the national and regional transport and communications systems in the former Soviet Union countries was closely linked to the geographic, economic, and political developments that shaped the Soviet era. It led to a hierarchical network of cities that were more evenly distributed by size than in other countries. In the post-Soviet era, the proximity to the EU market and the increased integration favored the emergence in CEE countries of urban centers closer to Western Europe and reinforced economic diversification in the capital cities. By contrast, agglomeration dynamics in Eurasia were attenuated by the long distance to leading world markets, which favored the consolidation of capitals and a few other leading cities, supported by the extension of public transportation. This agglomeration is not a handicap. Around the world, leading cities play a key role in production and trade by delivering a range of services, sustaining economic activities. Leading cities tend to be well connected domestically and externally—and tend to offer the most diversified production.

Small countries far from world markets, which make up part of Eurasia, face the stiffest challenges to economic growth and need a clear vision and strong commitment to cooperative solutions. These countries need to join "natural" groupings in which all participants support the objective of deep integration and adopt strategies for institutional cooperation and regional infrastructure (World Bank 2010). Enhanced regional cooperation could create a policy environment conducive to connectivity infrastructures, such as road corridors and broadband networks. A regional connectivity network depends on the functioning of the links and nodes in individual countries. Regional cooperation is thus vital.

As Russia has reoriented its economy from plan to market, spatial efficiency has improved. Between 1989 and 2004, almost all new firms chose to locate near Moscow and St. Petersburg, the gateways to international markets (Brown and others 2008). The sectoral composition of the economies of Moscow and St. Petersburg is more diversified than that in other locations, and the two cities are better positioned than others to lead Russia's diversification. Russia took a major step toward economic integration when it recently joined the World Trade Organization (WTO). Although special economic zone initiatives have failed to foster diversification, a new generation of special economic zones could provide a better business environment for foreign firms—if they are designed to promote agglomeration economies, are less distortional, and are better planned to stimulate investment in promising sectors.

By comparison, East Asian economies have become integrated through a dense array of regional production networks. These supply chains started with outsourcing by Japanese multinationals in the 1980s, as wages and land costs in the dense production area of Tokyo grew prohibitive for competitive manufacturing (Gill and Kharas 2007). Economic congestion in Japan; Hong Kong SAR, China; Korea; and Taiwan, China, has resulted in spillovers—first to middle-income countries in Southeast Asia and then to China, as the barriers of economic ideology were reduced. Recently, supply chains have

centered on China with its massive assembly operations in Guang-
dong and Shenzhen. As China has matured, it too has become an
exporter of intermediate goods and capital equipment. Because they
are landlocked, most Eurasian countries are at a large distance from
the booming Chinese eastern coast. But the Xinjiang Uygur region in
western China, with its nearly 21 million inhabitants, is an immediate gateway to China that is available particularly to leading cities in
Central Asia.

India's rise is also an opportunity for Central Asian countries. With
its domestic market of more than 1 billion people, India is attracting
an increasing share of industrial and service activities that may have
some spillover effects in Eurasian countries if adequate regional and
global integration policies are pursued by both India and these countries. However, stormy relations in South Asia after the end of British
colonial rule in 1947 prevented the region from taking advantage of
its market size: more than a fifth of the world's people. It took four
decades before trade volumes between India and Pakistan passed
those of the early 1950s (Nabi and Nasim 2001). In 2004, the two
countries engaged in a "composite dialog" on peace and security
issues, including terrorism and drug trafficking, confidence-building
measures, economic and commercial cooperation, and friendly
exchanges in various fields. On a broader regional basis, the South
Asian Association for Regional Cooperation is a forum to discuss
development challenges, such as collaboration in energy production
and water basin management. The greatest challenge for India, the
largest country by far in South Asia, is to take the lead in promoting a
common agenda (World Bank 2007b).

The competitive advantage of neighborhoods with big countries
such as China, India, and Russia is the size of their markets, the
breadth of their human capital, and the volume of remittances they
receive. Economic activities generating substantial economies of scale
benefit from being concentrated in countries with leading areas that
have strong agglomerations and better market access (Antweiler and
Trefler 2002). This tendency creates tensions, as most investment will
go to these countries, usually the largest in the region. The challenges
are to balance political and economic concerns between leading and
lagging countries—and to ensure spillovers of direct and indirect
benefits to lagging areas. Facing these challenges of division and distance requires institutions that can ensure policies and governance
that promote trade, factor mobility, and regional growth and infrastructure. The result will be to connect lagging and leading countries,
link regional economic centers, and favor regional production networks that are better integrated with the global economy.

Rethinking the Financing of Cities

Planning, connecting, and greening Eurasian cities will require finance (see table 1.4). In the transition era, funding for infrastructure maintenance declined dramatically, affecting the availability and reliability of services. The problem was heightened by the fact that the connective infrastructures were designed to cater to several republics that are now independent countries, sometimes with competing interests. The challenge is to find the resources to maintain, rehabilitate, and operate these large infrastructures. Several countries and cities are trying to develop cost-recovery mechanisms for the road transport sector. One focus is on road tolling, though work is being done on road funds, which have been instrumental in enhancing the sustainability of road maintenance financing elsewhere, notably in Africa.

The system for financing cities—and the infrastructure connections among them—have undergone a substantial transformation since the breakup of the Soviet Union. Although railroad transport continues to be the backbone of the long-distance transport system and to be largely self-financing, competition from trucks, buses, and

TABLE 1.4
Issues That Cities Face in the Former Soviet Union and Ways Forward

Period	Planning	Connecting	Greening	Financing
Soviet past	Master plans instead of zoning and central planners instead of urban planners; cities built around industrial areas and land misallocated	Hierarchical structure oriented toward Moscow, with limited horizontal links among lower order centers	Cost of externalities not considered in public policies; broad access to public transport; high rates of access to water and sanitation; recycling programs	System based on plan targets and intraparty negotiations; tariffs highly subsidized
Transitional present	High ownership rates and weak rental markets, with misallocated housing stock and missing or poorly enforced city planning regulations	Institutions established to manage connectivity infrastructure and develop sector plans, but progress moving at different pace across the region	Reduced pollution as firms went bankrupt; collapse of recycling systems; deterioration of public transit	Move to modern subnational finance with transparent systems of revenue sharing and equalization transfers, with some countries moving faster than others
Market future	Collaboration between local and central government to solve property issues, modernize land use regulations, and use public infrastructure development strategically	Promotion of a few cities well connected to world markets by road, rail, air, and telecommunication links; development of regional institutions for corridor management and interstate cooperation on connectivity issues	Preservation of positive features of the former Soviet Union; enforcement of existing regulations; improvement of livability by building cities for people and taking care of the environment	Increase in personal income tax rates; enforcement of payment of housing maintenance fees; increase in water tariffs; expanding of metering and raising of public transport tariffs; for big cities, exploration of public-private partnerships for large connectivity projects

private automobiles is slowly eroding the market share of rail transport, reducing the scope for cross-subsidies to loss-making business lines such as rail passenger transport. A large expansion in highway traffic has increased pressure for funding road network upgrading and maintenance. Private cell phone companies are now largely filling the gaps in the former landline-based telephone service.

Several Eurasian countries have encouraged more private sector involvement in transport and other infrastructure investments, reflecting the global trend that started in the 1990s. But private sector investments have been largely concentrated in a few countries, namely Armenia, Kazakhstan, Russia, Ukraine, and Uzbekistan. Over time, most investment has gone to Russia, though the single largest project was for the railway concession in Armenia. Most private sector investment projects in transport have been in two sectors, airports and seaports. This is not surprising, as these are the modes where most progress has been made in liberalization—and where revenue streams are easier to capture.

Changes have also occurred in the systems used to finance infrastructure services within cities, including the urban road network, water supply, sewerage, district heating, housing maintenance, and public transport transit. These services are generally the responsibilities of subnational governments. In the Soviet era, funding levels for subnational governments were determined largely through intraparty negotiations. In general, that system has been replaced by more objective and mechanical systems of subnational finance, though more so in some countries than in others. Even cities that have benefited from such reforms find themselves fiscally constrained, however, and unable to raise revenues from the most appropriate source—the consumers of urban services themselves.

Big cities in Eurasia have access to broad-based personal income taxes, but tax rates are low. These cities do not benefit from equalization transfers. And they bear enormous responsibilities in social sectors such as education, health, and the social safety net. Because an increase in central government transfers is not an option (given more urgent needs in smaller cities), it is important to find ways to make the people pay—through benefit taxes, tariffs, and fees—for using some types of urban infrastructure. Given the low rate of personal income tax in the former Soviet Union, there is room to increase these revenue sources to generate more funds for the needs of larger cities. Property tax, supposed to be the largest tax source for cities, could be revamped to simplify its administration and broaden its base. And tariffs and fees could be increased to approach cost-recovery levels, particularly for water and public transportation in large cities.

Looking ahead, three interrelated policy instruments are required to ensure the full participation of Eurasian cities in world markets:

- *Develop institutions to help integrate these cities into the world economy.* The most propitious change would be the accession to the WTO of the Eurasian countries that are not yet members, not just for the trade benefits but also for the related domestic economic and judicial reforms. Beyond that are opportunities to build institutions to improve the investment climate, strengthen the rule of law, and make national borders easier to penetrate by reducing trade barriers.

- *Improve infrastructure to connect to world markets.* Eurasia's trade facilities were built primarily around natural resource exports and intraregional trade. With the reorientation of markets, imports and exports can be facilitated by improving the infrastructure for integration with the EU, China, and India. Such improvements include seaport and airport development, construction of roads to Western Europe, and development of transshipment options through the Black Sea and Far East.

- *Concentrate incentives to attract capital and knowledge.* Special economic zones are a good starting point if they are designed to foster agglomeration economies and diversification rather than to provide rent-seeking opportunities to well-connected businesspeople. They also need to be more specifically targeted spatially so as to support the reform agenda. Useful lessons can be drawn from countries that successfully developed such zones, such as China, Malaysia, and Mauritius. Their experience suggests that successful zones can become strong catalysts for economywide change in just 15 years, rapidly transforming the entire economy (Farole and Akinci 2011).

As the *World Development Report 2009: Reshaping Economic Geography* illustrates, Eurasia (excluding Russia) is a 3D region—a region with low *density*, long *distance*, and many *divisions* (World Bank 2008). Securing accessibility to leading regional markets such as China, India, and Russia is thus critical. All three policy instruments suggested should be thoroughly applied: key institutions should be developed to unite the countries, key connective infrastructures should be established between domestic and regional markets, and targeted interventions should be undertaken to compensate countries for short-term losses from this deepened economic integration.

Policy makers at the highest levels in these countries should put accessibility at the top of their agendas. Indeed, the economic geography challenges facing 3D regions call for a bolder regional integration agenda to overcome economic divisions between trading partners, reduce the distance to major regional markets, and boost economic density domestically. If integration succeeds, the "home market effect" should help the region's major cities capture most of the benefits of agglomeration, thereby attracting increasing return to scale activities from other leading cities in the short and medium terms. With the largest cities in the region—outside of Moscow and St. Petersburg—Kazakhstan, Ukraine, and Uzbekistan should play a leading role in the cross-country implementation to secure accessibility to regional markets, thus balancing the unevenness of short-term gains from regional integration and securing long-term survival and success.

Notes

1. Other centrifugal forces (congestion, pollution, and crime) also influence city growth, but they are to some extent determined by land availability and values.
2. These are the "extra" people compared with population densities in Canada's remote frontier regions, where the economic geography has been largely market driven (Mikhailova 2005).

References

Antweiler, Werner, and Daniel Trefler. 2002. "Increasing Returns and All That: A View from Trade." *American Economic Review* 92 (1): 93–119.

Bergson, Abram. 1964. *The Economics of Soviet Planning*. New Haven: Yale University Press.

Broadman, Harry J., ed. 2005. *From Disintegration to Reintegration: Eastern Europe and the Former Soviet Union in International Trade*. Washington, DC: World Bank.

Brown, David, Marianne Fay, John Felkner, Somik V. Lall, and Hyoung Gun Wang. 2008. "The Death of Distance? Economic Implications of Infrastructure Improvement in Russia." Office of the Chief Economist, Europe and Central Asia Region, World Bank, Washington, DC.

Brülhart, Marius, and Pamina Koenig-Soubeyran. 2006. "New Economic Geography Meets Comecon: Regional Wages and Industry Location in Central Europe." *Economics of Transition* 14 (2): 245–67.

Canagarajah, Sudharshan, and M. Kholmatov. 2010. *Migration and Remittances in CIS Countries During the Global Economic Crisis*. Vol. 16 of *Europe & Central Asia Knowledge Brief*. Washington, DC: World Bank.

Cieślik, Andrzej. 2004. "Location of Multinational Firms and National Border Effects: The Case of Poland." Presentation at the conference of the Association de Science Régionale de Langue Française, Brussels, September 1–3.

Farole, Thomas, and Gokhan Akinci, eds. 2011. *Special Economic Zones: Progress, Emerging Challenges, and Future Directions*. Report 63844. Washington, DC: World Bank.

Fujita, Masahisa, Paul Krugman, and Anthony J. Venables. 2001. *The Spatial Economy: Cities, Regions and International Trade*. Cambridge, MA: MIT Press.

Gill, Indermit, and Homi Kharas. 2007. *An East Asian Renaissance: Ideas for Economic Growth*. Washington, DC: World Bank.

Hanson, Gordon. 1996. "Economic Integration, Intra-Industry Trade, and Frontier Regions." *European Economic Review* 40 (3–5): 941–49.

———. 1997. "Increasing Returns, Trade and the Regional Structure of Wages." *Economic Journal* 107 (440): 113–33.

———. 1998. "Regional Adjustment to Trade Liberalisation." *Regional Science and Urban Economics* 28 (4): 419–44.

Havrylyshyn, Oleh. 1994. "Reviving Trade amongst the Newly Independent States." *Economic Policy* 9 (19): 172–90.

Havrylyshyn, Oleh, and Hassan Al-Atrash. 1998. "Opening Up and Geographic Diversification of Trade in Transition Economies." IMF WP/98/22, International Monetary Fund, Washington, DC.

Hill, Fiona, and Clifford G. Gaddy. 2003. *The Siberian Curse: How Communist Planners Left Russia Out in the Cold*. Washington, DC: Brookings Institution Press.

Kontorovich, Vladimir. 2000. "Can Russia Resettle the Far East?" *Post-Communist Economies* 12 (3): 365–84.

Lewytzkyj, Borys. 1979. *The Soviet Union: Figures-Facts-Data*. Munich: K.G. Saur.

Lydolph, Paul E. 1990. *Geography of the USSR.* 5th ed. Elkhart Lake, WI: Misty Valley.

Mansoor, Ali, and Bryce Quillin, eds. 2006. *Migration and Remittances: Eastern Europe and the Former Soviet Union*. Washington, DC: World Bank.

Mikhailova, Tatiana. 2005. "Where Russians Should Live: A Counterfactual Alternative to Soviet Location Policy." Unpublished report, August 26.

Nabi, Ijaz, and Anjum Nasim. 2001. "Trading With the Enemy—A Case for Liberalizing Pakistan–India Trade." In *Regionalism and Globalization—Theory and Practice*, ed. Sajal Lahiri, 170–98. London: Routledge.

Sassen, Saskia. 1991. *The Global City*. Princeton, NJ: Princeton University Press.

Schiffer, Jonathan R. 1989. *Soviet Regional Economic Policy: The East-West Debate over Pacific Siberian Development*. Basingstoke, U.K.: Macmillan in association with the University of Birmingham, Centre for Russian and East European Studies.

Teignier-Baqué, Marc. 2010. "Economic Interactions amongst the Soviet Union Republics: Literature and Data Review." Background paper for this book.

Traistaru, Iulia, Peter Nijkamp, and Simonetta Longhi. 2003. "Determinants of Manufacturing Location in EU Accession Countries." Presentation at the 2003 European Regional Science Association Congress, University of Jyväskylä, Finland.

World Bank. 2007a. *World Development Report 2008: Agriculture for Development.* Washington, DC: World Bank.

———. 2007b. *South Asia: Growth and Regional Integration.* New Delhi: World Bank.

———. 2008. *World Development Report 2009: Reshaping Economic Geography.* Washington, DC: World Bank.

———. 2009. *Russian Federation—Regional Development and Growth Agglomerations: The Longer Term Challenges of Economic Transition in the Russian Federation.* Report 45486-RU. Washington, DC: World Bank, Poverty Reduction and Economic Management Unit, Europe and Central Asia Region.

———. 2010. "Reshaping Russia's Economic Geography." Unpublished report, World Bank, Washington, DC.

Zaionchkovskaya, Zhanna A. 1996. "Migration Patterns in the Former Soviet Union." In *Cooperation and Conflict in the Former Soviet Union: Implications for Migration*, ed. Jeremy R. Azrael and Emil A. Payin, 15–48. Arlington, VA: RAND Center for Russian and Eurasian Studies.

CHAPTER 2

Planning Cities

Spotlight—Planning Tbilisi, Georgia

Renewing a driving license used to take hours or even days in Tbilisi, Georgia, with long waiting lines and onerous paper-work. Perhaps informal payments would be required, too. But now the system is computerized, and residents report the process takes only a few minutes. It's a small part of daily life, but small parts add up to a larger whole. How has institutional change affected Eurasian cities, and what can be learned from successes?

Similar institutional reforms in Georgia go beyond driving licenses, improving key parts of Georgia's urban system. Urban land use regulations now include a "single window" mechanism for planning applications. Documents need only be submitted once, rather than in several places at several times to several government agencies. The government is then responsible for passing the application between relevant agencies. The new regulations also include a principle that "silence is consent": if an applicant for planning does not hear back from the relevant administrative bodies in a set period, he or she is permitted to assume the answer is positive. Government officials from Georgia have been invited to share their experiences with other Eurasian countries, including Armenia, Azerbaijan, the Kyrgyz Republic, Tajikistan, and Uzbekistan, where there has been some attempt to make similar institutional improvements.

Such reforms permit Georgia's cities to evolve with market demand rather than the wishes of central planners. But they also include safeguards to ensure that the needs of individuals and firms are balanced by some social values. For example, to maintain the aesthetic value of its old city center, Tbilisi limits the floor-area ratio[a] in some parts of the city to 2.2, even though more financial value could be derived from taller buildings. Tbilisi suffers from a severe lack of Class A office space[b]—its vacancy rates have effectively been zero since 2005—but large skyscrapers will not become a feature of Tbilisi's city center, to preserve its spectacular historic skyline.

The roles for city planning and institutional reform in Eurasian cities are the subject of this chapter, which reviews trends and recommends several priority measures.

a. The floor-area ratio is the limit imposed to the ratio of a building's total floor area to the size of the parcel of land upon which it is built.
b. According to Building Owners and Managers Association (BOMA), Class A office buildings are prestigious buildings competing for premier office users, have high quality standard finishes, state-of-the-art systems, exceptional accessibility, and a definite market presence.

Key Issues

• Eurasia's urban population has started shifting toward the norms of other countries, driven by a move from planning to the market. These changes are both within and between cities.

• But weak rental markets, misallocated housing stock, and missing or poorly enforced city planning regulations hinder the process.

• These bottlenecks in establishing efficient cities could be alleviated through collaboration between local and central governments to modernize land use regulations, solve property issues, and implement strategic public infrastructure.

In many circles in transition economies, *planning* continues to be a bad word, tied to the failures of the communist systems. It is considered a remnant, a relic, a communist tool—something to be avoided. Several Eurasian countries have been among the most vigorous opponents of planning in the past two decades. Following the demise of the communist systems in the early 1990s, many countries reversed course, adapting systems in which the market reigned supreme and planning played little or no role. With almost complete laissez-faire approaches, dwindling budgets, and minimal experience of decentralized city management, many Eurasian urban centers hit on hard times during the transition to a market economy.

Leaders in these countries failed to acknowledge that planning itself is not bad. Good planning is part of the basic toolkit of public interventions (along with regulation and fiscal measures) to enhance market efficiencies, while mitigating market inefficiencies. Urban planning is a key to ensuring economically efficient, socially inclusive, and environmentally healthy cities—what the international community increasingly refers to as "sustainable cities" (Suzuki and others 2010).

Soviet-style planning was primarily about standardization and the mitigation of inefficiencies in a system not run by market rules.[1] In dealing with market inefficiencies, the Soviets focused on markets' inability to ensure some social welfare outcomes (such as a more equal distribution of wealth), but paid little or no attention to issues pertaining to public goods, economic inefficiency, or environmental externalities.

This chapter describes the distortions created by central planning in cities, how these distortions were amplified (or only partly corrected) in the transition years of the 1990s and 2000s, and what needs to be done for more sustainable urban outcomes. By not letting cities develop based on market signals, central planning distorted the growth and location of cities; within cities, Soviet-style planning neglected the positive and negative externalities of urban growth. Eurasian cities have to address both the distortions from Soviet centralized planning and the market inefficiencies that affect them today. This chapter, looking at urban planning issues, identifies ways that they could be addressed to produce more sustainable outcomes.

The Soviet Past: The Era of Soviet Planning

Understanding the Soviet past is important to comprehending what happened in the transition years and solving problems and challenges. Most of the former Soviet Union countries underwent almost

70 years of central planning (longer than other centrally planned systems). The aftereffects of Soviet policies are thus both more pronounced and harder to undo than in other former communist countries. This section examines three key issues paramount to healthy city development in market systems: land, housing, and infrastructure and related public services.

Together with strong and clear property rights, the ability to price land is a major tenet of a well-functioning market economy (De Soto 2003). Urban spatial planning influences city development primarily through land and its price, location, ownership structure, and so forth.

Land in and around Soviet cities had two major idiosyncratic characteristics. It had no recognized value, in that Soviet planners did not factor land value in their city development decisions. And it was centrally owned, thus preventing local stakeholders from responding flexibly to local dynamics. Housing, and city planning in general, was defined by standardization, with a focus on quantity, not quality. What Ford did for car manufacturing, the Soviet *Glavmosstroy* (house-building combine) did for housing development. Public services were more widely available than in other countries of the same development level (for instance, almost universal potable water coverage in urban areas), though, again, the focus was on quantity, not quality, with poor maintenance, high subsidies, and low or nonexistent tariffs (which often encouraged resource wastage) undermining efficiency.

Master Planning versus Zoning, Central Planners versus Urban Planners

In the Soviet system, urban land was allocated at the whim of central planners. Master plans were devised for nearly all cities, and neighborhoods were designed and constructed wholesale. Individual preferences played no role, and housing was often allocated based on how close it was to the workplace.

One of the most striking misallocations of city land by Soviet planners was selecting prime areas for industrial uses. Newer cities and their urban structures often formed around industries. The location of industrial enterprises was often inefficient, with enterprises occupying land that could have yielded higher value from other uses. In addition, the size of this land was seldom optimal. Proper planning was not done for changing economic structures, increasing labor costs, or benefiting from new technology. To accommodate the shift from industrial production to services, flexible land markets in market economies have ensured a better reallocation of land for the most productive uses, inducing factories to relocate to cheaper land away from the center city, thus favoring more environmentally and economically sustainable land uses.

Whereas Soviet planners took a normative approach in designing urban structure, urban planners in market economies understood that cities cannot be optimally planned. As Bertaud (2010, 3) notes:

> Because of the complexity of the changing factors influencing labor mobility, it is not possible to design a city structure that would permanently optimize the mobility of labor and goods. Darwinian evolutionary forces are constantly putting pressure on urban spatial structures. As technology and economic parameters change over time, a city spatial structure would evolve toward increased efficiency only when households and firms are able to make multiple tradeoffs between location, the mode of transport, and the consumption of land and floor space. In a well-functioning market, the spatial distribution of real estate prices would reflect multiple and competing consumers' preferences. . . . To ensure that urban spatial structures stay efficient governments have to allow real estate markets to work with as few distortions as possible.

Land within a city should be allowed to be traded freely and transparently. Property rights should be guaranteed, and transaction costs within land markets (for example, the cost of identifying the owner of a parcel of land) should be reduced. A balance is necessary between publicly owned land (for parks and public spaces) and privately owned land (for the organic development of the city).

Urban planners try to enhance market efficiencies and reduce market inefficiencies. In doing so, they need to be guided by the political process, which reflects public choice regarding the balance between public and private interests—for example, determining how heavily to weigh protection of a city's cultural heritage in its development. Thus, city spatial plans and zoning regulations should be developed and updated openly, with extensive public input and communication, and plans and regulations should be monitored and enforced transparently and fairly, according to the rule of law.

In addition, urban planners often mediate between disagreeing parties within a city. They reduce transaction costs and increase information flow where property rights alone cannot ensure a compromise. For example, people in communities next to an airport might complain about airplane noise. City planners could work with the airport authorities to reduce the noise level (say, by changing the entry point for landing airplanes) or zone the land around the airport to prevent further housing construction.

Housing: Quantity Over Quality

If land is a critical raw material for city development, housing is one of the main products. Housing provides shelter for a city's lifeblood—its people. Ensuring the availability of good-quality housing is one of the fundamental challenges of city management, central to the well-being and satisfaction of residents.

But housing quality did not rank high on Soviet planners' agenda. Housing had to be built cheaply and quickly to accommodate the rapidly growing population and the massive population movements from rural to urban areas. As housing production technologies improved, housing quality fell. In the 1950s and early 1960s, government-built buildings had brick walls and were at most five stories, but with the *Glavmosstroy*, housing construction shifted to high-rise, prefab buildings made of concrete.

That these buildings were inexpensive was one of their only redeeming qualities—their shortcomings abounded. Most apartment blocks were built with a short planned life, some as little as 30 years. They were poorly insulated. The interiors looked shabby, even when fairly new. There was no common space. The hallways, staircases, and elevators were often unaesthetic and unsanitary. And building maintenance was in most cases handled by large state companies.

Housing Shortages

In former communist countries, one thing often remembered is that the government provided housing for the people. Disenchanted with the perceived impotence of the new democratically elected governments, residents of former Soviet Union cities see the neighborhoods they live in as evidence of the Communist might. Many fail to acknowledge that while Soviet cities were being built, capitalist cities were also growing—organically. In a capitalist city, land is allocated based on private value and public choice, and market demand guides housing development.[2] The cities that grow vigorously are ones where people want to live. Neighborhoods in the capitalist city tend to have some local character and a sense of place.[3] Soviet neighborhoods, for the most part, looked alike. Even so, by providing one of the most basic needs—shelter—Soviet planners left a long-lasting legacy.

Because demand guides housing development in capitalist cities, it is less likely that housing shortages plague urban development, though affordability is still a problem. In Soviet cities, "market" signals were readily ignored, and housing shortages were common—both in sought-after cities (those that the *Propiska* system was supposed to keep at a manageable size) and in completely planned cities (where housing was built only for the number of people that had to be moved there).

A particularly evocative example was the Soviet Union's most sought-after city, Moscow. Moscow's population grew steadily until 1989. Population losses caused by World War II were quickly made up, and growth was sustained until the fall of the Soviet Union. Attempts of central planners to halt and manage city growth succeeded only for short periods in the mid-1950s and early 1960s. Originally, Moscow's population was to be kept at 2 million. By 2002, it had ballooned to more than 10 million (Colton 1995).

To keep up with rapid population growth, planners built housing in Moscow at a breakneck pace after World War II. From 1946 to 1961, every year brought more square feet of housing than the previous year, as the population grew from 2.5 to 5.0 million. After 1961, the *Propiska* system was enforced more strictly, and housing construction continued on an even keel. But the population kept growing—by 2 million in the 1960s and another 2 million between 1970 and 1989 (Colton 1995).

After 1973, the pace of new housing development slowed, with fewer buildings erected than in the previous year. By 1988, almost half of Moscow's permanent residents were affected by citywide housing shortages, and more than 55 percent of "young families" (couples with the husband and wife ages 30 or younger) lived with parents or another relative (Colton 1995).

Lack of Housing Variety

In addition to underproviding housing, Soviet planners failed to consider people's inherent need for variety. Individual detached housing was seldom constructed in urban centers, and few concessions were made for housing space per individual—apartments were cramped, unattractive, and uncomfortable.

The highest demand for housing (which in itself is a general market signal for the economy) was in the cities' historic centers. In addition to providing access and prestige, such places offered a larger variety of housing units. Despite the availability of fairly new housing in peripheral neighborhoods, people overwhelmingly preferred housing close to the city center.

Housing units offered meager living spaces (table 2.1). In 1920, Soviet leaders promised to secure 9 square meters of living space for every citizen. By 1988, they were still some distance from fulfilling

TABLE 2.1

Housing Conditions in Selected Cities in the Former Soviet Union, 1988

City	Average per capita living space, square meters	Number of families and single people on waiting list, thousands	Percentage of all families on waiting list	"List norm," square meters
Almaty	8.9	49.7	15	6.0
Baku	7.9	68.7	26	5.0
Dnepropetrovsk	9.7	74.2	20	6.0
Kazan	9.2	112.9	34	7.0
Kharkiv	9.7	113.4	23	5.5
Kiev	9.6	208.4	26	5.0
Minsk	8.9	134.8	28	6.0
Moscow	10.7	344.8	12	5.0
Novosibirsk	9.0	111.6	25	8.0
Odessa	8.5	80.4	23	4.0
Rostov-on-Don	10.0	74.1	23	6.0
St. Petersburg	10.6	282.9	20	5.5
Tashkent	8.2	60.1	12	7.0
Tbilisi	9.5	59.0	19	5.0

Source: Pejovich 1990.

that promise. Overcrowding was common, with extended families living in a single unit.

A series of hurdles prevented people from moving to bigger or better housing. Cities had a "list norm," which dictated who was eligible for rehousing. Only people who had a small enough living space (say, 6 square meters per person in Almaty in 1988) were allowed to put their name on a waiting list for new housing.

The lack of variety in housing size was matched by a lack of variety in housing styles. Options were limited to similar-looking apartment units, most with fewer than four rooms. And apartments in Soviet neighborhoods were not only small, but most were not constructed efficiently. Thus, standard layouts for apartments and for buildings did not properly consider location and context. The same building type would go up on sites with different topographies (on a plain or at the bottom of a hill), in varying contexts (near the historic center or the rural outskirts), and in different types of communities (doctors and mechanical workers, professors and shop attendants).

Provision of Urban Infrastructure

The former Soviet Union was not the only country that took a normative approach to populating its vast territory. In *Cadillac Desert,*

Reisner (1993) details how U.S. authorities started massive water infrastructure projects to populate America's arid heartland. But Soviet central planners gave cities few levers for self-determination. Even when local authorities were interested in improving their resident's quality of life (which in a market system is stimulated by the electoral process), efforts to secure necessary funds often encountered insurmountable transaction costs and bureaucratic bottlenecks.

A public participation process to gauge the needs, desires, and preferences of people was lacking. Cities were allocated amenities based not on what people wanted but on what central planners thought they needed. The demographics of individual cities were often not understood, with services provided based on arithmetic, such as one hairdressing establishment per neighborhood.

Access Without Reliability to Communal Services

One of the communist mantras was that everyone should have access to decent living conditions. Soviet planners fell short of meeting this goal in at least two ways. First, they focused mainly on urban areas, spending little or no energy on rural areas. Second, as they attempted to provide services to all urban areas, they spread their efforts thin, regardless of actual demand. Providing services in an undifferentiated way meant that quality had to suffer. And providing services in a financially unsustainable way (through heavy subsidies) led to overall deterioration after the fall of communism.

District heating, one of the tenets of sustainable urban development in forward-looking cities like Copenhagen and Stockholm, was the norm in most Soviet cities. Entire neighborhoods or groups of apartment blocks were branched to district heating plants. Although district heating was a cost-effective and environmentally friendly way of delivering heat, it had four main shortfalls: the piping was subject to heat and water losses; heat was not always delivered when needed; households were not charged on the basis of actual heat consumption, but of the floor area of their apartment (meaning that some households ultimately subsidized other households, and all households subsidized a system prone to losses); and people could not adjust the temperature to their needs, receiving the level of heating the district heating plant deemed appropriate for everyone.

Water and waste removal services were available to most urban dwellers, but they were often delivered intermittently (people saved water in bathtubs and in pots and pans) and they were of poor quality. Brown tap water was the norm after every water shortage. Pipes burst in the cold winters. Power shortages were frequent. Solid waste management consisted largely of dumping waste in open landfills. Recycling centers for paper and metals were available in most cities, but they disappeared soon after the fall of the Soviet Union.

Where to Buy, What to Buy

If capitalist societies are consumerist, communist societies were the opposite—private enterprises in the retail sector played a minimal role (for example, subsistence farmers selling their extra yield), and central planners dictated access to foodstuffs and consumer goods. Supermarkets and retail stores, assigned proportionally to city districts, were severely undersupplied (in many cases only basic goods were available).

In many Siberian cities, even the most basic goods were heavily subsidized, as they had to be shipped over considerable distances. In their haste to develop new housing districts, Soviet planners often forgot to provide these areas with necessary amenities. And for the most part, the historic centers of cities that had previously grown organically had more retail space available than did the denser outskirts. In Moscow, central areas had three times more square feet of food stores than some underserved peripheral areas, and almost six times more square feet of consumer goods stores (exhibit 2.1). Soviet cities outside Moscow were severely underserved, especially in the 1980s when residents had access to few quality goods and services, and those available were of low quality.[4]

Public Transportation

Most urban dwellers had affordable public transit options. Soviet cities had good public transportation that still offers a good backbone for further development and extension. The two main shortcomings are its financial sustainability and its layout. Eurasian cities have public transportation networks that are often old and outmoded. These networks were designed to connect to large industrial areas, and many are no longer functional. Transit was designed to serve industrial enterprises, thus as cities shifted to a more service-based economy, many public transit lines ended up servicing dead zones.

However, infrastructure for private vehicles was undersupplied. Soviet policy makers discouraged private vehicle use and encouraged public transit. So, the urban and periurban infrastructure in the Soviet Union was not built to handle the drastic increase in private cars after 1991. Roads connecting to periurban areas were poor, as communities there were small; parking spaces were underprovided because car ownership was low. Thus, 10-story apartment blocks

EXHIBIT 2.1

Floor Area of Food and Consumer Goods Stores in Moscow, 1989

(sq. meters per 1,000 people)

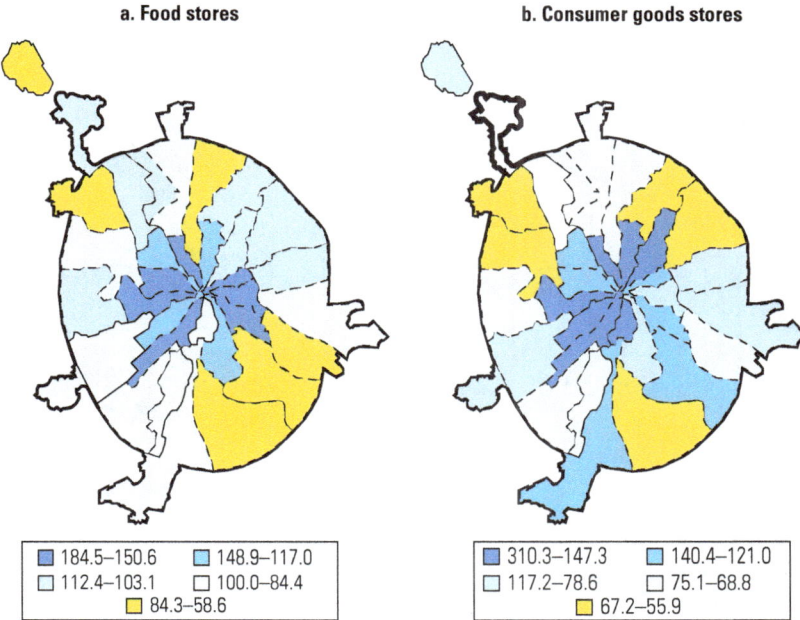

a. Food stores

b. Consumer goods stores

■ 184.5–150.6	■ 148.9–117.0
□ 112.4–103.1	□ 100.0–84.4
■ 84.3–58.6	

■ 310.3–147.3	■ 140.4–121.0
□ 117.2–78.6	□ 75.1–68.8
■ 67.2–55.9	

Source: Colton 1995.

often included parking spaces only in a small area around the building, and main roads in and out of cities often had no more than two lanes. The quality of infrastructure was also poor: the road surface was not built for large car loads, requiring frequent repairs.

The Transitional Present: Planning's Fall from Grace

The fall of the Soviet Union triggered different development directions in its former republics and different approaches to the new realities. Some countries reversed course, repudiating the precepts of central planning and trying to rely almost entirely on market systems. Others introduced elements of market systems but kept many Soviet institutions. And some remained entrenched in the Soviet-style planning system, not attempting to change.

One thing that all Eurasian countries had in common after 1991 was a direct or indirect adjustment to new market conditions. All former Soviet republics underwent an economic decline in the 1990s (figure 2.1), and many registered population decreases.

FIGURE 2.1

GDP per Capita in Selected Countries, 1990–2008

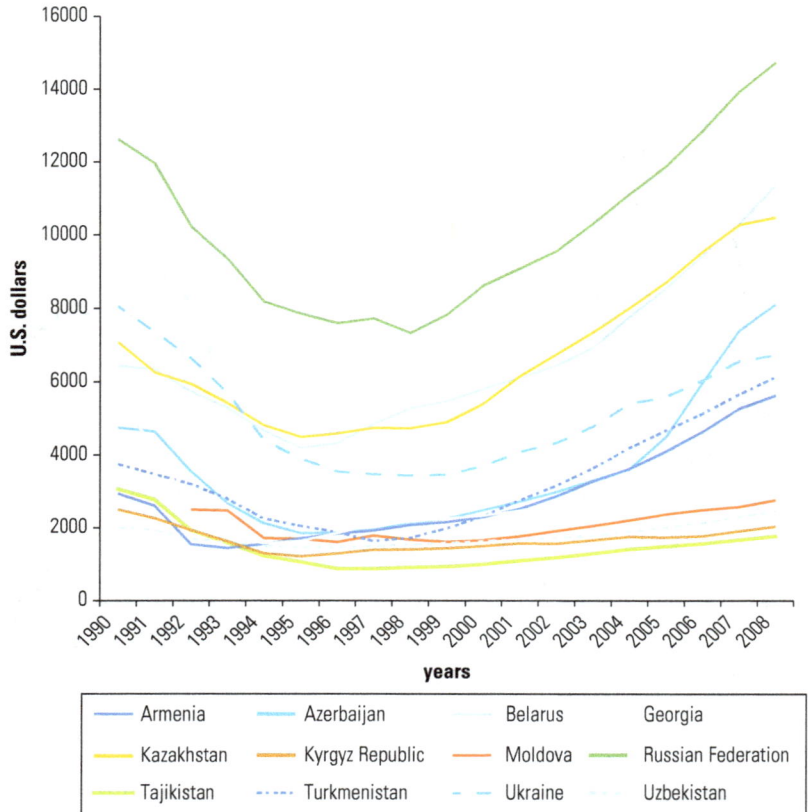

Source: World Bank 2011.
Note: GDP = gross domestic product.

The economic downturn of the 1990s had two marked effects on urban management and development. First, subsidies needed to efficiently run urban services were either cut or eliminated. Second, the infrastructure could not be properly maintained with the dwindling budgets, and it often fell into disrepair. These problems were not adequately addressed during the upswing of economic growth in the 2000s, and some deterioration continued.

As many of the key tenets of a functioning market system were not in place (clear property rights; functioning land, housing, and financial markets based on transparency and open to competition), the first challenge was to create institutions that could enhance market efficiencies. As societies became gradually more open to public opinion, and institutions for more democratic governance (news media, elected local government) were introduced or liberalized, the need to correct market failures, previously ignored or little understood, gained greater attention. In addition, as powers were increasingly devolved to local authorities, questions of efficient urban management arose. Without a tradition of market-oriented urban planning or a cadre of urban planners, most newly elected mayors and city councils learned how to run their cities through trial and error.

Land Markets Are Emerging

Private property was confiscated when the Communists came to power, and for several generations the Soviet Union had no real land market culture. Once countries switched to a market system, the lack of land markets created substantial problems, the most important being the lack of clear and irrevocable property rights.

After decades of public land ownership, it was difficult to establish who the original owners of land were. Land titles were uncertain or often missing. Many of the original owners had passed away. And divergences and misunderstandings often existed among their heirs. To further complicate matters, the land and property claimed by the previous owners (or their relations) were now occupied by other people and uses (such as schools, clinics, or administration buildings). Giving back these lands—even assuming all property title issues were solved—would have severely affected the urban centers' capacity to function efficiently. So much of the 1990s was plagued by failed starts, few property transactions, and little development.

As property issues are resolved, and urban institutions get better at reducing transaction costs, real estate markets have become more dynamic and flexible. The World Bank's *Doing Business* reports show that Armenia and Georgia have made impressive progress, particularly in registering property and obtaining construction permits, while Moldova, the Russian Federation, Tajikistan, Ukraine, and Uzbekistan still have some way to go.

Dealing with Misallocated Land

In a market system, land is allocated and developed based on perceived value—ideally, as revealed through innumerable transactions among well-informed players. Areas of high value tend to be developed more densely, while less valuable areas have lower densities. By contrast, in Soviet cities land was assigned no real market value, and development followed design norms rather than market norms. This approach skewed the density pattern in Eurasian cities, with higher densities in peripheral areas than in central areas.

In Western European cities, the density profile follows a more organic pattern, with central areas denser and outskirts progressively less dense (figure 2.2).[5] Without functioning land markets, obsolete or underused land is hard to redevelop, because demolishing buildings entails costs that cannot be offset by an increase in land value and higher revenues from higher density redevelopments.

Transformation takes time, but the density profile of some cities has already changed. Between 1992 and 2002, the density pattern in Moscow (Eurasia's most dynamic urban center) became more similar to that of major cities in developed market economies (Bertaud 2010).

Land Parcel Urbanism

Soviet neighborhoods were bereft of diversity; the neighborhoods of the transition years became too diverse and eclectic. Many new developments went up without proper construction permits. They were constructed with poor materials and poor craftsmanship. And they emerged before local authorities could respond. Municipalities were thus often positioned to react to changes rather than guide and anticipate them.

There was a lack of coordination between property rights and building rights. Faced with a new house that did not have the proper building permits, cities did not know how to respond. A built house represents a form of private property, and private property was becoming widely understood as the foundation of a market economy.

FIGURE 2.2

Density in Selected Cities and Their Peripheries, 1990

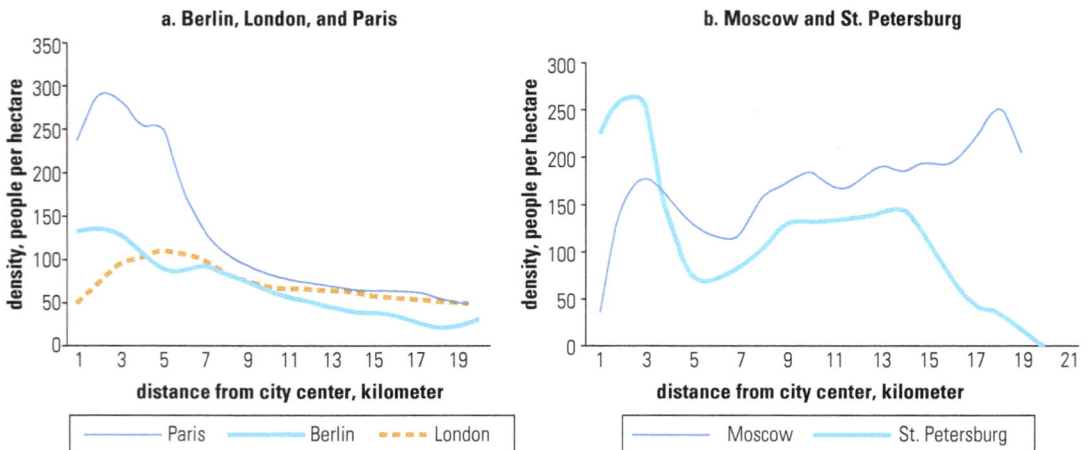

Source: Buckley and Mini 2000.

Local authorities were thus reluctant to demolish unlawful construc-
tions. Once one unlawful building or construction went up, others
took it as a cue to do the same—perpetuating "land parcel urbanism." This trend was supported by failures of governance—including
corruption—and an inadequate voice for citizens to protect their
interests in how the city developed for the general good.

The Challenge of Changing Land Use

Cities not only grow outward, but they also grow in place, recycling
used, underused, and abandoned land for new and more productive
purposes. Cities with strong property rights and dynamic land markets are in constant renewal. Office buildings take the place of housing units in busy central business districts. Higher density buildings
go up in sought-after neighborhoods. And new industries and services replace obsolete or aging ones.

Former industrial cities such as London and New York have shifted
to service industries, now with industrial areas that occupy less than
5 percent of their built area (figure 2.3). By contrast, large industrial
belts still dominate Moscow and St. Petersburg. Some of these industries are obsolete, and some are not working to their full capacity or
are on land that could be used more productively. Redeveloping
existing brownfields (including abandoned sites where soil is polluted from prior uses) is key to adding some dynamism to urban real
estate markets, especially in cities where idle land covers a large area
(World Bank 2010).

Redeveloping brownfields in Eurasian cities can be beneficial for
several reasons (exhibit 2.2). Brownfields are often in prime city
areas. They comprise large contiguous plots of land, which could
accommodate large-scale developments (such as a shopping mall).

Industrial Area as Percentage of Built-Up Area in Selected Cities, 2010

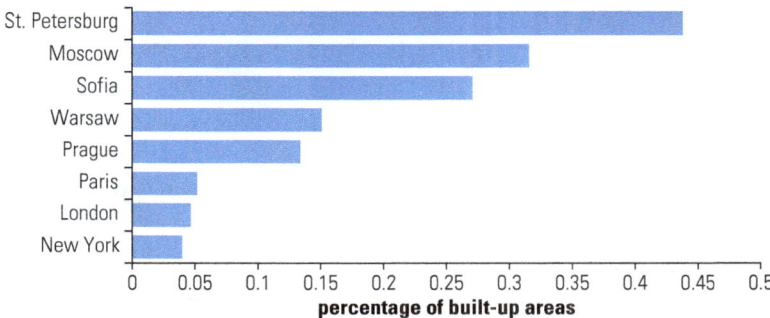

Source: Bertaud 2010.

EXHIBIT 2.2
Industrial and Similar Uses in Selected Cities in the Former Soviet Union, 2009
population

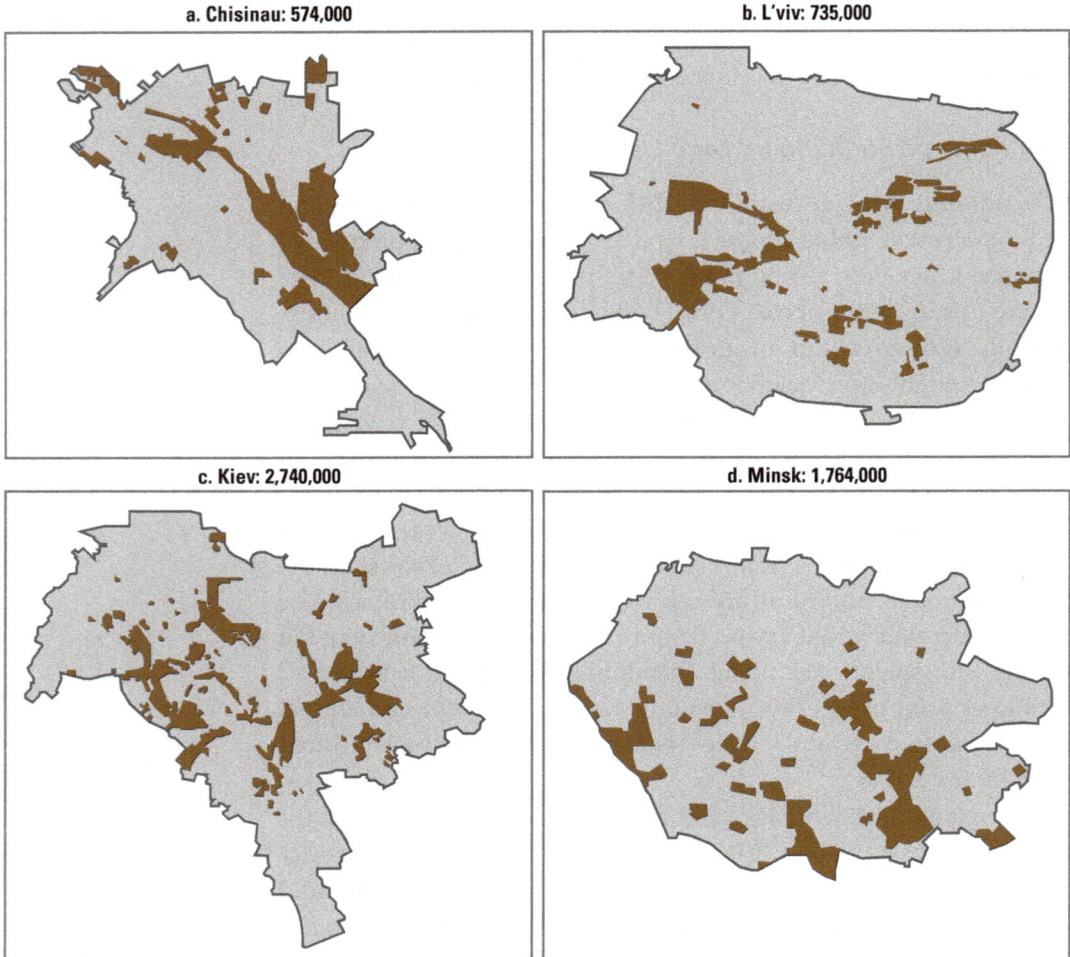

a. Chisinau: 574,000

b. L'viv: 735,000

c. Kiev: 2,740,000

d. Minsk: 1,764,000

Source: Corresponding city land use maps.
Note: The darker areas in this exhibit represent industrial or similar areas.

And they are already branched to urban infrastructure and often are on public transportation routes.

Traditional industrial enterprises remain vital economic players (sometimes even the only ones) at the local level, and their good economic performance should be encouraged. Where industrial hearts are no longer beating or beating very slowly, new life should be instilled by bringing in a mix of uses (housing, retail, entertainment, office, and light industrial) that generate activity throughout the day and yield higher productivity rates throughout the year.

Rethinking Housing When Things Fall Apart

When the Soviet Union disbanded, many cities suffered from housing shortages. As the economy faltered, fewer resources could be allocated for housing construction. In addition, as property began to be privatized, housing construction moved from the public to the private realm. But after many years of central planning and development, no experienced private developers could take on large-scale projects. Thus, housing construction declined dramatically in the 1990s, with projects mainly small in scale and financed with cash. As private developers gained experience, and credit markets started to mature, the number of new housing projects rose. New housing went up disproportionately (mainly due to speculation), with the major cities and regional growth centers taking the lion's share of new developments. In Armenia and Georgia, most new construction took place in the capital cities (figure 2.4).

These patterns represent a market correction, with most new construction in cities where people want to be and little construction in lagging cities. Construction in major cities rose rapidly even when transaction costs were high. The market often finds ways around some institutional rigidities, but others are more intractable. Developers will find creative ways to develop greenfields and abandoned land whose ownership and use is not clearly defined. But they will find it hard to redevelop land with (high-density) housing construction, where the title is likely to be disputed and possibilities for conversion are limited.

FIGURE 2.4

New Construction in Armenia and Georgia and Their Capitals

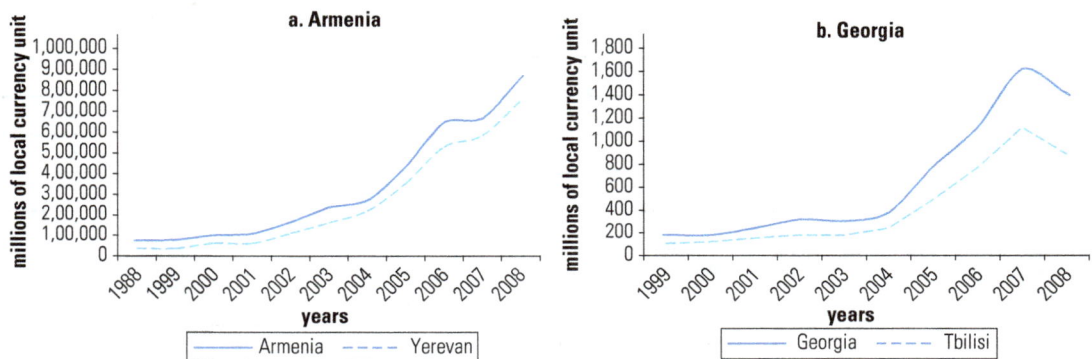

Sources: National Statistical Service of the Republic of Armenia; National Statistics Office of Georgia.
Note: Data for Armenia are between 1988 and 2008; data for Georgia are between 1999 and 2008.

The High Ownership Curse

If the market has found ways to realize new construction in sought-after urban locations, it has been less adept at dealing with one of communism's most visible legacies: Soviet neighborhoods, which have proven hard to redevelop or refurbish. After the fall of the Soviet Union, the resulting states undertook wide-scale privatization of housing, selling individual housing units at low prices (or outright giving away) to the people living there if they did not already have ownership rights. The belief was that rapidly creating private property would lay a foundation for an incipient market economy.

After this privatization, these countries found themselves with some of the world's highest homeownership rates (table 2.2). Because housing was one of the few forms of private property allowed under communism, most Eurasians highly valued owning a house, which gave them a sense of stability and certitude. Very high ownership creates market rigidities, however. It is harder to migrate if housing cannot readily be sold, and price differentials on housing are a substantial barrier to mobility for people without financial means (selling an apartment in Magadan could hardly generate the funds for buying a similar apartment in Moscow).

TABLE 2.2

Homeownership Rates in Selected Countries, 2005

percent

Country	Homeownership rate	Urban population	Share of urban housing	Poverty rate
Uzbekistan	98	36	—	47
Kazakhstan	97	56	—	11
Kyrgyz Republic	97	34	39	63
Armenia	96	64	60	46
Georgia	95	52	—	39
Moldova	90	46	41	39
Tajikistan	90	24	42	72
Belarus	84	72	66	12
Azerbaijan	83	50	57	17
Turkmenistan	79	46	35	—
Ukraine	75	67	64	19
Russian Federation	70	73	53	19

Source: Lipman 2010.
Note: — = not available.

When the housing stock was privatized at the start of the transition, most units went to already established households, despite widespread housing shortages—leaving young people out of the equation. They did not have access to housing, and there was no dynamic rental market (a standard feature of cities with market economies). High ownership rates, combined with the continuing inflexibility of the housing construction industry, discouraged a burgeoning rental market. So, most young people were tied to their families, continuing to live with parents and relatives until they could afford to move out.

Another rigidity has to do with the Soviet apartment blocks themselves. Because these buildings have many owners, they are nearly impossible to tear down (one would have to persuade all owners to move). They are also costly to redevelop because residents are rarely able to finance the work. In cities with market economies, the urban mass is in perpetual renewal and change. Market forces are reshaping Eurasian cities, but the cities' idiosyncratic legacy is not easy to change in a few decades.

Underdeveloped Rental Markets

Weak rental markets impede mobility. In developed market economies, rental markets enable young people to search for opportunities in places they choose. People look for a congenial living place, and cities look for people and firms that can ensure their sustainable development.

Long-term economic growth is a product of human capital (Romer 1990). The most resilient cities are those that manage to attract and keep the "creative class," which pushes technological change and innovation. To attract skilled people, cities need to have flexible and dynamic housing and rental markets, along with other amenities. Rental markets allow people to move without incurring high upfront costs. Sought-after cities will have higher rents due to higher demand, but also a wide range of rental offers to accommodate (almost) every budget.

In 2007, the monthly rent for a moderate one-bedroom furnished apartment was higher in Moscow than in Amsterdam; Rome; Stockholm; and Washington, DC; the monthly rents for a moderately priced three-bedroom apartment in Kiev, Moscow, or St. Petersburg were higher than in every European city except London; that same year, the average hourly cost of labor was more than 10 times higher in western cities than in Eurasian cities. The 2008 Mercer Cost of Living Survey found that Moscow was the world's most expensive city, thus putting it at a disadvantage for competing to recruit talent from across the world.

Unless Eurasian rental markets become more flexible, cities could price themselves out of the regional and global competition for talent. Rental market rigidities may be from land and housing market rigidities that constrain supply and raise transaction costs. They also may be from a lack of clear tenancy laws, prevailing tax regimes for properties, or a lack of incentives for developers. In addition, it is likely that a large share of rental activity is undocumented to evade taxes and bureaucracy.

Dealing with Housing Shortages and Surpluses

Most Eurasian cities emerged from communism with strong local demand for housing. The market demanded both more units and a larger variety of housing options, with quantities varying greatly across the region. In Eastern Europe (particularly Moldova, western Russia, and Ukraine), demand for new housing was soon dampened by widespread population declines caused by lower fertility rates, higher mortality rates, out-migration, and reverse migration to rural areas. In many areas, demand for low-quality and poorly located apartments fell, and some cities (especially industrial cities with fledgling manufacturing) faced housing surpluses. By contrast, demand for single-family detached homes rose in most places (Buckley and Tsenkova 2001).

Meanwhile, some Central Asian cities (particularly major ones) faced absolute housing shortages as their populations soared. In Tajikistan, population rose 16.5 percent over 1998–2005, while the housing stock grew only 9 percent. Rapid migration to Dushanbe led to a housing deficit there of more than 100,000 units. In the Kyrgyz Republic, the population grew from 4.4 million in 1990 to 5.3 million in 2008, with Bishkek, which absorbed 200,000 migrants from rural areas in recent years, suffering from acute housing shortages.

Without a government safety net, the transition to a market economy left many urban dwellers, especially those in vulnerable groups, in a precarious economic situation. National and local authorities need to think of efficient ways of creating social safety nets for the cities' poorest people. A lack of access to affordable housing can lead to the proliferation of slums in cities with acute housing shortages and sustained population growth. According to the United Nations Human Settlements Programme, 56 percent of people in Tajikistan, 52 percent in the Kyrgyz Republic, and 51 percent in Uzbekistan were in slums in 2007 (UN-HABITAT 2007).

The Tragedy of the Commons: In and Around
the Apartment Block

People in Eurasian cities own the apartments they live in, but all other elements of the apartment block, interior and exterior (including the land it is on), are in either common or public ownership. The stairwells, hallways, roof, elevators, heating and electrical systems, and surrounding land—common elements of the building affecting its comfort, convenience, and value—are still owned and maintained by local government entities or are in common ownership without a formal binding commitment for action.

Because of the lack of formal binding commitment, it is unclear who is responsible for maintaining and managing these elements. As public goods, these areas are subject to the "tragedy of the commons." Residents of apartment buildings do not always take it upon themselves to maintain common areas. In addition, common areas, such as grounds and attic spaces, are sometimes taken over by individuals for personal use. Without strong homeowner associations, these buildings often fall into disrepair.

The legacy of the Soviet era makes it hard to form and sustain homeowner associations. Because most apartment blocks house a mix of social classes, some people are more able than others to pay the needed building maintenance and improvement costs. In developed economies, the housing markets often sort residents based on income—people who cannot live in a building or an area seek more affordable options. Note, however, that even in developed markets, disagreements over expenditures occur in condominiums. But condominiums in market economies generally tend to be governed by clear rules and regulations.

The lack of strong planning rules to govern shared goods leads to aesthetically distasteful outcomes and often to safety violations. City regulations need to be reinforced by landlord-tenant contracts or homeowner association rules that dictate what external and internal modifications to the building can be made, how costs are to be shared, and what the penalties are for noncompliance.

These norms follow more than just aesthetic considerations. Landlords know that the value of their buildings will fall if the buildings are not properly maintained. And city officials know that they are likely to lose their tax base in a neighborhood where housing is falling apart. Further, poor maintenance of a single building can lead to property value losses for surrounding buildings, which can drive people out of the neighborhood, leading to even more deterioration.

The Challenges of Providing Urban Infrastructure

Providing urban infrastructure in Eurasian cities faces many challenges, including poorly developed amenities, clogged roads and a shortage of parking spaces, aging utilities networks, and dramatic demographic shifts. The persistent problem is the lack of zoning, especially for mixed use in most cities. Moreover, without clear urban development and minimal design standards, the resulting buildings sometimes contribute to the already poor look of neighborhoods. Basic incentives could be put in place to encourage builders to consult architects and professional designers before erecting a new structure or modifying a current one. The poor materials and appearance may also reflect entrepreneurs' unwillingness or hesitancy to invest without greater certainty about the direction of the neighborhood, given the absence of formal planning and zoning for mixed-use development. Public information, oversight, and enforcement of urban plans and basic development regulations could lead to more coherence in newly developing areas without squelching initiative and local color.

Poorly Developed Amenities

Soviet neighborhoods were not designed with many amenities. Soviet planners designed most neighborhoods to be cost-effective and to look good from above (aerial photos of Soviet neighborhoods show "clinical" design patterns)—they were not built for comfort and convenience. Thus, cities lacked many things that improve people's lives, from neighborhood shops to cafes, pubs, and other entertainment venues.

During the transition years, Soviet neighborhoods have been transforming, responding more closely to residents' needs and desires. But these adjustments have had to be on already existing urban infrastructure, which is hard to alter. Buildings were already in place, with new amenities having to find a way to fit in.

In many apartment blocks, the first floor was converted into office, retail, or entertainment space or a combination of these uses. Housing units became neighborhood supermarkets, barbershops, bars, banks, insurance companies, pharmacies, and doctors' offices. The space around and between apartment blocks was often devoted to new uses, from shops and private kindergartens to hotels and restaurants, sometimes curtailing ease of access for pedestrians, vehicles, and green spaces.

Soviet neighborhoods were not built for cars. They were criss-crossed by good public transportation networks, but not designed to handle the dramatic increase in private car ownership since the collapse of the Soviet Union (table 2.3; see table 2A.1). In many former Soviet Union countries, the number of passenger cars per 1,000 people almost tripled over 1993–2007. This rapid growth in motorization improved mobility for vehicle owners and their passengers, but caused or heightened traffic congestion, reduced road safety, and substantially increased air pollution and the deterioration of public transport services in some cities. Traffic gridlocks occur daily in Moscow and are considered one of its most pressing problems (Gessen 2010).

The rapid increase in private car ownership and use, combined with a sharp drop in financial support from central governments for public transport systems, has posed considerable challenges for providing acceptable transport services. The private sector has provided passenger transport in most places, but through substandard, small, or old vehicles, typically uncomfortable and often overloaded and unsafe.

The ownership structure of public transport providers is typically fragmented, with many operators serving each urban area. Integrated services, which allow passengers to transfer between operators, are the exception rather than the rule. Publicly operated "electric transport" systems are often in a poor state of repair or are being considered for abandonment.

TABLE 2.3
Number of Passenger Cars, by Country, 1993 and 2007
per 1,000 people

Country	1993	2007
Belarus	76	240
Russian Federation	78	207
Kazakhstan	61	141
Ukraine	81	128
Armenia	84	96
Georgia	90	95
Moldova	38	92
Turkmenistan	54	81
Azerbaijan	35	72
Kyrgyz Republic	41	44
Uzbekistan	39	43
Tajikistan	36	29

Sources: World Bank 2011, United Nations Statistics Division.

And the limited space around apartment blocks is choked with garages and cars parked wherever a space is available. Makeshift garage structures often fill already limited space between apartment blocks—space that could be used for other purposes (such as playgrounds).

Aging Utilities Networks

The Eurasian urban population has good access to key services. Access to water in urban areas is close to universal, and the waste-water connection rate is nearly 95 percent in all countries. The Soviet urban water policy was transformed into a system with some market elements in Armenia, Moldova, and Russia as well as, to a lesser extent, Kazakhstan and the Kyrgyz Republic. Water policy in Azerbaijan, Belarus, Tajikistan, Uzbekistan, and especially Turkmenistan is resolving public health concerns, and their governments are willing to provide subsidized water and wastewater services.

Although access to water systems is high in all Eurasian countries, the performance of these systems is not impressive—and sometimes it worsens. The major cities overwhelmingly provide 24-hour service, but service delivery in urban areas can be spotty, especially in smaller cities and towns in Armenia, Azerbaijan, Georgia, and Moldova (table 2.4).

Wastewater collection has not expanded in Eurasian countries. Wastewater treatment is even getting worse, with only Russia having a fully operational system. Wastewater investment programs have been completed or are ongoing in Bryansk, Moscow, Rostov, St. Petersburg, Ufa, and a few other large Russian cities. In other countries, wastewater treatment was discontinued (Armenia and Georgia), reduced to mechanical treatment (Belarus, Kazakhstan, and Ukraine), or never existed.

The poor operating status of utilities in Eurasia relates to their having been built around the same time (1960–80) and not having been expanded or updated since. These systems were designed based on population projections and norms of water use that overestimated demand. Thus, utilities operate well below capacity, resulting in excessive electricity use and asset depreciation, since rising costs cannot be covered by reduced revenue flow. Declining population adds to the problem in many cities.

There is also the problem of enterprise-run utilities. Many cities were developed around industrial enterprises, which subsidized the utilities. After 1991, some of these industrial monoliths became economically unviable and could not continue to offer financial and

TABLE 2.4

Average Daily Hours of Operation of Water Services, by Country

Country (last year observed)	Average for country	Average for capital
Armenia (2008)	13.2	18.1
Azerbaijan (2009)	15.0	18.0
Belarus (2008)	24.0	24.0
Georgia (2008)	14.7	24.0
Kazakhstan (2008)	23.0	24.0
Kyrgyz Republic (2006)	23.6	24.0
Moldova (2009)	16.0	24.0
Russian Federation (2009)	23.9	24.0
Tajikistan (2005)	21.3	24.0
Turkmenistan (2009)	—	24.0
Ukraine (2007)	22.0	24.0
Uzbekistan (2007)	17.3	24.0

Source: IBNET database and World Bank staff.
Note: Data for the capitals of the Kyrgyz Republic, Tajikistan, and Ukraine are for 2009. — = not available.

technical assistance to sustain the systems. Even for profitable companies, city utilities tend to be a social component of their activity
that does not generate profit, because tariffs are kept artificially low.

Dramatic Demographic Shifts

The fall of the Soviet Union was followed not only by the widespread
deterioration of infrastructure and services, but also by dramatic
demographic shifts. These demographic changes will shape future
infrastructure and services.

One of the most important shifts is the imbalance between men
and women in some Eurasian regions. Because of the jobs the Soviets
created in the cold, harsh regions of Siberia, men mainly inhabit
these areas (in some cases, men account for more than 70 percent of
the population; exhibit 2.3). By contrast, women disproportionately
inhabit the more densely populated areas of the west and the center,
partly reflecting the internal migration of women, who are better
prepared than men to perform service and professional jobs in the
more dynamic cities in these regions.[6]

The aging of the population is another important demographic
shift. The populations of all Eurasian countries aged between 1991
and 2008 (figure 2.5). Ukraine, Russia, and Belarus fared worst,
with dwindling young populations and rising numbers of old people.[7] As these countries prepare to handle the growing share of
retired people (by adjusting the pension system), their cities have to

Distribution of Males in the Soviet Union, 1989

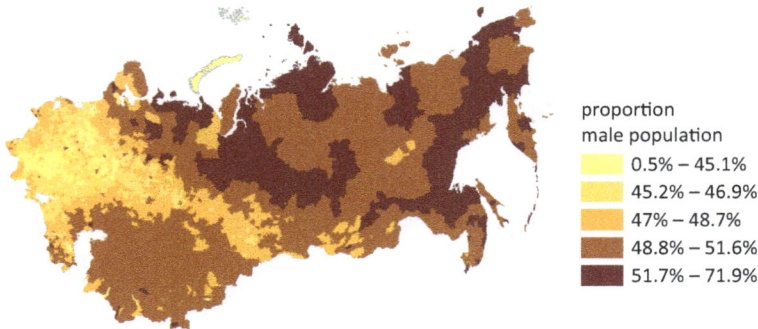

proportion
male population
- 0.5% – 45.1%
- 45.2% – 46.9%
- 47% – 48.7%
- 48.8% – 51.6%
- 51.7% – 71.9%

Source: Federal State Statistics Service 2009.

FIGURE 2.5
Young and Old People, by Country, 1991 and 2008

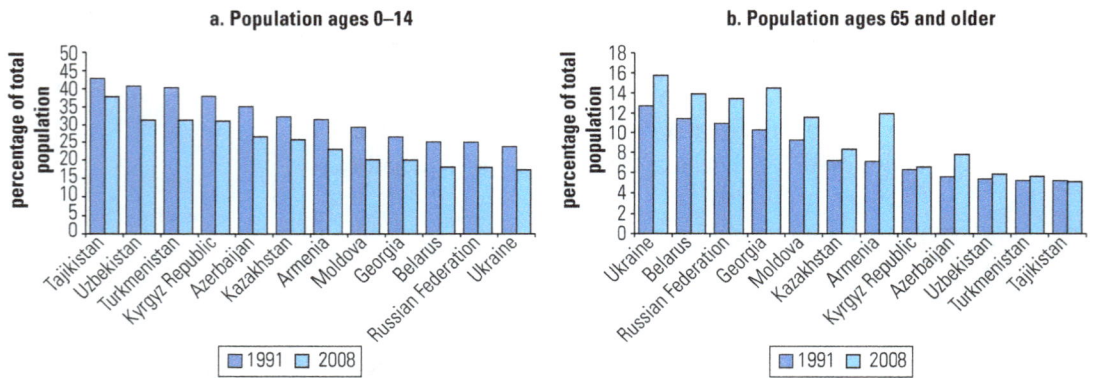

a. Population ages 0–14

b. Population ages 65 and older

Source: World Bank 2011.

change as well (by changing how they deliver services and infra-structure). Urban planners in Eurasian cities thus have to learn how to plan for cities that are different in many ways from other urban areas around the world.

A Sustainable Future: The Rebirth of Planning

In the transition years Eurasian cities experienced considerable changes: birth rates fell (below the population replacement level); out-migration rose (within and out of Eurasia); life expectancy at birth for men dropped, particularly in urban areas; and reverse-migration to rural areas accentuated the deurbanization. So the population of most cities, large and small, fell over 1989–2009, some declining rapidly (5 percent a year), others just facing a stagnating population.

It is hard to predict what will happen to these cities, but in the short and medium term many cities have to plan for a shrinking population base. This prospect requires that local authorities think outside a growth paradigm. The way infrastructure is dimensioned and maintained, and the way services are delivered and financed, has to be adjusted based on new socioeconomic realities. Neighborhoods have to be consolidated as the city as a whole loses density. Public services, designed for a larger population, that end up running below installed capacity have to be redimensioned. Abandoned houses and apartment blocks have to be maintained or demolished to prevent crime and disease.

Fostering Efficient Land Markets

Whether their populations are declining or growing, most Eurasian cities will expand geographically. They have to make up for the housing shortage and uniformity inherited from the Soviet era by creating new spaces to host the new economy. Dynamic and efficient land markets can create an environment conducive to growth by allocating land efficiently to its most productive use. Good urban planning—such as encouraging in-fill development and discouraging sprawl—can ensure that land markets develop sustainably. At the same time, attention should be paid to urban development practices that seem sustainable but may conflict with other sustainable practices—such as with in-fill development in historical neighborhoods, which has happened in many Eurasian cities, such as Tbilisi (Salukvadze 2009).

Land for city development is available both in and outside cities. Redeveloping in-city land can take many forms, such as demolishing old buildings and constructing new ones, making use of unused or underused land, and converting land (such as old rail yards) to new uses. Eurasian countries have started to redevelop from within, but they face major challenges.

First, apartment blocks take up much of the prime real estate in city centers. Designed primarily as dormitories, these apartment blocks lack space for the amenities a functioning market economy needs (such as large neighborhood supermarkets). Many dominate areas that could benefit from a mix of functions (such as office and retail space). Redeveloping these apartment blocks is difficult because of the large number of owners that have to be persuaded to move somewhere else. In the meantime, new offices have to be built in peripheral city areas, increasing commuter traffic and city congestion. Converting apartment buildings to other uses is not always desirable, as it can rob city centers of vitality and dynamism (like in many U.S. cities). But mechanisms should be in place that enable more economic activity to occur in prime locations without unduly affecting city life.

Second, brownfields—former industrial estates that are idle or underused and suffer from real or perceived contamination—scar the area that could be redeveloped. They often cover prime city locations (in St. Petersburg, for example). They are already connected to the urban infrastructure. And they are often large, allowing for complex and large-scale redevelopments, including mixed-use complexes. But site contamination is often difficult and expensive to remove, ownership is not always clear, and local expertise in dealing with brownfields is lacking (World Bank 2010).

If brownfields and Soviet-era apartment blocks are some of the main obstacles to inward city expansion, overly fragmented or coagulated periurban land (for example, large parcels of land that are either public or private property) is one major barrier to outward city expansion. Periurban land that is too fragmented creates high transaction costs and spawns land parcel urbanism and scatter-pattern suburban development. Assembling land for larger projects is often difficult, forcing cities to expand unsustainably. But land that is too coagulated introduces land market rigidities and portends collusion and corruption.

Given that the population in most Eurasian cities is falling, many cities, particularly the one-company monotowns, will also have to deal with shrinking footprints. Just as some cities will have to learn to expand sustainably, some will have to learn to contract sustainably. Land markets are likely to become weaker, and local authorities will have to manage large tracts of idled urban land.

Reducing Transaction Costs in Land Markets

One of the most effective ways to foster more dynamic land markets is to reduce the transaction costs buyers and sellers of land incur. A first step is to reduce the need for intermediaries by transparently making land information available. Croatia created an online "geoportal" that enhances people's access to land information and related services, already reducing the time it takes to register land by 90 percent. And Georgia, the Kyrgyz Republic, and Moldova have similar geoportals.

The information available online varies. Ideally, all land information should be available in an online database. An investor interested in finding a land parcel for a new production facility should be able to access a geographic information system database that shows not only how the land is parceled, but also who owns the land, how the owners can be contacted, and possibly how much the owners are asking (if they are interested in selling). In Tbilisi, such information, as well as the master plan and zoning details pertaining to a specific plot, is accessible through the city's website.

Bringing more transparency and dynamism to local land markets is obviously tied to a functioning institutional framework. The basics of such a framework are clearly enforced property rights (and a complete inventory of land and landowners), an absence or low incidence of corruption, and clear urban planning regulations (what can be constructed, where, and how). The last is important because it will better guide where people buy land and for what purposes.

Modernizing and Enforcing Land Use Regulations

The challenge in modernizing land use regulations is to mitigate negative externalities efficiently without being overly restrictive. Master plans and detailed regulatory plans, witnessing a resurgence in many Eurasian cities, are trying to catch up with the realities of urban development (both institutionally and legislatively). These plans have to make way for clear land use regulations that guide city development rather than prescribe it. Land use regulations should be flexible, dynamic, and not overly restrictive, allowing cities to develop sustainably with minimal distortional effects.

Bertaud (2010), comparing the land use regulations in St. Petersburg and Perm, Russia, finds regulations in St. Petersburg to be more detailed than needed, with 54 land use categories and fairly rigid floor-to-area ratios. By contrast, Perm has only 34 land use categories, and its floor-to-area restrictions are more lax.

International experience shows that if land use regulations are overly specific (stating, for example, that a plot of land can be occupied only by a school rather than zoning it generally for services), land development is likely to be slow and costly, delaying the supply response and raising the cost of housing and real estate. Moreover, as cities become dynamic, rigid land use regulations go out of date and prevent land from being allocated to its most productive use or the uses the community values most.

Every city that develops organically needs clear, flexible, and dynamic land use regulations. The lack of such regulations can lead to a surge in illegal construction and squatter settlements, contribute to the persistence of land parcel urbanism, or both.

Encouraging Citizen Participation in the Planning Process

In most developed countries, citizen participation is inherent in planning. Good urban planning is about facilitating the myriad individual plans crafted by a city's people, businesses, and organizations (Jacobs 1961). Engaging citizens is beneficial not only from a political standpoint, but also from an economic one, as an engaged citizenry takes a stake in the city's future, providing creative and novel ideas for problems the city is facing.

But Soviet planning discouraged citizen participation. Since the transition, most Eurasian countries have undergone a tenuous learning process to determine how best to engage citizens. Some countries have progressed in the area, but others have actually regressed. In Russia, regulations have been changed to encourage more transparency in urban planning. In addition, three key avenues for citizen participation have been created: public hearings on draft master plans (local governments are responsible for specifying the rules for civic engagement in their charters); public hearings on land use regulations and zoning requirements; and public hearings on land subdivision and building requirements. Draft master plans need to be available for public scrutiny in accessible places, and local authorities and design agencies are encouraged to use multiple media sources for official presentations of these plans.

Yet, citizen participation in master plan development for Russian cities remains limited. So far, it includes only very rudimentary consultations, largely for informing the citizenry. Most local government managers believe that no special skills are required to facilitate public hearings and obtain constructive feedback from citizens, rendering these forums far less useful than they could be.

At the same time, there is no culture of civic engagement and participation among the citizenry of Eurasian cities. Many talk about mentalities that are hard to change. But Eastern European countries show that when local authorities engage people, they can help shape a dynamic civil society.

Encouraging In-Fill Development while Preserving Historical Heritage

Eurasian cities have large tracts of misallocated land—some are now abandoned, some are underused, and most are not used productively. In-fill development can allow cities to develop sustainably by "deepening" inward rather than expanding outward.

St. Petersburg's historic core is surrounded by an industrial belt, separating it from its housing neighborhoods. This industrial belt not only acts as a buffer between people and the urban core, but also represents prime real estate often not used to its potential. Much of this land is being redeveloped with high-density, mixed-use buildings (Bertaud 2010). Where such sites have been polluted or otherwise degraded, redevelopment often requires partnerships between local government and private investors, as well as support from central or regional governments.[8]

In-fill development should not come at the price of destroying historical heritage (including industrial heritage), regardless of how run-down a building might be. In Russia, more than 400 designated historical cities face the challenge of safeguarding their historical neighborhoods from encroaching development.

Preservation strategies vary widely across municipalities, but without clear preservation laws (and a roster of historic buildings to be protected), buildings disappear in a city's development and redevelopment (Myers 2003). Citizen engagement in projects undertaken in historical areas should support strong preservation regulation, especially if some of the buildings designated to be redeveloped are not among a country's historical monuments but are of great importance to the communities surrounding them.

Managing Urban Sprawl or Decline

In-fill development is key for preventing sprawl, but outward city growth is inevitable. Development in periurban areas can be guided by strategic infrastructure and efficient taxation and regulation. Local authorities have to be careful to choose the least distortional tools that will have the greatest expected impact. Highly normative approaches, such as the growth boundary established in Portland, Oregon, in the United States, have proven suboptimal in the long term because they do not prevent "leap-frog" development outside the boundary.

Whenever possible, local authorities should try to integrate infrastructure investments and service provision with planning regulations and with land and property taxation to achieve consistent urban sustainability objectives, such as facilitating density and reducing congestion. For example, the planning of urban public transport routes and services can help reduce private vehicle traffic by commuters, and housing developers can be obligated to finance the extension of secondary infrastructure networks in new neighborhoods. In effect, local authorities should provide infrastructure in areas where more development would be desirable (such as brown-fields or areas around public transit hubs) and offload the responsibility on the developers when new developments are planned in less desirable areas (such as suburbs).

By contrast, some Eurasian cities face a double challenge posed, first, by population decline (from demographic shifts) and population loss (from economic shifts, particularly the loss of manufacturing jobs), and second, by the declining quality of life. This shrinking city phenomenon affects not only the monotowns, but also cities with fairly dynamic economic bases. A smaller population inevitably leads to a smaller urban footprint, as parcels of land once occupied by businesses and people become vacant or underused. So, local authorities have to switch from a paradigm of planning for growth to one that considers urban decline and stagnation. Such a shift requires thinking about ways to consolidate housing and infrastructure and better manage city land.

The possibility that a city will stagnate or even decline in the short to medium term has to be reflected accurately in city development strategies. A clear grasp of current and future perspectives is more likely to generate sustainable solutions to complex challenges. Three of the most important issues are dealing with urban land that becomes idle or is underused; consolidating neighborhoods and urban cores (for example, offering incentives for relocation from sparse peripheral areas into denser central neighborhoods); and scaling down infrastructure to reflect reduced demand.

Managing City-Owned Land

Local authorities are not always clear about what they own, and they often fail to lease or sell properties strategically (to influence the shape and character of the city), even when they have the authority to do so. Former owners of publicly owned land sometimes claim property titles, and the central government often owns and manages local public land.

Local governments should inventory and manage their own property assets, to facilitate local economic development and mobilize municipal revenues. Land owned by local authorities can be used for key local investments, or it can be rented to generate revenues for the local budget.

This situation is better illustrated by the Kyrgyz Republic case. To spur better municipal property asset management, the Kyrgyz Republic government adopted a new land code in 1999 (revised in 2001), mandating that all land not owned privately or publicly be transferred into municipal ownership. As part of decentralization, it also transferred an array of centrally owned properties (schools, kindergartens, clinics, cultural centers, and city halls) and municipal service facilities (water and sewage, solid waste management, and street cleaning) into municipal ownership.

Initially, this move had ambiguous results, as local governments were new to the concept of asset management and fairly weak, given their limited experience of self-government. In addition, municipal land management faced many issues common to most former Soviet Union countries:

- Unclear institutional competencies (three different agencies had the right to allocate land rights for new construction)

- Unreliable land information (no one had a clear picture of the number or location of sites in municipal ownership)

- Dubious land transactions (for example, allocation of parkland for private development)

- Corruption (for example, allocation of municipal property to private interests at below market values)

- A lack of proactive land management (local governments were poorly motivated to excel in this area)

To unlock some of these municipal land market rigidities, a U.S. Agency for International Development project set out to inventory all municipal land in major Kyrgyz cities and propose policy solutions based on actual landholdings (Kaganova, Akmatov, and Undeland 2007). The study found that estimates by central agencies often differed substantially from actual numbers. It also found that not all cities can rely on municipal land as a valuable asset. For instance, Karakol owns 20 percent of the land within its boundaries (most of it vacant), whereas Osh owns just 0.4 percent.

Creating Livable Spaces and Neighborhoods

A city's success is tied to how well it creates good living conditions for its people and improves the overall quality of life. If people have access to good quality and affordable housing, they are more likely to be happy about where they live and to be more productive.

At the beginning of the transition, most Eurasian cities had an undersupply of housing, and Soviet planners could not keep up with demand. The 1990s did not bring an upswing in housing offerings—indeed, quite the opposite happened. The fall of communism led to the dismantling of many institutions responsible for housing design and construction. And market enterprises slowly took their place.

Thus, new housing development declined in most cities. Only the principal cities with very high housing demand managed to sustain more dynamic housing markets.

As markets started to mature, construction booms began in more cities. Many new developments emulated what people in the region were accustomed to—high-density apartment buildings. More recently, with increasingly dynamic housing markets, developers started to respond to a wider range of tastes. More people have started to ask for the housing type they could not access during the Soviet era, such as detached homes with custom designs and floor space. Most of these homes went up in peripheral areas with available land. And many were constructed in areas with no or poorly enforced building guidelines, leading to land parcel urbanism. Thus, the suburbs of many Eurasian cities developed in a checkered and unsustainable pattern, requiring higher energy costs for service delivery (water, sewage, transport, solid waste management) and generating more congestion and pollution.

By unlocking land markets, local authorities can ensure that housing markets become more dynamic. By encouraging strategic infrastructure investments (in, say, public transit lines), they can help guide sustainable new developments. In addition to unlocking housing markets, local authorities should unlock and formalize rental markets, which make city-to-city migration easier and allow a broader spectrum of people to find housing (including people who lack the means to buy).

Revitalizing Homeowner Associations

Many households in Soviet-era apartments own their homes. By contrast, common spaces and property (land around apartment blocks, stairwells, elevators, roofs, water systems, and electrical mainframes) have uncertain ownership. Municipal maintenance companies (*Zheks*) often continue to manage these shared spaces and utilities, but they do so inefficiently and without direct accountability to homeowners (they rely on state transfers and subsidies to operate).

In the developed world, homeowner associations efficiently maintain and improve multifamily housing units with individually owned dwellings. Homeowner associations not only ensure improved and more cost-efficient service provision, but also enable access to municipal and other sources of funding and encourage businesses geared toward building maintenance, management, and ancillary services.

Eurasian countries have attempted to encourage homeowner associations, with uneven results (table 2.5). One main problem is

TABLE 2.5

Reported Numbers of Homeowner Associations in the Former Soviet Union, by Country, 2010

Country	Reported number of homeowner associations
Armenia	700 (two-thirds of multifamily buildings), many from mergers of buildings without consent of owners; associations are not true homeowner associations, however—they have no clear role in dealing with *Zheks*
Azerbaijan	Almost none; no legislative basis for their formation
Belarus	566, most in new, privately constructed apartment houses; about half in Minsk
Georgia	2,600 in Tbilisi
Kyrgyz Republic	500 (18 percent of all multifamily housing, about 25 percent of units in cities)
Kazakhstan	10,133
Moldova	Less than 20 percent of multifamily housing in Chisinau
Russian Federation	66,933
Tajikistan	100
Ukraine	(6 percent of multifamily housing)
Uzbekistan	4,969

Sources: Lipman 2010; national statistical agencies.
Note: No information was available on Turkmenistan.

the mix of households found in these apartment blocks, where households of widely different incomes live side by side, and better-off families often subsidize capital repairs and maintenance for lower income families. The sheer size of these apartment blocks and the transaction costs required to get all residents to agree can be daunting. Thus, repairing a roof leak can turn into a drawn-out war between residents on the upper and lower floors.

Facilitating Property Sales and (Re)Development

In incipient real estate markets, many people struggle to come up with enough money to buy or refurbish a home. In booming urban centers, outside investors often distort the real estate market (with speculators buying housing units with the intention of reselling them at higher prices), making housing prices much higher than what average local salaries would permit. The housing market is the first to be affected in an economic downturn. It is also important to a vibrant and healthy urban economy. In Tbilisi, the Georgian Developers Association came up with an innovative way of instilling some dynamism in a construction sector hard hit by the global financial crisis (box 2.1).

In incipient real estate markets, where development capital is often difficult to access and housing tends to be undersupplied, local

BOX 2.1
_____

Housing Swap Scheme in Georgia

The global financial crisis left many development companies with unfinished and unsold buildings and large bank credits (in mid-2008, developers accounted for 35 percent of banks' loan
portfolio), severely affecting Tbilisi's economy. More than 7 percent of Georgians and many businesses depended directly or indirectly on construction (most concentrated in the capital). To
avoid an economic standstill, the Georgian Developers Association proposed a housing swap
scheme, offering people from the historical part of Tbilisi (more than 50,000 families in badly
maintained and overcrowded historical housing) the chance to move to newly constructed housing. For its part, the municipality offered to cover the developers' debts to banks (both old debt
and new loans required to finish buildings) in return for the full cadastral units cleared by the
people who moved to new developments. The historical buildings acquired by the city were put
out to tender for developers to refurbish and sell. Since the program started, more than 2,000
families have moved to newly finished apartments.

Source: Shavishvili 2010.

authorities can facilitate an organized framework for bartering
between landowners and developers. This second-best approach can
be a solution where land sales are constrained legally. Such bartering
can help transform informal settlements into formal ones, using sites
better by improving housing quality and making housing denser
(World Bank 2007). In this approach, informally developed land
(without proper building permits, for example) is offered to developers, who in exchange offer the residents apartments in a new building on the same site. So, the developer avoids overly high upfront
costs for land purchase (or, if purchase is not yet possible, land acqui-
sition). The informal residents benefit from improved and formalized
housing in new apartments. And the city can resolve the previously
unmonitored land parcel urbanism. But such arrangements can be
problematic if developers do not live up to the agreement.

Local authorities can also promote densification through zoning regulations and incentives. In Copenhagen, high-density developments
are approved only within a 600-meter radius of a public transportation hub. This measure curbs the reliance on private vehicles and
encourages public transportation, thereby reducing congestion,
improving air quality, and creating a more pedestrian-friendly environment (transit-oriented developments also encourage walking and
biking, which promote health). Such measures help provide more

ridership for the public transportation network, and they offer more people easy access to affordable transportation. But in their attempts to gain efficiency from higher density, local authorities should not fall into the trap that Soviet planners fell into. Density is good—but not at any cost. Very dense areas can lead to congestion, pollution, and a lower quality of life.

Improving Public Spaces and Building Façades

Strong urban design guidelines should outline the changes that people can make to the exterior and interior of apartment buildings and shared spaces. Without such rules, neighborhoods will be subject to continued deterioration. Indeed, private property has a public component. Apartments and housing units do not exist in a vacuum; they influence the way neighborhoods around them develop. In France, local authorities require that building façades be repainted every five years.[9] In New York City, dealing with the "broken window syndrome" (removing graffiti and repairing abandoned or run-down buildings) formed part of a strategy that reduced the city's crime rate over a very short time.

The deterioration of the exterior of Soviet-era apartment buildings worsens every year, gradually reducing the quality of life of the people in these neighborhoods. By offering the right incentives, local authorities and central governments can transform such neighborhoods. A program proven successful throughout Eastern Europe is the thermal insulation of buildings. It is particularly well received by residents, because insulating their apartments both reduces their heating bills and improves the visual aspect of the neighborhood.

For example, Romania started its thermal insulation program in 2009, which offered grants to homeowner associations to improve the thermal performance of their buildings. The central government covered 50 percent of final costs, local authorities 30 percent, and end beneficiaries 20 percent. Initially, the program met a muted response because people were reluctant to try an unfamiliar program. But after the first pilots, more people bought into the program. Eventually, waiting lists got so long that many households performed the thermal insulation work on their own, without any public assistance. In Cluj-Napoca, for example, a quarter of the city's apartments (20,047 of 83,779) were thermally insulated from March 2009 to June 2011. Of these, 4,848 were insulated with the help of public funding, and the rest were rehabilitated with fully private funding. The program infused life into a construction sector hit hard by the economic crisis, with 14 construction companies being involved in thermal insulation work.

Unlocking Rental Markets

Eurasian countries have very high homeownership rates and fairly rigid rental markets. The private sector is moving to create more rental spaces, but the pace is slow, and a large share of rental activity takes place outside formal channels (to avoid income taxation).

The real estate market is geared toward ownership rather than renting, for several reasons. A finished unit can garner high returns on investment (much higher than in mature western markets), the costs of owning an apartment or house are low (because property taxes are low), and people in the region prefer to own rather than rent (a remnant of Soviet times). But not everyone has the capital to buy a new home. Young people are most affected, with many continuing to live with parents well into their 30s (Robila 2004).

Local authorities have to take an active role in unlocking rental markets. One way is to require that private developers building on publicly owned land set aside units with affordable rents, which can be rented to individuals and families in a particular income bracket. Such measures can complement more widespread subsidies and grants for affordable homeownership. In turn, local authorities can put in place tenancy laws that protect renters and provide incentives for developers to invest in rental housing.

Providing Affordable Urban Services Efficiently

In truly sustainable cities, efficient and affordable urban services are paramount. Efficiency translates into economic viability and environmental consciousness. And affordability takes the social aspect into consideration, ensuring that all people in the city, regardless of income, have access to quality services. Improving infrastructure access can include the assessment of demand for specific services, understanding of the market structure (feasibility of competition and natural monopolies with price regulation implications), choice of regulatory framework (pricing rules and legal framework), and ownership options.

The transition has taken its toll on city infrastructure and the quality of urban services. Improving this infrastructure and these services needs to be accompanied by improved local or regional self-government (with less reliance on subsidies and transfers from the central government) and higher accountability to citizens. Service providers should have the tools for recovering costs, both from charges paid by users who are well served and from governments for service that is a public good or delivered to users unable to pay.

Ensuring Sustainable Water and Sanitation Services

Offering quality municipal services comes at a price. During the Soviet era, services were heavily subsidized. This method of financing municipal services carried over to recent times.

In the long run, depending excessively on public subsidies can contribute to deteriorating service quality (World Bank 2004). Running utilities sustainably requires balancing economic and social efficiency. Ideally, utilities should be able to recuperate operating costs through a viable tariff structure and ensure that everyone has access to quality services. Service providers should be accountable to their customers, who are also represented by the municipal owners. This role of local government as an agent should be separated from undue (short-term) political influence.

Low tariffs are an important element of social policy in Azerbaijan, Belarus, Tajikistan, Ukraine, and especially Turkmenistan (where communal services are free) and Uzbekistan (where water tariffs have not changed since 2002; table 2.6). Local authorities argue that low tariffs help keep services affordable, but given the development situation in the region, these authorities lack the resources to provide good services. Moreover, doing so would be an inefficient use of government resources. The United Nations Development Programme

TABLE 2.6

Water Tariffs and Cross-Subsidy Rates in Regions' Capital Cities, 2010

Capital city	Posted residential tariff, dollars per cubic meter	Cross-subsidy rate, ratio
Chisinau, Moldova	0.74	1.41
Moscow, Russian Federation	0.54	1.31
Yerevan, Armenia	0.35	1.00
Baku, Azerbaijan	0.19	4.67
Kiev, Ukraine	0.16	2.11
Astana, Kazakhstan	0.15	1.81
Tbilisi, Georgia[a]	0.14	3.75
Minsk, Belarus	0.13	2.23
Bishkek, Kyrgyz Republic	0.10	1.77
Dushanbe, Tajikistan[b]	0.08	5.07
Tashkent, Uzbekistan	0.04	2.09

Source: IBNET database.
Note: Data on Ashgabat, Turkmenistan are not available.
a. Tariff set on a per capita basis of GEL 2.40 per cubic meter and a consumption norm of 350 liters per capita per day.
b. Tariff set on a per capita basis of SM 2.47 per cubic meter with a consumption norm of 250 liters per capita per day.

office in Kazakhstan reported that water tariffs were just 25–33 percent of affordability level, encouraging the wasting of water. Not much has changed since 2004, when the report was published, with tariffs changing only symbolically, despite inflation and rising energy costs.

This state of affairs poses a financial paradox. Almost all utilities receive subsidies (either subsidies for operations or transfers for investments) and provide services below costs, by running down their assets and accumulating debt. Many utilities find this approach simpler than taking measures to introduce better management practices, since they are confident that local governments will not allow services to be suspended. So, water service quality is declining, and utilities may be unsustainable without substantial reforms in tariff policy and a financing mechanism for municipal infrastructure.

Encouraging Intermunicipal Cooperation

Municipalities often run services in a vacuum, focusing mainly on their constituents. But many public services are much better organized regionally, where the benefits of economies of scale can be reaped. For instance, solid waste management systems could be run more efficiently if they were organized regionally, by having one major landfill close to the major regional center and transfer stations close to smaller cities, rather than having each city served by its own landfill. Higher efficiency can also translate into higher profitability and more participation from the private sector.

Rethinking District Heating System

District heating was the norm in most Soviet cities. If these systems were run efficiently in the transition years, they could have continued to be a reliable and environmentally friendly means of delivering heat and hot water to households. But a lack of care and investment (because of poor cost recovery and little accountability to consumers) led to the deterioration of networks, thus increasing costs. Water losses registered because of bad piping are transferred to households, which have become increasingly resistant to paying for water and heat they did not receive and for bad service (heat levels often cannot be adjusted, and heat is delivered regardless of need).

Thus, many people have disconnected themselves from the system and installed individual heating units. In Armenia, most of the district heating systems stopped service in 1992. The few that remained were taken out of service in 2003, when the government stopped subsidizing them. Many Armenians have switched to individual gas-operated heating units or local solutions, such as boilers that serve an apartment building or entire block. Low-income households, and many public institutions, that could not afford individual heating units have been literally left out in the cold.

To address this issue, Armenia's government, with the World Bank and the Global Partnership on Output-Based Aid, put together a grant scheme that offers incentives for adopting cost-effective heating. By 2009, more than 10,000 poor urban households, and several schools, had benefited from this program, receiving heat and hot water efficiently.

In other situations, district heating could become viable again. Forward-looking cities, such as Copenhagen and Stockholm, have widely adopted district heating as a way of shrinking their carbon footprint. But these cities can afford to charge higher tariffs. Many former Soviet Union cities house vulnerable groups, which are very sensitive to tariff fluctuations. For these groups, as well as for the middle class, individual heating solutions may prove more effective. Local authorities should weigh social, economic, and environmental considerations and decide what options are best in the long term.

Extending Services to Peripheral Areas

Peripheral areas are underserved in many Eurasian cities, and urban infrastructure extension often does not keep pace with land developments, forcing new developments on the outskirts of towns—particularly single-family detached homes—to provide their own infrastructure. Lacking water and sewerage pipes, many people have drilled their own wells and constructed individual septic tanks. And lacking organized trash collection, many people simply throw their garbage into nearby waterways or dump it into makeshift landfills. In some instances, slums have formed in those peripheral areas.

This is not a safe or sustainable way for a city to develop. Local authorities should monitor all new developments, ensuring that zoning regulations are respected and that builders have the necessary permits. The infrastructure network can be extended appropriately, based on actual requirements. To some extent, the municipality can anticipate infrastructure extension needs by putting clear zoning regulations in place. Thus, if an undeveloped area is zoned for low-density, single-family detached homes, new infrastructure requirements will be more modest than what a high-density neighborhood would require.

Annex 2A

TABLE 2A.1

Car Registration in the Former Soviet Union, by Country

Country	Population, 2007, millions	Percent urban, 2008	GDP per capita, 2008 dollars	Base year of registration	Number of vehicles in base car registration year	End year of registration	Number of vehicles in end car registration year	Annual vehicle registration growth between base year and end year, percent
Russian Federation	142.1	73.4	11,832	1993	11,518,900	2007	29,405,000	6.9
Kazakhstan	15.5	57.9	8,513	1993	995,873	2007	2,183,131	6.3
Belarus	9.7	73.5	6,230	1993	773,582	2007	2,329,450	8.2
Azerbaijan	8.6	51.9	5,315	1993	263,315	2007	616,853	6.3
Ukraine	46.5	68.0	3,899	1993	4,235,700	2007	5,939,244	2.4
Armenia	3.0	63.9	3,873	1993	282,448	2007	296,877	0.4
Turkmenistan	4.9	48.6	3,039	1993	214,100	2007	404,015	4.6
Georgia	4.4	52.7	2,970	1993	468,763	2007	416,106	−0.8
Moldova	3.7	41.8	1,694	1993	166,440	2007	338,944	5.2
Uzbekistan	26.9	36.8	1,023	1993	861,000	1994	971,800	12.9
Kyrgyz Republic	5.2	36.3	958	1993	188,200	2007	229,807	1.5
Tajikistan	6.7	26.5	751	1993	200,700	2007	192,403	−0.3

Sources: World Bank 2011, United Nations Statistics Division.
Note: GDP = gross domestic product.

Improving Transit Infrastructure and Services

The dramatic changes in urban transport conditions in Eurasian countries resulted in many issues that governments have not fully addressed at either the national or local governmental levels. Government actions will be particularly important in addressing the lack of appropriate laws and regulations, which impedes effective responses to improve urban transport conditions. Part of the problem is that cities need changes in national legislation, which is out of their control, to act as needed. For example, charging for on-street parking is illegal in some countries. Where it is legal, the fees charged or fines levied are restricted in some cases, making viable parking programs difficult to administer. Another example: there are too many exemptions for various classes of public transit riders, which are not matched with compensation from the central governments to the cities that operate the systems.

The urban infrastructure from the Soviet era was not designed to handle the current car load and use, and it has to be completely revamped. Today, a disproportionate amount of urban transit expenditure in former Soviet Union cities goes to new road development, often at the expense of current infrastructure, which is left to deteriorate.

Additional traffic also creates congestion. Most large Eurasian cities face traffic congestion–related issues—some can be solved through strategic and efficient traffic management, but others require targeted policies. London tackled its congestion problems by introducing charges for all vehicles entering the urban core.

To rid cities of unsightly makeshift garages built on public land around apartment blocks, policy makers should encourage privately managed underground or above-ground neighborhood parking garages, which would remove cars from street curbs.

Eurasian cities are fairly well served by public transit, though there is a need to increase efficiency and financial sustainability. Moscow's metro is one of the most heavily used systems in the world. And several other Eurasian cities also have working metro systems or are in the process of building them (see table 2A.2). The performance and efficiency of public transport services can be improved by consolidating the number of bus service providers (to encourage economies of scale and reduce the complexity of system integration); lengthening and making other alterations to concession agreements (to encourage or require that private operators invest in better vehicles and provide better services); engaging in better route planning, extending service, and integrating modes of transit; and selectively increasing fares and reducing passenger exemptions (to improve cost recovery of service providers).

TABLE 2A.2

Length and Capacity of Metro Systems in the Former Soviet Union, by City, 2010

City	Population	Annual number of passengers, millions	System length, kilometers	Annual number of passengers per kilometer, millions	Annual metro trips per capita
Moscow, Russian Federation	10,509,592	2,573	292.2	8.81	244.8
St. Petersburg, Russian Federation	4,502,991	878	110.2	7.97	195.0
Kiev, Ukraine	2,740,312	642	59.9	10.72	234.3
Kharkiv, Ukraine	1,459,908	278	35.4	7.85	190.4
Baku, Azerbaijan	1,202,258	176	32	5.5	146.4
Tbilisi, Georgia	1,140,408	91.8	26.4	3.48	80.5
Minsk, Belarus	1,763,899	252	30.3	11.5	142.8
Nizhny Novgorod, Russian Federation	1,256,488	33	15.3	2.16	26.2
Yerevan, Armenia	1,091,235	17	13.4	1.27	15.6
Kazan, Russian Federation	1,120,320	7	8.0	0.88	n.a.
Tashkent, Uzbekistan	2,194,272	164	37.5	4.4	57.9
Novosibirsk, Russian Federation	1,372,332	70	14.3	4.9	55.4
Samara, Russian Federation	1,143,346	27	10.2	3.5	23.2
Yekaterinburg, Russian Federation	1,308,441	20	8.6	3.9	22.1
Dnipropetrovsk, Ukraine	1,044,770	15	7.8	2.1	14.3
Almaty, Kazakhstan	1,372,660	Under construction	8.6[a]	n.a.	n.a.
Astana, Kazakhstan	750,000	Construction of elevated light rail system planned for 2010	35	n.a.	n.a.
Omsk, Russian Federation	1,123,395	Under construction; 69 million passengers annually projected	n.a.	n.a.	n.a.
Donetsk, Ukraine	987,453	Under construction	70.0	n.a.	n.a.
Chelyabinsk, Russian Federation	1,089,328	Under construction	6.7	n.a.	n.a.
Krasnoyarsk, Russian Federation	931,536	Under construction	8.5	n.a.	n.a.
Sochi, Russian Federation	330,156	Under construction	86.4	n.a.	n.a.
Rostov-on-Don, Russian Federation	1,044,852	Planned	n.a.	n.a.	n.a.

continued

TABLE 2A.2
Continued

City	Population	Annual number of passengers, millions	System length, kilometers	Annual number of passengers per kilometer, millions	Annual metro trips per capita
Krasnodar, Russian Federation	702,427	Planned	n.a.	n.a.	n.a.
Volgograd, Russian Federation	975,150	Existing metro tram serves 50 million passengers a year	13.5	3.7	n.a.
Kryvyi Rih, Ukraine	730,739	Existing metro tram	17.7	n.a.	n.a.

Sources: World Gazetteer, http://world-gazetteer.com/MetroSoyuza, www.metrosoyuza.net/; individual websites of transit authorities in selected former Soviet Union cities.
Note: n.a. = not applicable.
a. There is a big construction project underway that will bring the length to 45 kilometers.

Notes

1. Indeed, Soviet planners worked under the assumption that the market was inherently incapable of generating the right outcomes for the economy and society.
2. Housing markets are subject to market inefficiencies in capitalist systems. Where people cannot afford housing, public measures, such as housing subsidies, are needed. Land allocation by planners for public purposes, such as parks and infrastructure, considers land values but balances the demand for profitable uses against the public need.
3. One could argue that many mass housing (tract) developments in capitalist city suburbs are no more appealing than Soviet neighborhoods—and sometimes even worse, in the costs of extending infrastructure networks and encouraging private cars.
4. In 2007, after years of market development, former Soviet Union countries were still far behind Western European countries in available retail space. Russia had 39 square meters of gross leasable shopping center space per 1,000 inhabitants, and Ukraine just 19 square meters. These figures are an order of magnitude lower than in the Netherlands (448 square meters), Sweden (408), the United Kingdom (266), or France (245) (see Dijkman 2009).
5. This density pattern is not equally strong in all developed cities. Many factors affect the way land is valued. In the United States, cars and low fuel costs have often made land more valuable in suburban areas, leaving central cities devoid of people and flattening the density profile across the city radius, as low transport costs encourage higher consumption of land in the periphery.
6. For a discussion of a similar phenomenon in Germany in the 1990s, see World Bank (2009). This dichotomy between what planners wanted and what people wanted is well illustrated by events in Germany after reunification. The Federal Republic of Germany was in the midst of developing a service-based economy, while the former German Democratic Republic

remained heavily industrialized. Over a short time, women—who adapt much more rapidly to a service-based economy than men do—migrated from the former German Democratic Republic to the Federal Republic of Germany, leaving a largely male population behind.

7. In Russia, there is also a large gap in life expectancy at birth between men and women: during the transition years, women lived on average 12 years longer than men.

8. The World Bank prepared a guidance note—*The Management of Brownfields Redevelopment* (World Bank 2010)—for cities in Eastern Europe and Central Asia, highlighting the benefits, issues, and procedures of reusing already developed land.

9. Such a policy for apartment buildings assumes that some entity (such as a homeowner association) takes responsibility for the exterior and that the cost can be funded by the residents collectively.

References

Bertaud, Alain. 2010. *The Development of Russian Cities: Impact of Reforms on Spatial Development*. Draft report. Washington, DC: World Bank.

Buckley, Robert M., and Federico Mini. 2000. *From Commissars to Mayors: Cities in the Transition Economies*. Washington, DC: World Bank.

Buckley, Robert M., and Sasha Tsenkova. 2001. "Housing Market Systems in Reforming Socialist Economies: Comparative Indicators of Performance and Policy." *European Journal of Housing Policy* 1 (2): 257–89.

Colton, Timothy J. 1995. *Moscow: Governing the Socialist Metropolis*. Cambridge, MA: The Belknap Press of Harvard University Press.

De Soto, Hernando. 2003. *The Mystery of Capital: Why Capitalism Triumphs in the West and Fails Everywhere Else*. New York: Basic Books.

Dijkman, Marinus, ed. 2009. *Retail Space Europe: Assets, Trends, and Market Players*. The Hague, the Netherlands: Europe Real Estate Publishers.

Federal State Statistics Service. 1995–2009. *The Demographic Yearbook of Russia*. Russia: Federal State Statistics Service. http://www.infostat.ru/eng/catalog.html?id=309&page=info.

Gessen, Keith. 2010. "Letter from Moscow. Stuck: The Meaning of the City's Traffic Nightmare." *The New Yorker,* August 2.

Jacobs, Jane. 1961. *The Death and Life of Great American Cities*. New York: Vintage.

Kaganova, Olga, Abdirasul Akmatov, and Charles Undeland. 2007. "Strategic Land Management Plans in Kyrgyzstan's Cities: Promoting Transparent Local Public Policy and Efficient Utilization of Public Land." Paper presented at the Fourth Urban Research Symposium, World Bank, Washington, DC, May 14–16.

Lipman, Barbara J. 2010. *Homeowner Associations in Cities in the CIS: Stalled on the Road to Reform*. Washington, DC: World Bank.

Mercer Cost of Living Survey. 2008. http://www.mercer.com/costofliving.

Myers, Steven Lee. 2003. "Moscow Journal: Landmark Buildings Tumble, Creating a Dust-Up." *New York Times*, October 16.

Pejovich, Svetozar. 1990. *The Economics of Property Rights: Towards a Theory of Comparative Systems*. Dordrecht, the Netherlands: Kluwer Academic.

Reisner, Marc. 1993. *Cadillac Desert: The American West and Its Disappearing Water*. New York: Penguin.

Robila, Mihaela, ed. 2004. *Families in Eastern Europe*. Vol. 5 of *Contemporary Perspectives in Family Research*. Amsterdam: Elsevier.

Romer, Paul M. 1990. "Endogenous Technological Change." *The Journal of Political Economy* 98 (5): S71–S102.

Salukvadze, Joseph. 2009. "Market versus Planning? Mechanisms of Spatial Change in Post-Soviet Tbilisi." In *City Culture and City Planning in Tbilisi: Where Europe and Asia Meet*, ed. Kristof Van Asche, Joseph Salukvadze, and Nick Shavishvili. Lewiston, NY: Edwin Mellen Press.

Shavishvili, Nick. 2010. "The Tbilisi Model: A Unique Four-Tier System of Urban Regeneration: A Program for Crisis Management in Historical Cities Worldwide." Unpublished report.

Suzuki, Hiroaki, Arish Dastur, Sebastian Moffatt, Nanae Yabuki, and Hinako Maruyama. 2010. *Eco2 Cities: Ecological Cities as Economic Cities*. Washington, DC: World Bank.

UNDP (United Nations Development Programme) online database. http://data.un.org/.

UN-HABITAT (United Nations Human Settlements Programme). 2007. *State of the World Cities*. Nairobi: UN-HABITAT.

United Nations World Development Indicators.

World Bank. 2004. *World Development Report 2004: Making Services Work for Poor People*. Washington, DC: World Bank.

———. 2007. *Albania Urban Sector Review*. Report No. 37277-AL. Washington, DC: World Bank.

———. 2009. *World Development Report 2009: Reshaping Economic Geography*. Washington, DC: World Bank.

———. 2010. *The Management of Brownfields Redevelopment: A Guidance Note*. Washington, DC: World Bank.

———. 2011. *World Development Indicators*. Washington, DC: World Bank.

———. Doing Business online database. http://doingbusiness.org.

CHAPTER 3

Connecting Cities

Spotlight—Connecting Tajikistan

The whistle of a gentle breeze, and the faint buzzing of a bee in the sky. It was a sunny day at the border post between Tajikistan and Uzbekistan, but there wasn't much action. The large metal gate across the road was locked, and the border post seemingly deserted. We began banging a brick on the gate to get someone's attention. The Uzbek border guards were inside their hut watching football.

This was certainly not the thriving border crossing one might expect from its location between Tajikistan's second largest city (Khujand; population 193,800) and the prosperous Uzbek cities in the Ferghana Valley (Andijon, Fergana, Kokand, Margilon, and Namangan; combined population 1.3 million). The reason appears to be political rather than physical: the border is "thick" with time-consuming paperwork, proce-dures, and arbitrary delays. Traders in the Tajik marketplace in Khujand source their fruit juice from the Kyrgyz Republic and their figs from Afghanistan, but avoid Uzbek imports wher-ever possible. Our simple journey on foot—two people with one small suitcase each—entailed more than 90 minutes of waiting while paperwork was filled out and processed and documents checked. The contrast to the border between Tajikistan and the Kyrgyz Republic a few miles away was striking: several cars and a small truck passed through in quick succession, and the whole process took 10–15 minutes. But in Tajikistan's cities, industries are visibly constrained by thick international borders.

Compare this situation with the fluid passenger and cargo movements taking place in the world's more economically dynamic regions. In the Pearl River Delta, one can "work in Hong Kong and live in Macao; live in Hong Kong and trade in Shenzhen; live in Zhuhai and work in Zhongshan; work in Foshan and live in Guangzhou; live and work any place at all, yet still have a weekend residence in Nansha" (Gutierrez and Portefaix 2005). In the Ferghana Valley, why can one not work in Kokand and live in Khujand; live in Kokand and trade in Batken; live in Isfara and work in Ferghana; work in Margilon and live in Osh? Why cannot the cement and brick factories on the Tajik side of the border expand their production by selling to Uzbekistan, and why cannot the UzDaewoo car parts production lines in Asaka and Andijan benefit from selling more of their speedy and efficient cars to Tajikistan and the Kyrgyz Republic? These cities are mostly connected by good roads, but separated merely by bureaucratic boundaries. Indeed, Tajiks now need a visa to cross into Uzbekistan.

Cities and countries elsewhere in Eurasia also face connectivity challenges, especially because of the complex issues that need to be worked on regionally. For example, the economic impact of Georgia's new highway to its Black Sea ports, or a new railway to Turkey, will be constrained unless its neighbor Azerbaijan also mirrors its border reforms and transport investments and unless Turkmenistan and Kazakhstan unblock their congested monopoly on Caspian Sea ferry transport. Georgia will be hoping that its successes are strong enough to demonstrate economic benefits to its neighbors.

The power of connectivity to bring economic benefits is demonstrated within countries, too. In Kazakhstan the population of Karaganda shrank dramatically from 614,000 in 1989 to 436,000 in 1999, but has now turned around, rising to

460,000 in 2009. It shrank because of the rapidly declining demand for steel, coal, copper, and machinery from Karaganda (and neighboring Temirtau). Its renaissance—with higher real wages and grand city plans for a new sports hall and leisure facilities—has been prompted by a new road with two lanes in each direction to Astana, the capital (reducing the journey from 4 to 2 hours), and its place on the country's new express train line, which links Karaganda to Almaty (Kazakhstan's largest city) and Astana.

Key Issues

- Eurasia's physical infrastructure is gradually shifting from a hierarchical structure oriented toward Moscow, to a more multipolar structure reflecting the emerging economic importance of Europe and Asia.

- Big gains could come from better interstate cooperation on land transport corridor management, as borders and bottlenecks hamper trade. Cities could better connect by introducing less restrictive international aviation policies, encouraging competition in air transport markets, and promoting information and communications technology (ICT) connectivity.

- Institutions have been established to develop, manage, and regulate connectivity infrastructure and services, but progress is slow in some countries.

Soviet planners did not figure the "cost of distance" in their decisions. They created large industrial towns in remote areas to serve single industries or in locations with multiple industries. Output and plan fulfillment dominated the system, with little regard to the cost of a particular region. Because transport costs were subsidized, Soviet enterprises were located in remote regions regardless of their distance from input sources and potential markets.

The result: a system with too many dispersed cities that underexploited agglomeration economies, along with excessive trade volumes among the Soviet republics. The 1989 census for the Soviet

Union reports more than 2,500 towns with fewer than 5,000 residents. Trade within the Soviet Union exceeded its trade potential by about 43 times, if potential is taken as proportional to the gross domestic products (GDPs) of the trading countries and the distance between them (Fidrmuc and Fidrmuc 2000).

This chapter explores the factors that shaped interurban and international connectivity between cities in Eurasia and beyond. It emphasizes the policy and institutional dimensions of transport and telecommunications as the connecting systems that ease the movement of goods, people, and information across cities and countries.

The Soviet Past: Connecting to a Preeminent Center

Two main forces affected the development of transport systems between cities in the Soviet Union: a state-driven dispersive force, which sought to distribute urban life across the country to eradicate inequality across regions—and a central bureaucracy, which channeled power and subordination along the administrative chain of command. The interaction of these forces led to a hierarchical network of cities that were more evenly distributed by size than in other countries. And relations between the cities were governed by this hierarchy. Governments of lower level cities were constrained by and dependent on cities at the next level in the political hierarchy for planning. Interactions, and thus transport links, were designed and centered on this geographical chain, creating hierarchical pyramids that lacked or had very limited horizontal links.

The massive size of the Soviet Union influenced its transport system. The Russian Federation alone is the largest country in the world (17 million square kilometers), with almost 40,000 kilometers of coastline and long distances between the eastern and western extremities (almost 10,000 kilometers separate Vladivostok and St. Petersburg). Moreover, Central Asia has the second-highest concentration of landlocked countries after Africa, and one of the most difficult terrains on Earth. Some 70 percent of Turkmenistan and large portions of Kazakhstan (the world's ninth-largest country and its largest landlocked country) and Uzbekistan are deserts, and their border areas are mountainous. Long distances and lack of accessibility created substantial transport challenges.

Railways were the most important transport mode in Soviet times, carrying some 89 percent of freight volume before World War II (Khachaturov 1945). Waterborne transport came next, carrying only 8 percent, a very low figure explained partly by the limited access to the region's frozen waterways during wintertime. To worsen matters, international sea trade was limited to specific commodities (petroleum, coal, wood, and grain) and a handful of partner countries—and handled by a monopolistic freight forwarding agency. Road freight services were used as feeders for railways and in short-haul distribution, comprising only 3 percent of the total freight volume. The remaining freight was transported by air, though marginal at the time.

As the average length of freight hauls grew (due to greater regional specialization and the depletion of nearby deposits of raw materials) and transport costs rose (due to inefficiencies in transport management), savings had to be achieved through higher efficiency in operations, disagglomeration, higher regional self-sufficiency, and alternative transport modes, such as the underused system of inland waterways. The attempted diversion of a large portion of the rail trade between Central Asia and European Russia to Caspian Sea routes increased inland navigation, with new route operations and vessels (such as train ferries from Krasnovodsk to Baku). Also, the completion of the Trans-Kazakh line linking the Karagandy coal reserves to the Urals and western Siberia—and its connection in 1953 to the Turkestan-Siberia line—reduced the average regional length of haul by strengthening interdependence between Central Asia and Kazakhstan (Taaffe 1962).

Railways Throughout the Empire

Connectivity during Soviet times was largely about railways. Partly due to the dispersion of production across a vast territory, the transportation of cargo in the Soviet economy represented a larger share of GDP than in western economies (Raballand 2004; Strong and others 1996). In western Russia, cities sprung up where they did for the same reasons they did elsewhere in Europe: to insulate the capital from military threat, and because of their proximity to waterways. In the east and elsewhere, railways were the most influential factor behind cities' expansion.[1] Cities were created along railway lines either to support the national economy by extracting resources or to promote the socialist ideology. The railway network in the western part of the empire had the densest structure and radiated from Moscow, but in the east and elsewhere, its configuration was mainly linear. The system became so extensive that most cities were within 10 kilometers of a railway line (Iyer 2003).

Soon after World War II, vast stretches of the Soviet railway system were electrified to increase efficiency and industrial potential. This allowed the railways to use more locally generated energy and

avoid petroleum products, which had to be hauled over long distances (Wohl 1945). The lines chosen for electrification were those
that carried high volumes of traffic, passed through mountainous
areas, or traversed deserts, where steam locomotives were inadequate. Electrification also extended to urban commuter systems.
Cities—mainly in Russia and the western part of Eurasia—saw their
systems electrified first.

By 1990, the Soviet railway system was one of the world's most
extensive and complex transport systems. It comprised 151,000 kilometers of industrial or "own account" railways (such as industrial
conglomerates operating their own trains and wagons), integrating
operations across 11 time zones. Its 60,000 locomotives managed
almost 1.5 million freight wagons and more than 50,000 passenger
cars, carrying half the world's freight traffic. Russia had the largest
share, with almost 60 percent of tracks and 68 percent of ton-
kilometers. Ukraine accounted for about 16 percent of tracks and
13 percent of ton-kilometers, and Kazakhstan for 10 percent of
tracks and 11 percent of ton-kilometers.

The Role of Trucking

Long distances, heavy cargoes, and the government's reluctance to
invest in highway transport meant that trucking was less effective
than rail transport. Even so, before the breakup of the Soviet Union,
about 3.2 million trucks were engaged in commercial road transport
activities, most assigned to a few giant, vertically integrated organizations operating as monopolies within each republic. Agroprom—the
second-largest operator, with more than 700,000 trucks, for the
roughly 26,000 state and collective farms—hauled agricultural products among farms and to food-processing plants; its trucks were also
used in some intercity transport. For-hire trucking, overseen by
Rosavtotrans, transported 18 percent of all tonnage moved by truck
in Russia.[2] Its constituent organizations were trucking associations
that operated 30–40 enterprises, which collectively owned an average of 200 trucks and enjoyed a commodity-specific or geographic
monopoly within the oblast.

Air Transport Behind the Curtain

By the time of the breakup of the Soviet Union, air transport was one
of the most popular transport modes (Sagers and Maraffa 1990). As
with other transport modes, geography was a key driver behind the
expansion of Aeroflot, the Soviet centrally planned airline. Given the

enormous distances in the former Soviet Union, time savings from air travel were larger than those from other transport. Technological advances made aviation even more attractive for passengers when scheduled jet services became available in the 1950s. Moreover, climatic conditions barred physical infrastructure beyond the permafrost line, leaving a large part of Eurasia isolated during wintertime (Porch 1964). Thus, capital expenditures to develop airport and air navigation infrastructure were deemed minimal compared with those for other transport.

Another factor contributing to air travel's popularity was its lower cost for domestic services (Kish 1958). Land and air transport fares were set to curb congestion in trunk railway lines by diverting long-haul passenger rail traffic to airplanes. For example, Aeroflot fares between cities with a railway connection were discounted 40 percent (Jenkins 1963; MacDonald 1975).

In the early 1950s, Eurasia was isolated from international commercial air transport. Only a few western airlines introduced services to Eurasia after 1954, and in each case, Aeroflot flew a parallel service to the corresponding capital on a strict reciprocal basis.[3] As part of the Soviet policy to minimize foreign penetration, all airlines from non-Eurasian or satellite republics were restricted to "gateway points" near its borders. And they were not permitted to cross any major portion of Soviet territory, much less to continue to third countries (Heymann 1958). Even so, Aeroflot introduced interline agreements to facilitate flight connections with western carriers at specific points to ease luggage check-in and ticketing at the origin point for the entire trip.

Until the early 1960s, air transport planners favored expanding direct services from Moscow to the Soviet capitals and many major cities. Air services were divided into two kinds. "All-Union" air services comprised trunk routes from Moscow to the capitals of the 14 other republics and more than 100 regional administrative centers (accounting for 60 percent of passenger traffic in 1973). These services were operated according to Aeroflot's central timetable, presumably after extensive research by the Ministry of Civil Aviation. "Local" air services had scheduled regional and local flights within the boundaries of a republic, region, or district. From local administrative centers, 29 different Aeroflot directorates had regular services to about 3,500 towns and villages throughout Eurasia, accounting for a large share of feeder traffic onto trunk "all-Union" routes (MacDonald 1975).

As for cargo, Aeroflot established regular freight services interlinking up to 44 cities in the early 1960s, using mostly turboprop aircraft based in Moscow. Seasonal requirements for carrying perishables from main producing areas of southern Eurasia to central and northern Eurasia were counterbalanced by fish products and seafood flying the opposite way. Air freight services were essential in Eurasia's most isolated regions (such as Siberia), providing necessary services during wintertime and performing air-bridge (rail or sea to air) operations from nodal points along the Trans-Siberian railway line, ports in the Okhotsk Sea, and northern parts of the former Soviet Union (MacDonald 1975).

By 1990, air transport comprised almost 35 percent of all intercity passenger travel. The staggeringly low fares and huge popularity of air travel transformed Aeroflot into the world's largest airline, with more than 130 million passengers a year. After the breakup of the Soviet Union, regional Civil Aviation Directorates that had served under Moscow were separated. Aircrafts, airports, and air traffic control facilities were allocated to each directorate in different geographical locations, where air passenger operations were later resumed under newly created airlines ("Baby-flots") in different Eurasian republics (World Bank 1993).

Government Control over Communications

Like other infrastructure in the Soviet Union, communications systems were controlled by the government, primarily from transmit decisions affecting the economy, national security, and administrative functions throughout Eurasia. The Ministry of Communications was responsible for telegraph and telephone transmissions, communications satellites, and the postal service. Postal and telegraph infrastructure was spread widely across the country.

The Soviet Union was a world leader in developing advanced communications technologies. In 1965, it inaugurated the Molniya satellite communications system, linking Moscow to towns and military installations throughout the country. The system enabled retransmission of radio and television broadcasts originating in Moscow. Several other satellite communications systems were also launched in the 1970s and 1980s. Since the breakup, the republics have struggled, facing huge costs to replace Soviet-era systems.

The Transitional Present: Living in a Multihub World

The aftermath of the breakup was marked by a series of challenges. Among the most important was the absence or weakness of institutions for managing transport, aggravated by the abrupt changes in traffic and transport use that followed. However, the

Soviet Union's fragmentation as a whole had immediate consequences. While most operations had been centralized, the multiplication of intervening entities quickly highlighted the lack of an alternative mechanism for coproducing policies with neighboring countries. Difficulties with funding, maintaining, and improving transport and communications systems also emerged.

Establishing New National Institutions and Policies

One of the immediate legacies of the breakup was that the centralized bodies no longer available could guide policy formulation and implementation. As in other sectors, a vacuum was left in institutions responsible for planning and managing transport. And filling the institutional and planning gaps remains one of the more important challenges Eurasian countries face as they seek to better manage their transport both locally and nationally.

Institutional development took two forms: establishing ministries and agencies responsible for the transport sector—and designing strategic plans for its development. Several Eurasian countries had to establish ministries for transport. Countries started with—and still have—different capacities, and they reformed at different paces. Azerbaijan, for example, established a ministry of transport in 1998 and has progressed substantially since then to encourage the private sector to provide transport services.

Before the ministry, the Cabinet of Azerbaijan handled all transport matters. The government also separated the regulatory and operational responsibilities of state agencies in the transport sector. Azeravtonagliyyat, the former parastatal, now handles regulatory activities, acting as a de facto ministry in the road sector. Since a presidential decree in 2000, the former Caspian Shipping has been vested with all shipping authorities of the Ministry of Transport, even though it continues to act as an operator in the sector. Policy for the transport sector comprises laws, decrees, and regulations, including the Law on Transport, Law on Communication, Law on Road Traffic, and Law on Roads. The sector's institutional fragmentation hinders coordination across modes and strategic management. There has been some privatization, with most road transport operations now run commercially and most road haulage firms run by private operators.

The Changing Face of Land Transport

Rail transport dominated passenger and freight transport during the Soviet era. Its continued importance depended on the long distances between centers and the fact that the commodities carried were largely bulk, such as raw materials. In addition, countries were likely to continue to favor railway transport for strategic reasons. It is not surprising, then, that this sector suffered the most after the breakup. But new trade patterns greatly increased the demand for road freight services, creating new challenges to provide adequate infrastructure and regulation for the sector.

Organizing, Downsizing, and Redirecting Railways

In 1992, the railway system was disbanded and succeeded by 19 regionally autonomous railway administrations. Whereas a single management team previously ran the railways, 19 teams now run individual national systems, complicating coordination. Moreover, controls at new international borders forced trains to stop to change crews and locomotives. To prevent the total disintegration of rail operations, a Railway Transport Council was established early in 1992 to coordinate functions (World Bank 1993). It reflected the realization very early on that railway transport would continue to be important to most of the newly independent republics.

Railway performance since 1992 has varied across the region. Output and incomes declined dramatically through the 1990s, causing demand for railway services to decline (figure 3.1). The railways of Belarus, Kazakhstan, and Russia rebounded quickly, however: by about 2007, output in these systems had returned to 1992 levels. In other countries, notably Azerbaijan and the Kyrgyz Republic, volumes recovered much more slowly, now accounting for less than half of what they were before the breakup. The different recovery paces reveal the extent to which capacity was overdesigned in places, leaving some railway systems with excessively large workforces and massive underused infrastructure that are costly to maintain.

Until the late 1980s, the bulk of Eurasia's rail traffic went to or through Moscow, reflecting not only a by-product of the capital's influence, but also the lack of connecting links with bordering economies to the east and west. Since the early 1990s, some trade volumes have been redirected and new connections developed—such as between the Turkmen and Iranian networks in 1996—driven by both economic imperatives and geopolitical considerations. In general, there has been growing emphasis on Central Asia. Kazakhstan, and Almaty in particular, has become an important node in the continental railway system. New lines wholly within Russia run between the east and St. Petersburg.

FIGURE 3.1

Railway Traffic Volumes in the Soviet Union and Successor Countries, 1985–2007

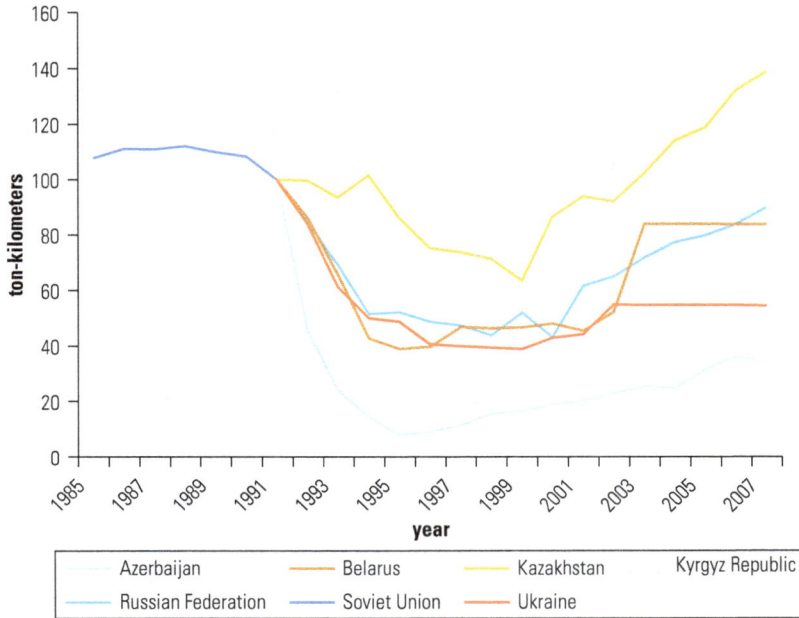

Source: World Bank 2009a.

Meeting the Growing Demands on Roads

Changes in transport patterns reflect changes in the volumes, directions, and types of trade flows within Eurasia. Most Eurasian countries export bulk commodities and import manufactured products from Western Europe—the latter better suited for road transport. So, one of the most important trends has been the rapid growth of road transport, affecting individual cities, entry points, and expenditures. Negatively, the increase in road transport has reduced road safety in most countries (box 3.1).

Although rail transport still comprises a large share of traffic in ton-kilometers, road traffic has grown rapidly. However, Eurasian roads were designed to carry a maximum single-axle load limit of 10 tons, and many roads were even designed for axle loads of only 6 tons. These limits are well below the international standards in Europe, where the gross vehicle mass is about 40 tons. This situation has led to a rapid deterioration of roads in nearly all Eurasian countries, raising the demand for funding for road rehabilitation and maintenance.

BOX 3.1

Declining Road Safety

As road transport has grown, road safety has declined. Countries enjoying rapid economic growth since the breakup (such as Kazakhstan and Russia) have increased motorization rapidly—without adequate infrastructure. Over 1990–2003, the number of cars per 1,000 people grew 120 percent in the Commonwealth of Independent States (World Bank 2009b).

Most vehicles in former Soviet Union countries are old, with substandard safety features. For this and other reasons, road safety is dire. The average mortality rate from road traffic accidents in the former Soviet Union is 21.8 per 100,000—nearly three times that of major Western European countries (7.9 per 100,000). Kazakhstan has the highest mortality rate (30.6 per 100,000), followed by Russia (25.2) and the Kyrgyz Republic (22.8). Russia led the world in deaths from road accidents, at more than 33,000 in 2007. The vast majority of fatalities are suffered by urban pedestrians, according to the World Bank (2009b). This study attributes the deteriorating road safety environment to three main risk factors:

- Road design features, including those that expose pedestrians to vehicles.

- Lack of effective regulation and enforcement of laws about vehicle condition, risky behavior, and driver education and training.

- Driver behavior, including speeding; driving recklessly; drinking and driving; not using seatbelts, helmets, and other protective equipment; and using mobile phones, especially for texting.

Source: World Bank 2009b.

Although after the breakup the central government had no formal price-setting mechanism for motor freight tariffs, there was some de facto regulation of rates at the municipal level and oblast in for-hire trucking. But as countries became more connected to Western Europe, they were exposed to more developed and sophisticated transport services—and adhered to international conventions. For instance, all Eurasian countries have ratified the Convention on the Contract for the International Carriage of Goods by Road of 1956, and all but Uzbekistan have ratified the Convention on Road Traffic of 1968 as well as the Convention on International Transport of Goods under Cover of Transit International Routier Carnets (TIR Convention) of 1975. Considerable road transport operations now take place through Turkey, for example.

Constraints on Water Transport

Given the limited extent of navigable rivers, most of the river transport system remained under Russian ownership following the breakup. Government policy in river shipping fostered the free negotiation of contracts, the removal of regulated tariffs, infrastructure financing through user fees rather than subsidies, and the spinoff of shipping companies from other enterprises, among other features (Strong and others 1996; World Bank 1993).

Eurasia depends on only a few seaports for external trade. The old maritime shipping system was organized under specialization, with each carrier and port developed to manage a specific part of Soviet trade, leaving disjointed water transport and infrastructure assets. Each shipping company in the merchant marine fleet was assigned ports to serve, with little overlap or competition (the shipping lines owned the ships). Russia's major seaports were owned by the regionally based national ship carriers. The central authorities determined the ships and cargo that went to each port. As a result, most ports became highly specialized (Strong and others 1996; World Bank 1993).

Water transport was already losing traffic before the breakup. And by 1992, the international ocean, national sabotage, and river transport's share of total freight tonnage had fallen to only 2.6 percent, down from 8.0 percent during World War II.

The disruption of seaborne trade links has been minimal, mainly because many Eurasian countries are landlocked, forcing them to rely on their coastal neighbors for sea access. The largest port remains St. Petersburg, which handled about 1.3 million 20-foot equivalent units in 2009 (table 3.1). The other major ports and port cities are also in Russia, though the ports in the Caucasus provide the shortest route between Central Asia and Europe. Batumi and Poti on the Black Sea in Georgia, Baku and Dyubendi in Azerbaijan, and Ilyichevski in Ukraine are critical for the landlocked republics. Eurasian countries also use ports in the Islamic Republic of Iran and Turkey, and some major regional trade corridors have been designed to promote these trade routes.

Opening Air Transport

Air traffic in the former republics fell sharply after the breakup. Passenger flows across the former Soviet Union declined to about one-sixth of the volumes prior to the collapse. But airfreight and passenger demand have grown rapidly since 2001. According to different estimates, air traffic will almost triple within the Commonwealth of

TABLE 3.1

TABLE 3.1

Maritime Port Volumes in the Former Soviet Union, 2009

20-foot equivalent units

Port	Volume
St. Petersburg, Russian Federation	1,341,850
Novorossiysk, Russian Federation	307,188
Ilyichevsk, Ukraine	256,825
Odessa, Ukraine	255,461
Vladivostok, Russian Federation	227,978
Poti, Georgia	172,800
Kaliningrad, Russian Federation	94,516
Vanino, Russian Federation	22,991
Batumi, Georgia	8,813
Mariupol, Ukraine	4,412

Source: Containerization International. http://www.ci-online.co.uk/.
Note: Table shows volumes of largest ports only.

Independent States in the next 20 years (Boeing Commercial Airplanes 2011). A major source for this projected growth is the expansion of Russia—Eurasia's most diverse and wealthy market. Russian aeronautical infrastructure and related activities range from state-of-the-art airports moving more than 20 million passengers annually, to local airfields in isolated regions with limited access to air services and faulty airside facilities. Russia is also where market dynamics are most vibrant: more carriers compete, and more carriers go out of business while others enter the market. In the rest of Eurasia, aviation markets are mainly concentrated in the capital's airport, and one or two major cities at best. In some cases, their flag carriers are still the descendants of the Aeroflot Regional Directorate fleets, which were spun off and later reabsorbed by the newly created republics.

After the breakup, institutions had to be rebuilt (sometimes with limited material and human resources), including bilateral agreements to govern international air travel. While some countries chose to adhere to international standards and market principles, others continued with centralized planning and state monopolies for air transport. With such diverging patterns of development in air transport, cities across the region also endured radically different access to air services.

Moscow's Everlasting Centrality

Since the deregulation of aviation markets in the 1970s, researchers have applied elements of graph theory and social network analysis to airline schedules to measure the interconnectedness of cities and their main airports (Bowen 2002). This approach often focused solely on the geographical aspects of connectivity (the number of cities covered by air services, clustering within a specific region).[4] Regulatory regimes were also studied because they defined the terms under which carriers could provide cross-border air services. But the rising importance of global hubs for connecting passengers and cargo has led to further study from a temporal perspective in the past 15 years (Burghouwt 2004).

Node centrality, one of the most popular concepts for evaluating air transport connectivity, is a measure of the average "distance" (not geographical, but in number of flights) between cities within a network—the closer the distance with other elements, the more central a point is (table 3.2).[5] As such, Moscow remains the most dominant and central city in Eurasia's aviation network, followed by Kiev, St. Petersburg, and Tashkent, consistent with previous empirical evidence (Derudder, Devriendt, and Witlox 2007).[6] This also reflects disparities in air transport development among the different Soviet republics since the breakup, not only in traffic generation (seat capacity departing from all capital cities accounts for only half of that in Moscow), but also in infrastructure, technology, human capital, and regulatory and institutional capacities.

As in any transition, demographics and the concentration of economic, political, and government functions influence market reorganization. This was true in the reconfiguration of airline routes in the past 10 years, especially in Central Russia, where networks lost considerable density after the domestic was deregulated. Most notably, routes flying astride Moscow that connected cities in the Southern and Central districts with the North-Western, Ural, and Volga Federal Districts were affected. A plausible explanation is that regional carriers offering nonstop services between second- and third-tier cities faced growing competition from the larger carriers' connecting flights through Moscow, which offered more flexibility and more destinations. The introduction of narrow bodies has also extended the range of operations (and the catchment area of major hubs), raising the number of aircraft turnarounds compared with turboprops and the number of available flights a week. As these point-to-point routes ceased, available seat capacity at these cities was lost, replaced by major airlines' flights to their own hubs or taken over by other regional carriers that were part of the major airlines' networks.[7]

Airline networks in the region have become increasingly concentrated in space and time (see table 3A.1). Seat and belly-hold capacity

TABLE 3.2

Centrality Indicators for Capital Cities in Eurasian Aviation Network

City	Number of destinations served, degree[a]			Closeness centrality (0 = min; 1 = max)		Weekly outbound seat capacity, thousands	Reachable network cities with direct flight, percent	Main destinations percentage of total seats
	1958	2000	2011	1958	2011	2011	2011	2011
Yerevan	3	37	44	0.21	0.50	18.4	15	Moscow (40), Dubai (6)
Baku	8	34	50	0.25	0.48	31.1	9	Moscow (24), Istanbul (20)
Minsk	7	20	30	0.29	0.48	14.9	6	Moscow (23), Vienna (10)
Tbilisi	5	25	34	0.24	0.46	14.3	3	Istanbul (24), Kiev (13)
Almaty	6	32	43	0.24	0.47	44.5	4	Astana (19), Moscow (9)
Chisinau	3	24	22	0.28	0.48	12.6	7	Moscow (21), Istanbul (17)
Bishkek	5	19	16	0.25	0.47	12.1	5	Osh (30), Moscow/Istanbul (13)
Moscow[b]	26	177	243	0.38	0.85	601.8	83	St. Petersburg (14)
Dushanbe	3	3	31	0.24	0.47	15.3	7	Moscow (16), St. Petersburg (9)
Ashkhabad	4	15	21	0.25	0.48	21.0	6	Dashoguz (19), Turkmenabad (15)
Kiev	11	50	93	0.29	0.54	81.3	28	Moscow (11), Tel Aviv (4)
Tashkent	9	57	59	0.31	0.48	38.5	10	Moscow (11), Istanbul (5)

Source: Authors' calculations based on Data In Intelligence Out (DIIO) data on combined passenger/cargo services, March 2011.
a. Number of links or nonrepeated connections that a particular city has.
b. Accounts for Sheremetyevo, Domodedovo, and Vnukovo airports.

is thus more unevenly distributed across cities, and the time gap between arrivals and departures is smaller. From the perspective of the largest cities near major airline hubs, concentration can have benefits through wider network coverage and greater flight availability. But evidence indicates that smaller, more remote cities do not always benefit from concentration. Indeed, smaller airports in the United States and Europe endured substantial losses in the number of destinations and frequency of service (mostly to other small airports) from the deregulation and intensification of "hubbing" practices (GAO 1997; Graham 1995, 1998; Reynolds-Feighan 1995). Yet, even when the number of direct destinations or flight frequencies (direct connectivity) declines for smaller airports, available connections (indirect connectivity) through major hubs may rise.

About a quarter of the cities in Eurasia's aviation network suffered a net loss of scheduled air services in both destinations and flight frequency in the past 10 years (see table 3A.2). Still, 80 percent of them have gained connections at other hubs and traffic stations, while only a few small airports have lost both direct and indirect connectivity. But 95 percent of the increase in smaller airports' indirect connections became available through Moscow's three airports. In other words, for the possible peripheralization of smaller cities in response to changes in network structure, some counterbalancing forces come into play. Even so, relying more on a few central transfer points or hubs can have inherent costs for travelers, through delays and higher hub premiums (Evans and Kessides 1993; Holloway 2007). Indeed, one of the most debated subjects in air transport relates to the degree of market fragmentation (nonstop hub bypass routes) that may develop due to congestion and passenger preferences.

Do All Flights Lead to Moscow?

Hubs add a temporal dimension to airline networks concentrated in a single traffic station or a few. They exist not only as a virtue of network design, but also as a result of scheduling decisions by the carriers themselves (Holloway 2007). Major airlines developed hubs by scheduling integrated "waves" or peaks of incoming and departing flights to maximize the volume of connecting traffic. While a connection with a wait of several hours may be less attractive for the business travel segment (not necessarily for the leisure segment), shorter connecting times may not be long enough for passengers and cargo to transfer to connecting flights.

The number and quality of onward connections at an airport depend on several factors. They are not only determined by the hub's "wave" system, the frequency of inbound and outbound services, and the availability of conveniently timed arrivals (or *landing slots*), but also by other operational aspects, such as interline agreements to allow seamless connections.[8] Although some Eurasian capitals are served by local and major airlines offering flexible schedules to major airport hubs (for example, Baku to Istanbul), other cities have limited access to these transfer points. This is because flights from these locations are either operated infrequently—sometimes thanks to restrictive aviation policies—or are performed by local carriers without agreements to interline or code-share with other airlines, as with Dushanbe.[9]

Major hubs like Frankfurt, Istanbul, and Moscow account for half of the onward connections available for the 10 selected Eurasian capital cities (table 3.3).[10] These hubs compete for transit traffic in different submarkets, where patterns of geographical specialization emerge depending on the hub and origin city. Frankfurt, Istanbul, and Moscow are best scheduled to connect the selected cities with major markets in Western Europe, European Russia, and the United States (see table 3A.3). And alternative markets are best served through Istanbul and the Emirates' hubs in Dubai or Abu Dhabi to reach African and Middle Eastern networks—and through Bangkok; Dubai; Hong Kong SAR, China; or Seoul to connect with Asia and the Pacific.

The notion of connecting traffic is not restricted to hubs in Europe or the Middle East. Given its geographical centrality, the region has locational advantages for transit passengers and cargo. In theory, these airports can increasingly become switching points for connecting passengers to the extent that carriers establish more definite hub-type operations, when combining 3rd and 4th freedoms of the air on short-, medium-, and long-haul routes.[11] In addition to the hub's geographical centrality, other factors contribute to its quality, including (Holloway 2007):

- The "feed" strength of inbound services (regional and long-haul from alliance partners, as well as intermodal flows of passengers or cargo), sometimes limited by restrictive aviation policies.

- The volume of "local" traffic originating or finishing its journey at the hub (origin and destination traffic).

- Its efficiency for connecting traffic (speedy ground handling and short terminal transfers).

- Its attractiveness for passengers (geographic scope and scheduling of connections, availability and quality of facilities, and convenience of transportation to the city's center).

TABLE 3.3

Number of Weekly Direct Services and Indirect Connections at Main Hubs

Hub	Moscow				Dubai		Frankfurt		Istanbul		Others		Total	
	Domodedovo		Sheremetyevo											
	WC	DS	WC	DS	WC	DS	WC	DS	WC	DS	WC	DS	WC	DS
Almaty	121 (1)	14 (1)	196	14 (1)	—	—	795[a]	17 (1)	225	11 (1)	1,212	287	2,549	343
Ashkhabad	47	7 (2)	—	—	41	2 (2)	182	1 (2)	314	14 (2)	298	120	882	149
Baku	188	30 (4)	177	14 (1)	306	23 (3)	137	3 (1)	552	39 (3)	1,032	142	2,392	251
Bishkek	50	6 (2)	181	10 (1)	26	2 (2)	—	—	187	9 (2)	308	91	752	118
Chisinau	237	19 (2)	—	—	—	—	178	5 (1)	217	14 (2)	838	85	1,470	123
Dushanbe	3	7 (1)	—	—	17	2 (1)	104	2 (1)	61	4 (2)	178	116	363	131
Minsk	135	21 (1)	111	14 (1)	—	—	416	9 (2)	91	7 (2)	1,383	121	2,136	172
Tashkent	127	17 (2)	52	5 (1)	22	2 (1)	90	2 (1)	190	10 (2)	1,071	229	1,552	265
Tbilisi	40	8 (2)	—	—	31	2 (1)	119	3 (2)	227	23 (2)	908	106	1,326	142
Yerevan	209	25 (2)	208	21 (1)	67	8 (2)	—	—	0	1 (1)	636	91	1,120	146
Total	1,157	154	925	78	511	43	2,021	45	2,064	132	7,864	1,388	14,542	1,840

Source: Authors.

Note: Based on schedule of first week of March 2010. Number of carriers in parentheses. WC = (weighted) indirect connections, DS = weekly number of direct flights, — = not available.

a. About 60 percent of the indirect connections can be explained by dedicated freight services of Lufthansa Cargo from Almaty to Frankfurt, about 20 percent corresponds to available connections of dedicated cargo services, and the rest is for passenger and cargo services.

By computing the number of available connections at each city, we can classify them by stage length—a measure of flown distance by departure (see table 3A.4).[12] Some airlines in the region can offer suitable connections that mimic the "hinterland" or "regional" hub model.[13] The "hinterland" model feeds short-haul traffic to international or long-haul trunk routes (and vice versa) departing in different geographical directions. And the "regional" model mainly offers short-haul to short-haul connections in all directions. Note, however, that connections between the nonalliance, non-code-share services of two or more airlines are increasingly infrequent. Instead, they rely more on alliance partners and the *hub carriers* themselves (such as Aeroflot at Moscow) that exploit "natural 6th freedom" rights.

Thus, airlines based in the smaller capitals may have limited opportunities to provide long-haul directional connections between the Western Hemisphere and Asia. Although some of the smaller carriers offer these connections, sometimes they are not marketed through traditional distribution channels. Instead, they appeal to lower booking-class segments willing to sacrifice service attributes (in-flight services, shorter waiting times, convenient routing) for discounted fares. Even so, there is evidence that Ashgabat and Tashkent serve as gateways for long-haul international markets (Derudder, Devriendt, and Witlox 2007).

Moscow's airports—especially Sheremetyevo—are natural "all-around" hubs, providing international connections with major Eurasian cities and with different continents. A main reason for Moscow's dominance as a transfer point is that 6th freedom traffic is generally less vulnerable to competition when supported by a high level of 3rd and 4th freedom traffic (and thus high quality of service). Moscow not only depends on hub carriers' *online* connections, but also on the feed strength provided by their alliance and regional airline partners.[14] But Muscovite airports face competition for transit or *through-traffic* in the same markets (though with different route overlays) from other European hubs. For traffic originating in Europe or the United States, Moscow competes against all Star Alliance's connections to Central Asia through Istanbul (continuing with the Turkish Airlines' routes to Dushanbe, Ashgabat, and Tashkent), Frankfurt or Munich, among others.[15] It also competes for directional traffic to Oceania or East Asia with the Middle Eastern and Asian "hourglass" hubs and their carriers, such as Emirates and Singapore Airlines (Hanlon 2007).

Access Barriers to Air Services

The vertical integration of airports and air carriers may give way to anticompetitive practices to displace entrant airlines at an airport (Serebrisky 2003). During the Soviet era, airports and airlines were fully integrated. This vertical integration was also common during the postbreakup transition and still exists in some Eurasian countries, despite regulatory reforms to separate airlines from airports, most notably in Russia (Lukyanov, Tissen, and Kislyak 2009; World Bank 1998, 2005).[16] Other forms of integration—for instance, among the policy-making, regulatory, and oversight functions of the government in civil aviation—were also frequent in the region's smaller countries, creating blatant conflicts of interest and posing operational safety hazards. State presence in air transport is still common in Eurasia. About 40 airlines in Russia had some form of national, state, or municipal government participation until recently—a number that grows to 75 when including the rest of Eurasian countries.[17]

Regulations can limit the entry of new operators to the market in many ways besides including single designation provisions in bilateral agreements, such as when exclusive traffic rights are provided to a single operator on a "long-term exclusive basis."[18] In other countries, antitrust and competition policies have not been fully enforced to ensure the equal access of carriers to airports. This seems to be more problematic in smaller regional airports with strong vertical links to local airlines that usually deny access to new carriers based on technical regulations or an alleged lack of proper infrastructure and human resources. Even so, there have been some advances to accommodate new airlines, with a noticeable impact in the number of carriers per route.[19] For instance, in Russia, 43 percent of the seat capacity in 2011 is allocated to routes operated by three or more carriers, compared with 11 percent in 2000. In other cases, more definite reforms dissolved state monopolies on aviation, as in Tajikistan (World Bank 2005).

Airlines in the region operate one of the oldest fleets in service, where rapidly aging Russian-built aircraft are very much present (Embraer Commercial Jets 2009). This poses not only environmental concerns through lower fuel efficiency, higher emissions, and more noise pollution, but also safety concerns.[20] While the largest carriers in Russia have successfully passed the International Air Transport Association's (IATA) Operational Safety Audit, "safety concerns remain with the continued operation of some Russian-built equipment that does not comply with ICAO [International Civil Aviation Organization] standards" (IATA 2011).

Further, a large number of operators have been banned from the European Union (EU) skies altogether or limited to using specific aircraft types within their fleets.[21] The particular situation of technical regulators—those bodies responsible for observing the safety standards in air transport and complying with internationally accepted regulations—is quite heterogeneous. For instance, in the Caucasus region, Armenia shows fair levels of compliance based on ICAO's Universal Safety Oversight Audit Programme and the European Aviation Safety Agency's Safety Assessment of Foreign Aircraft, while Azerbaijan and Georgia are lagging. But they are far from some Central Asian countries (such as the Kyrgyz Republic), which still do not conform with the minimal safety regulations for international air travel.[22]

Although many airports are managed by corporatized operators or have been fully privatized, competition in infrastructure services can be limited. For ground handling services, charges in the region can be up to four times higher than in comparable European airports.[23] Monopolistic practices in airside services such as airport fuel provision are common, possibly representing a large source of savings for air carriers if more competitive mechanisms were introduced.[24] Moreover, foreign operators can be charged up to 25 percent more than domestic carriers through "commercial handling" fees for no apparent reason.

Aeronautical charges in the capitals' airports also appear to be above international benchmarks (see table 3A.5).[25] Based on total turnaround cost computations, Baku and Yerevan stand out as the most expensive airports in the region (with charges between 50 and 100 percent higher than the average of those in Istanbul, Dubai, and Frankfurt), followed by Tashkent, Almaty, Ashgabat, and Tbilisi. These charges are not exclusively borne by air carriers—they are largely transferred to passengers. Research is needed to determine why aeronautical charges in most capitals—except Moscow—seem to be at comparable or higher levels than those in selected major hubs. Particular questions requiring investigation include the extent of the cost-recovery mechanisms used and the prospects for regulating airport charges on congestion and other externalities (such as noise and emissions) and service quality. The last aspect is one of the most contentious issues for users transiting through the smaller capitals, because the quality of services and infrastructure in some airports is still far from the minimum IATA level of service standards for comfort and convenience (World Bank 2005).[26]

The expansion and modernization of infrastructure will continue to play a central part in developing the sector, because of the varying needs of the different countries. Some countries have already started a major overhaul of their main airport terminals, runways, and airside facilities, but others are still struggling with years of neglect and immediate priorities that public funding cannot entirely cover.[27] Good practices can be replicated to encourage private capital participation in infrastructure funding, as with St. Petersburg's Pulkovo airport. But hard infrastructure is not a sufficient condition for the complete modernization of the sector. "Soft" components like the regulatory framework for airport operators, institutional reform of civil aviation bodies (especially in regard to safety), and streamlining of procedures (e-freight paperless systems for cargo) are still lagging in some Eurasian countries.

A Sustainable Future: Moving toward Better Integration

The foregoing review of connectivity in Eurasian cities points to a distinct pattern of leading cities well connected nationally, regionally, and internationally—and a large number cities connected only through the leading cities. If the core cities offer poor service, it will burden all the other centers. This section provides some options for improving the city connectivity with international markets and with leading Eurasian cities.

The Future of Transport Connectivity

Funding for infrastructure maintenance declined dramatically during the transition, adversely affecting service reliability and availability. The infrastructure itself, which tended to be large and designed to serve several republics rather than individual countries, heightened the funding problem. The challenge was to find the resources to maintain, rehabilitate, and operate assets.

Several countries and cities are trying to develop cost-recovery mechanisms for road transport, though the prospects seem limited due to continuing low traffic volume on key roads. Many are focusing on road tolls, though some work is happening on road funds, which have been instrumental in putting road maintenance financing on a more sustainable footing elsewhere, notably in Africa.

Meanwhile, other countries have been encouraging more private sector investment in transport and other infrastructure investments, as part of a global trend that started in the 1990s. But private sector investment has been largely in Armenia, Kazakhstan, Russia, Ukraine, and Uzbekistan, with most investment going to Russia (though the single largest project was the railway in Armenia). Most private sector investment projects for transport have been in airports and seaports, the modes that have been liberalized most and in which revenue streams are easiest to capture.

Strong institutions and coordination mechanisms—critical in fostering collaboration between countries—are missing in Eurasia. Although numerous regional initiatives link the main economic centers, no institutions based in the region drive this effort, nearly all initiatives are coordinated from the outside. Evidence from Africa suggests that institutions are needed to coordinate the various players instrumental to improving services within trade corridors (Arvis and others 2011). In other regions—and several Eurasian countries—national committees play this role, but most are not effective. Corridor-level management and engagement across countries needs to be strengthened to address trade constraints.

Measures have been taken to address some of the problems, especially with funding road transport and services. So far, the private sector has shown little willingness to finance road and rail infrastructure, preferring instead to develop seaports and airports. Initiatives on road tolling and other mechanisms for cost-recovery that could improve the quality of connecting infrastructure are increasingly common, though they still remain limited in some countries, such as Russia. The challenge is greatest in countries that have not reformed fast enough and may continue to have poor infrastructure. The whole region may suffer because many economies depend on their neighbors for access to export markets.

Funding mechanisms to tackle the growing menace of road traffic accidents are needed. Some of the measures policy makers could consider include the following:

- Improve road design standards to protect vulnerable road users when mixing with traffic (most fatalities are pedestrians).

- Develop and enforce regulations for vehicle condition, driver education and training, and risky behaviors.

- Improve driver training to curb speeding, recklessness, drinking and driving, and use of mobile phones, especially texting while driving—and to increase the use of seatbelts, helmets, and other protective equipment.

Looking ahead, the most promising transport appears to be road and air.

Establishing New Trade Routes

Eurasia has an intricate network of trade routes linking major economic centers—a legacy of the past as well as a reflection of a new equilibrium among trade flow dynamics, demographics, and economic growth. The dismantling of the Council for Mutual Economic Assistance, which governed trade with the rest of the world and between the Soviet republics, left a void in coordinating foreign trade policy and heightened the general policy and institutional vacuum in Eurasian countries. Filling this institutional vacuum is critical, especially for the landlocked countries, which depend on their neighbors for infrastructure and border facilities for trade.

Some countries have political difficulties that affect transport connectivity. Uzbekistan cannot use links through some of its neighbors, with whom relations are not cordial. Armenia's border with Turkey is closed, forcing the two countries to use transport links in Georgia. Conflict in the border region of Moldova hampers its access to Ukraine. The 2008 Georgia-Russia conflict resulted in the elimination of direct airline connections between Tbilisi and Moscow, though this activated daily connections between Tbilisi and Kiev.

Despite these problems, there have been considerable efforts to define and develop a network of trade routes across Eurasia. Several routes have been formalized through regional agreements, programs, and development projects, supported by governments and bilateral and multilateral development agencies. Prominent initiatives include efforts by the United Nations Economic Commission for Europe (UNECE) and the United Nations Economic and Social Commission for Asia and the Pacific (ESCAP) to enhance Euro-Asian transport links; the International Road Union's New Eurasian Land Transport Initiative (NELTI); the Central Asia Regional Economic Cooperation (CAREC) corridors, coordinated by the Asian Development Bank; the EU's Transport Corridor Europe-Caucasus-Asia (TRACECA) initiative; and the EurAsian Economic Community transport corridors program. More than 40 trade route initiatives link more than 130 major cities across Eurasia. The numerous trade routes give countries alternatives, which remain important because some countries have unfriendly relations with others. But the multiplicity of initiatives portends duplication and waste (Pomfret 2010).

Some countries have extended their transport infrastructure. In 1997, China, the Kyrgyz Republic, and Uzbekistan agreed to develop road and rail links connecting the centers of Ardijan, Osh, and Kashgar. And although Kazakhstan and China share more than 1,600 miles of borders, the Kazakh railway network was only connected to the Chinese network in the late 1980s, because of the dispute between Moscow and Beijing. But the connection is now a significant interface between the Chinese and Eurasian railway networks.

To reintegrate the region, Eurasian countries have worked through several bodies, including the Eurasian Economic Community (formerly the Commonwealth of Independent States [CIS] Customs Union), the Central Asian Cooperation Organization, the Economic Cooperation Organization, the Shanghai Cooperation Organization, and GUUAM (Georgia, Ukraine, Uzbekistan, Azerbaijan, and Moldova).

The former Council for Mutual Economic Assistance (COME-CON) Organization for Railways Cooperation—which included all former Soviet Union countries and several others interested in rail traffic between Europe and Asia—is using the system known as the Agreement on International Railway Freight Communications for an integrated movement. At border points separating neighboring railway organizations that are part of the agreement, the waybill was rewritten from one format to the other. Recognizing the harmful impact of this arrangement on the efficiency of international rail movements, railway operators have sought ways to harmonize the procedures. Russia has spearheaded efforts to define a new transit document, the GPBRT bill of lading, for container block-trains between Germany and Russia. The services run through Belarus and Poland under the Ostwind container services between Berlin and Moscow (ESCAP 2001). Such an arrangement could also benefit the rail container movements of other countries in the region.

Various initiatives have been taken to cooperate subnationally, especially between border regions in neighboring countries. But such initiatives continue to be governed by bilateral agreements between states rather than subregions (Kaminski and others 2010). A World Bank study (2011a) shows that promoting a corridor management institution for the north-south corridor linking Kazakhstan, the Kyrgyz Republic, and Tajikistan along the Petropavlosk-Astana-Almaty-Bishkek-Osh-Batken-Isfara-Khujand-Dushanbe-Nijny Pjanj roads connection could boost intraregional trade and agribusiness exports to Russia, China, and India.

Improvements in transport infrastructure across Eurasia have highlighted problems at the border, especially regarding road transport. New international borders have added considerable delays and additional costs to land transport (figure 3.2). The latter largely reflect informal payments as well as frequent stops and checks by authorities in different countries.

Delays and monetary costs could be avoided at least partly by adhering to and implementing the TIR Convention—and abolishing customs escorts of normal, nonsuspicious cargo. Harmonizing border procedures on roads and railways across countries and transit fees could increase predictability by considering the interests of the transit country as well as the landlocked country, along the lines of the work under the TRACECA initiative. But these reforms would not be possible without enhancing trust building and public-private dialogue

Time, Cost, and Distance of Transport along the Almaty-Berlin Trade Route, circa 2003

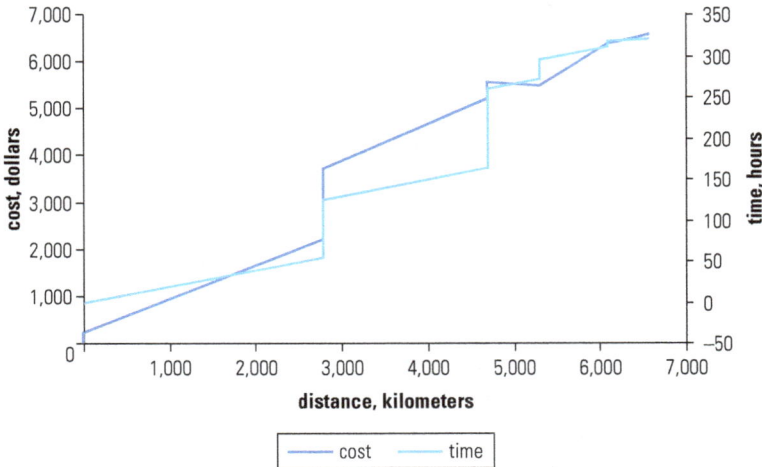

Source: Authors' estimates, based on ESCAP data.

and cooperation—and, equally important, without systematically monitoring the main international transport corridors.

Liberalizing Air Services and Connectivity

Provisions in bilateral air service agreements (ASAs) can affect connectivity in many ways.[28] One provision is the customary use of airport designation under the ASA negotiating framework, in which both signatory parties may determine the number of entry and exit points in each country.[29] Connectivity can also be affected by restricting frequency and capacity allocation in general or for particular routes, limiting the number of airlines allowed to operate (single or multiple designation), and restricting the extent to which parties can access extended networks by reciprocally granting traffic rights beyond the 3rd or 4th freedoms.[30] Other provisions that may affect connectivity and traffic flows include nationality clauses in ownership, tariff-setting mechanisms, and the possibility of entering into cooperation agreements between designated airlines (such as code-sharing).

The World Trade Organization's Air Liberalization Index is based on a scorecard system that ranks ASAs according to their provisions, with a higher score indicating a more liberal bilateral regime. According to the index, bilateral agreements in Eurasia are among the most restrictive compared with those in other regions.[31] Single airline designation,

substantial ownership and control provisions, and double approval of
tariffs are common features in bilateral agreements negotiated by most
countries in this region.

Most ASAs for Eurasian countries include capacity predetermina-
tion clauses, with only a few very liberal "Open Skies" agreements
(for example, Armenia and Uzbekistan with the United States).[32]
Due to historic migration flows, and its size and higher purchasing
power, the Russian market—and especially the routes to Moscow—
attracts considerable business and "Visiting Friends and Relatives"
traffic from other Eurasian countries. Even so, bilateral agreements
with Russia usually include capacity restrictions in terms of frequencies (table 3.4).

Smaller countries often show less interest in relaxing the capacity
restrictions of agreements (or negotiating new ones) to protect their
national carriers from increased competition, especially when they
face financial distress (World Bank 2011b). These restrictions can
burden passengers with higher airfares, limit the number and availability of connections, and diminish the opportunities for airlines to
build commercially profitable traffic levels—especially in business
class, where time flexibility is central. Restrictive aviation policies can
also hinder the prospects for the smaller countries' airlines to carry
6th freedom traffic through their own hubs.[33] A notable exception is
Georgia, which fully liberalized its air transport market in 2005, with
sizeable impacts on traffic growth.

In general, the negotiation of 5th freedom rights has been protracted in international aviation bilateral agreements (Hanlon 2007).
There are fewer Eurasian carriers flying passenger intra-regional
routes with full 5th freedom rights than in other parts of the world.
Third-country airlines that fly scheduled 5th freedom sectors within
Eurasia are also quite rare, apart from a few cases.[34] And to a lesser
extent, the same occurs for Eurasian carriers flying 5th freedom sectors outside the region.[35] But 5th freedoms are much more common
in other regions (such as Africa), where liberalization has advanced
further. Up to 43 percent of the routes African carriers fly in the con-
tinent are 5th freedom flights, though with wide variations by the
Regional Economic Community (Schlumberger 2010).

Some carriers in the scheduled dedicated cargo segment exploit a
network of 5th full freedom rights to schedule multistop "ring"
routes. Since airfreight flow imbalances in Europe-China trade generate excess capacity on eastbound operations, carriers have added
more stops in the Middle East and Caspian Sea regions—for example,
Cargolux's "5th freedom hub" in Baku—to increase load factors on
the routes to Asia.[36] Meanwhile, other scheduled cargo operators use

TABLE 3.4

Selected Bilateral Agreements with the Russian Federation

Country	Provisions	Capacity, percentage of total seats		Use of capacity restriction, percent
		Russian Federation	Moscow	
Armenia	Agreement has multiple designations (the Russian Federation has designated Aeroflot and Siberia Airlines; Armavia on the Armenian side) with capacity limitation to 42 flights a week on the Yerevan-Moscow route, and no more than two carriers per city-pair. Russia may operate Yerevan, Gyumri, Stepanovan, and two other points in Armenia.	64.7	41.9	116
Azerbaijan	Agreement limits Baku-Moscow services to 32 flights a week, Moscow-Ganja to 12, and St. Petersburg-Baku and St. Petersburg-Baku to 4 for each country's carrier. No limits are on the number of carriers.	39.3	78.5	71[a]
Kazakhstan	The Almaty-Moscow route is limited by the bilateral agreement to 14 flights a week for each country's airlines (two for freight transport). Similar restrictions apply for Astana (seven a week), Aktau (three), Shymkent (two), and Karaganda (three) to Moscow. St. Petersburg has a maximum of two daily flights from most cities in Kazakhstan.	11.3	8.6	100[a]
Tajikistan	Tajik airlines may go to four points in Russia (Moscow, Novosibirsk, Ekaterinburg, and one more TBD), from any point in Tajikistan. Airlines designated by Russia can fly from any point in Russia to Dushanbe, Khujand, and one more point TBD. The Dushanbe-Moscow route is treated separately, limited to 14 flights a week, with aircraft not bigger than TU-154M, according to World Bank (2005).	66.3	23.8	100[a]
Ukraine	The parties agreed to increase the number of air carriers to 4 a week and flights to 49 a week between Moscow and Kiev by June 2011—and to have 10 flights a week on a contract between Moscow and Odessa, for each of the parties. Previous restrictions limited to 35 flights a week and three designated carriers for Kiev-Moscow on the Russian side. For other points from Russia, except Moscow, there were to be 20 designated points by Ukraine and 4 TBD by Russia, limited to two designated carriers on a pair of cities per side, with no other restriction.	17.7	15.1	100[b]
Kyrgyz Republic	Limitations are imposed on Moscow-Bishkek route of 10 flights a week.	20.5	15.0	110[a]
Uzbekistan	Designated points include intermediate points, and Tashkent, Samarkand, Bukhara, Ferghana, Andijan, Namangan, Urgench, Nukus, Termez, and Karshi, Kokand, and Navoi for Russia. Moscow and St. Petersburg are limited to 14 and 2 flights a week for each party, respectively. Moscow-Bukhara is limited to three flights a week.	33.1	18.1	100[a]
Moldova	Moscow-Chisinau route is restricted to 14 flights a week, with a maximum of two carriers per side. Points in Moldova include Chisinau, Balti, Cahul, and additional points. Beyond points include items in Africa, Asia, Europe, and the Middle East. For the rest of the routes, no more than one carrier per city-pair.	22.8	22.8	71[a]

Source: Authors, based on Rosaviatsiya, Russian Federal Air Transport Agency, www.favt.ru/favt_new/?0=dejatelnost/mezhdunarodnaja_dejatelnost/dvustoronnie_dogovorennosti.
Note: All 5th freedom routes are subject to a separate agreement between the aeronautical authorities of the contracting parties. TBD = to be decided.
a. Moscow routes.
b. Includes code-share flights marketed by Aerosvit and operated by Aeroflot.

the region's geographical centrality to combine 3rd and 4th freedoms to bridge cargo between Europe and the Far East.[37]

For Russian cargo carriers, routes from Moscow to Beijing are restricted to 21 flights a week, Shanghai to 28, and Tianjin to 14. For "triangular" services, points are restricted to Almaty, Asia, Africa, the Middle East, the Far East, and North America, with seven flights a week without full 5th freedoms and three with full traffic rights.[38] Some extra-regional cargo carriers use Almaty and Krasnoyarsk or Karaganda as en route technical stops to Asia (Osaka; Tianjin; Shanghai; Hong Kong SAR, China; Guangzhou) and on the way back to Moscow or Europe. For airports, this involves higher revenues from flight operations and aircraft handling, as well as air traffic control fee collection from overflights.

Improving ICT Connectivity

Efficient information and communications technology (ICT) leads to substantial productivity gains, and such ICT is critical to economic growth and international competitiveness. Continuing deficiencies in the telecommunications infrastructure, especially the lack of broadband connectivity, will prevent Eurasia from fully exploiting ICT to improve productivity, foster sustainable development, and link its landlocked countries with the world.

ICT development and productivity

The benefits ICT can have for individuals, businesses, cities, and countries depend on the availability of broadband.[39] Eurasian networks—designed for traditional telecom services, not broadband communications—may not be able to accommodate the growing needs for reliable, robust, and reasonably priced broadband connectivity.

Across the region, Internet access continues to be provided largely as a dial-up service, at speeds very low by global standards. Since the breakup of the Soviet Union, Central Asian countries have particularly struggled with poor telecommunications infrastructure and ineffective regulatory systems. Access to ICT services in these countries lags the rest of Eurasia. In 2010, Internet penetration was 39.3 percent in the Kyrgyz Republic, 34.1 percent in Kazakhstan, 26.8 percent in Uzbekistan, 9.2 percent in Tajikistan, and just 1.6 percent in Turkmenistan (figure 3.3).

Broadband access is even lower (figure 3.4). Broadband subscribers comprise only a small proportion of total Internet users. In Uzbekistan, 83 percent of Internet connections in 2010 were in the

FIGURE 3.3

Internet Penetration Rates in Selected Countries, 2010

Internet users as a percentage of total inhabitants

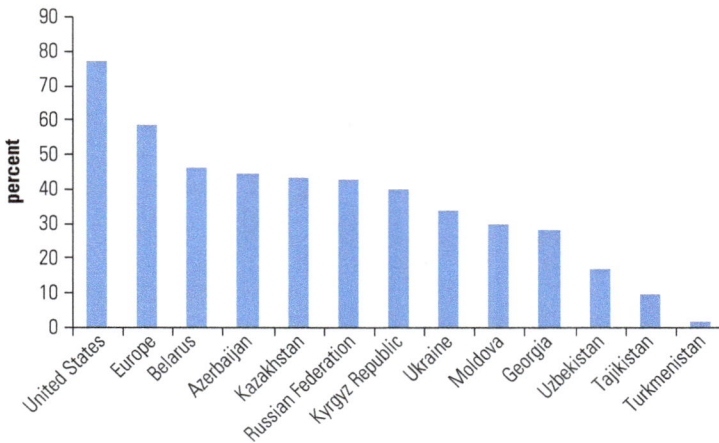

Source: Internet World Stats, www.internetworldstats.com.
Note: Internet penetration is computed as the number of Internet users as a percentage of total inhabitants. An Internet user is defined as someone age 2 and older who went online in the past 30 days.

FIGURE 3.4

Share of Broadband Subscribers per Capita in Selected Countries, 2009

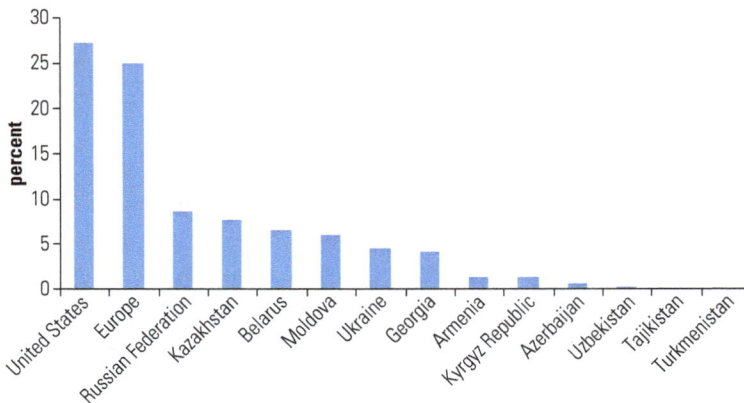

Source: ITU 2009.

narrowband range (Akamai 2010). By the end of 2008, the region as a whole had reached a 4.6 percent fixed and 0.9 percent mobile broadband penetration, a long way from Europe, where both fixed and mobile penetration exceed 20 percent (figure 3.5).

Several studies document the importance of broadband penetration for economic growth. A World Bank (2009b) report finds that a 10 percentage point increase in broadband penetration is correlated with a 1.3 percentage point increase in economic growth. Similarly,

FIGURE 3.5

Number of Fixed Broadband Connections in the Former Soviet Union and the World, 2000–08

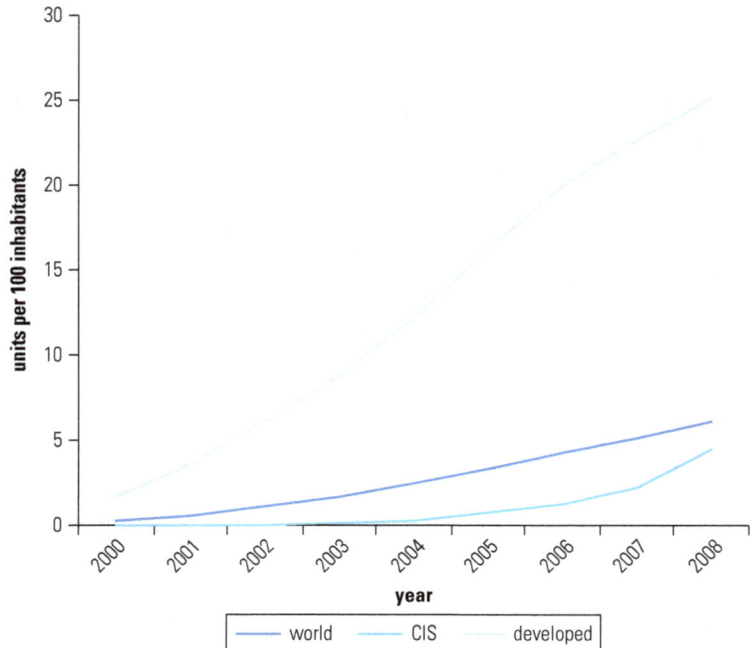

Source: ITU 2009.
Note: CIS = Commonwealth of Independent States.

Buttkereit and others (2009) find that a 10 percent increase in broadband household penetration leads to an increase in gross domestic product (GDP) of 0.1–1.4 percent. And Friedrich and others (2009) find that a 10 percent increase in broadband penetration is correlated with 1.5 percent higher labor productivity over the following five years.

A key factor inhibiting broadband connectivity in many Central Asian and Trans-Caucasian republics is the lack of competition in regional backbone networks. Although telecommunications services in these countries have been formally opened to competition, significant market dominance is still present. For example, Kyrgyztelecom dominates the fixed segment of the market in the Kyrgyz Republic, with a 96 percent share and unequalled territorial coverage. And Ukrtelecom dominates the fixed-line sector in Ukraine.

Policy and regulatory impediments and other constraints on competitive service provision (for example, slow licensing) have inhibited domestic backbone networks. Potential fixed-line infrastructure providers continue to face barriers to entry. In the Kyrgyz Republic, only two companies (Saima-Telecom and Sapatcom) other than Kyrgyz-telecom operate in the national market, despite that some 44 licenses have been issued (ITU 2009).

On paper, countries in the region have progressed considerably in overhauling the archaic post-Soviet legal system and establishing the institutional requirements for effective, independent regulation. But in no country is the regulatory agency free from political interference or able to meet its responsibilities given the financial and human resources. Telecommunications reform has been blocked by well-organized interest groups. The political elite and segments of the business elite have worked together to preserve the monopolies of government-controlled telecommunications industries and delay their competitive restructuring and privatization (Ure 2005).

Incumbent operators whose business has been historically dominated by traditional telecommunications services have resisted the regional push and demand for broadband services. Their opposition is understandable, given the threat that expanding and rolling out broadband access poses to traditional voice and data revenue streams and investment in legacy infrastructure. But international experience reveals that it is not possible to fight the powerful forces of technological convergence. The region is thus at a turning point. As its Internet service provider markets are deregulated and new competitors and a strong demand for high-speed Internet services emerge, incumbent operators are under pressure to rethink and revise their strategies.

Secondary Internet hubs have emerged in Asia to complement the larger global hubs of North America and Europe. Many less developed countries and transitional economies can benefit from this hub-and-spoke architecture through bilateral and regional cooperation. Indeed, the very character and essence of the Internet require such cooperation among countries (especially neighboring countries) to improve ICT effectiveness and efficiency through communication networks. The effectiveness of enhancing the capacity of national networks is sensitive to regional and international cooperation. The efficient development of regional broadband networks also depends on integrated and harmonized development of national networks in individual countries.

Enhanced regional cooperation is critical because it can create a policy environment that fosters the development of broadband networks, expedites the financing and implementation of ICT projects, identifies pressing needs and priority objectives, and creates a solid foundation for mutually beneficial relations. The performance of a regional network consisting of links and nodes in different countries depends on how well the links and nodes function. Indeed, one of the salient features of a network is that any missing links or malperformance of individual nodes can affect its overall efficiency. Thus, regional cooperation is vital.

After the breakup of the Soviet Union, the Central Asian and Trans-Caucasian republics inherited outmoded telecommunications infrastructure with failing wire and cable systems. Upgrading this backbone telecommunications infrastructure requires substantial new investment, difficult to find due to the constrained fiscal space in most countries of the region and deteriorating global financial conditions. In addition, governments continue to fail to commit credibly to specific regulatory and other sectoral policies. Even given the right policies, these countries still may not attract large-scale foreign investment because of the smaller size of their telecommunications systems. Regionalization could help these countries overcome some or most of these problems.

An important driver of cooperation in telecommunications in post-Soviet countries is the Regional Commonwealth in the field of Communications (RCC), formed in December 1991 in Moscow by the heads of national telecommunications administrations. As a regional body, it implements International Telecommunications Union policy. The RCC comprises Armenia, Azerbaijan, Belarus, Georgia, Kazakhstan, the Kyrgyz Republic, Moldova, Russia, Tajikistan, Turkmenistan, Ukraine, and Uzbekistan.

The RCC's main goals are to develop a strategy for cooperation among its member countries and to integrate the region into the global information community. The action plan for regional ICT development and cooperation includes the following components:

- Establishing a favorable environment for cooperation in ICT

- Harmonizing laws and developing regulations and standards

- Developing new ICT segments

- Developing the ICT sector

- Enhancing information security and implementing measures for preventing cybercrime and cyberterrorism

    Projects being implemented include the following:

- Creating a network for an information and marketing center for promoting products and services to national markets in the region

- Establishing compatible remote medical consulting and diagnostic systems

- Developing information technology parks to help diversify the economy, boost its innovative development, and address pressing social issues, such as employment and high-skill job creation

- Providing information security for newly created public systems and resources, especially information and telecommunications systems used for interstate data exchange

The Silk Road was the information superhighway of its age. It served as a conduit for goods as well as for the transmission of knowledge and ideas between east and west. Merchants and others traversed this ancient trading link between Asia and Europe, carrying with them culture, art, philosophy, beliefs, and ideas. More than 2,000 years later, projects have been launched that seek to create a "virtual silk highway" to connect Eurasia to the global information economy.

The Trans-Asia–Europe Line

The Trans-Asia–Europe (TAE) fiber-optic cable system, the world's longest overland fiber-optic system (27,000 kilometers), connects Asia and Europe with modern telecommunications facilities along the ancient Silk Road (exhibit 3.1). The TAE was designed to carry voice telephony and data traffic with a 155 megabits per second (Mbps) capacity.

Construction of the TAE system was initiated in 1992 by China's Ministry of Posts and Communication. In 1993, China, Germany, Kazakhstan, the Kyrgyz Republic, Poland, Ukraine, and Uzbekistan signed the agreement, committing each country to the construction of its own TAE segment. In January 1994, the Islamic Republic of Iran and Turkmenistan joined the agreement, followed by Afghanistan, Austria, Belarus, Hungary, Pakistan, and Romania in 1995. TAE's international traffic service was inaugurated at the end of 1998, transmitting the entire range of telecoms for hundreds of cities along its route and carrying voice telephony and data traffic with a 155 Mbps capacity (equivalent to between 13,000 and 15,000 simultaneous telephone calls) at an estimated cost of about $560 million.

The Black Sea Fiber Optic Cable System

When it came online in September 2001, the Black Sea Fiber Optic Cable System (BSFOCS) became one of two new multigigabit submarine cables providing high-quality connectivity in the Black Sea region (the other is the Georgia-Russian system, or Geo-Russ). BSFOCS connects Bulgaria (Varna), Russia (Novorossiysk), and Ukraine (Odessa). The system's landing points (where the cable

EXHIBIT 3.1

The Trans-Asia–Europe Optical Fiber Cable Network

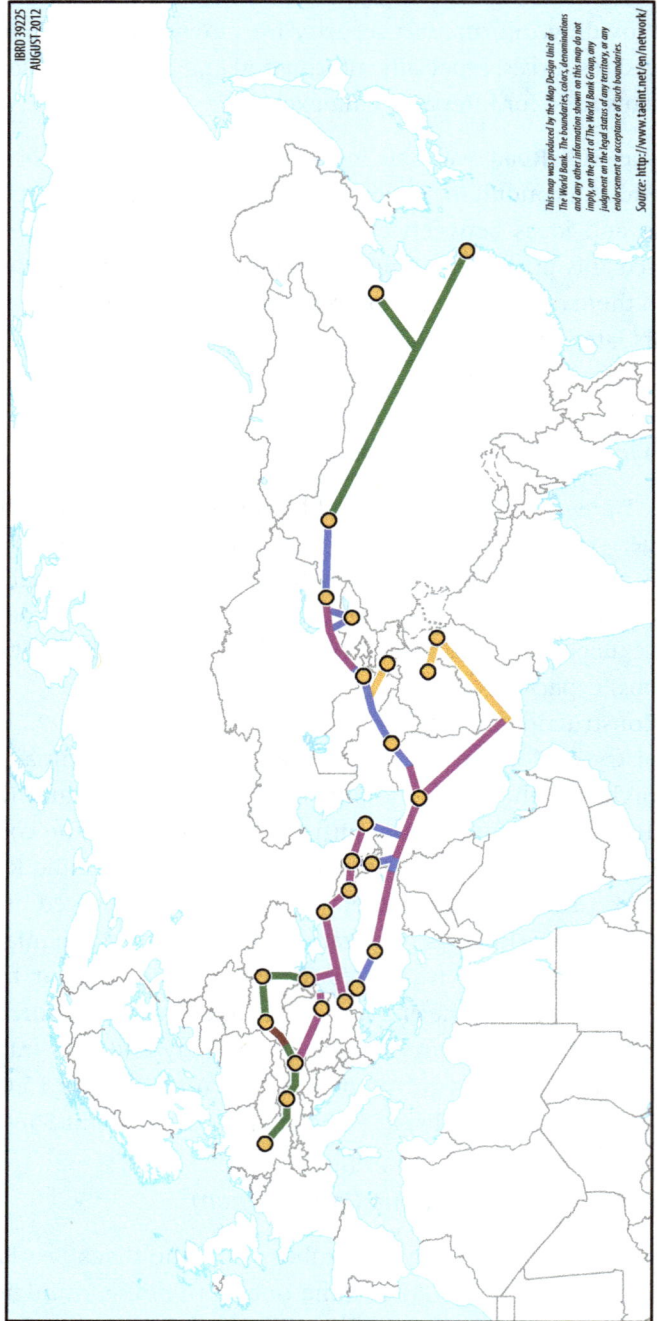

IBRD 39225
AUGUST 2012

This map was produced by the Map Design Unit of
The World Bank. The boundaries, colors, denominations
and any other information shown on this map do not
imply, on the part of The World Bank Group, any
judgment on the legal status of any territory, or any
endorsement or acceptance of such boundaries.

Source: http://www.taeint.net/en/network/

Source: Trans-Asia–Europe Optical Fiber Cable Network, www.taeint.net/en/network/.

makes landfall) provide direct access to Georgia-Russia (Geo-Russ), Karadeniz Fiber Optik Sistemi (KAFOS), Italy-Turkey-Ukraine-Russia (ITUR) and other destinations in northern Europe, the former Soviet Union, and Asia. In 2001, TAE's segments in Armenia, Azerbaijan, and Georgia were brought online. At Poti, Georgia, the TAE cable connects to the undersea Geo-Russ system KAFOS, which then connects to BSFOCS. TAE's interconnection with BSFOCS and Geo-Russ allow the transmission of international traffic from Europe to the Caucasian countries and Asia.

The explosive growth of Internet applications led to rapid growth in the volume of international data traffic on TAE. This growing demand outpaced the network's bandwidth. In particular, there was a lack of spare capacity at cross-borders. Thus, many countries the TAE covers launched major network upgrading and expansion programs. In 2005, they started upgrading cross-border equipment from Synchronous Transport Module (STM)-4 to STM-16 and converting the national networks to Dense Wavelength Division Multiplexing (DWDM) technology.[40]

The TAE has enhanced Eurasia's backbone infrastructure substantially. But it suffers from some disadvantages (Klyueva and Volkova 2008):

- It runs through many countries, complicating traffic control and increasing costs.

- Some of the countries (Afghanistan, Georgia, Tajikistan) are politically unstable.

- Most of its Asian section lacks parallel emergency lines, a prerequisite for successful competition in the transit market.

The SilkSat Project

In 2000, leaders from the countries (Armenia, Azerbaijan, Georgia, Kazakhstan, Moldova, Romania, Ukraine, and Uzbekistan) that span the ancient Silk Road met in New York to commit to a new form of regional cooperation. A key objective of the plan was to enhance the telecommunications infrastructure of the participating countries by introducing and integrating fiber-optic, wireless, and small communications satellite technologies throughout the region.

The proposed SilkSat project will reconstruct the ancient Silk Road by replacing the physical road with a communications highway. Given the project's large scale and its huge financing needs, the plan envisaged forging partnerships among governments, private investors and corporations, and international organizations—and using experts and infrastructure in the countries. By facilitating greater communication and informational flows, the Silk Road broadband highway could reduce misunderstanding and discord between countries. Experience in regional cooperation gained through SilkSat could also further regional cooperation in other areas (Berger 2001).

The SilkSat system contains a network of ground stations and terrestrial sites that connect satellites to local telecommunications networks. It employs a Very Small Aperture Terminals (VSAT) system to connect the National Research and Engineering Networks in Central Asian and Caucasus countries and Afghanistan to the Internet. The first satellite dish was installed in Tashkent in August 2002; the last hookup, to Ashgabat, was completed in August 2003. The hub of the VSAT system is in DESY at Hamburg, Germany.

A New Silk Road Broadband Highway

With the growing importance of broadband technologies, ESCAP organized a regional workshop "Broadband and ICT Development for Improved Communication in Central Asia" in Tashkent in July 2007. More than 100 ICT experts from Central Asia and other countries attended the meeting, which raised awareness among participants of the limits and inadequacies of the regional telecommunications infrastructure (at the time of the conference, the route from Asia to Europe and the countries in the Middle East depended on submarine cables and the TAE system).

The TAE system was not designed for high-speed broadband connectivity. It comprises a single route, with route diversity provided only locally. Its reliability is thus questionable. Given the rapid growth in Internet traffic in Eurasia and TAE's acknowledged limits, the New Silk Road Broadband Highway was proposed during the workshop.

This broadband highway would provide a key reliable route from Europe through Central Asia to East Asian countries. It would have enough spare capacity and provide route diversification with fiber-optic cables to reduce network vulnerabilities and enhance reliability. Moreover, it would use next-generation networks, thus providing end users with a more complete set of applications. The next generation network platform would allow for the fast formulation of new ICT services without introducing new infrastructure. ESCAP decided to undertake national feasibility studies in four countries to examine whether a regional broadband network would fit into an overall development of the ICT sector.

The Trans-Eurasian Information Superhighway

The Trans-Eurasian Information Superhighway (TASIM) initiative was proposed by Azerbaijan in 2008 to give Eurasian countries low-cost, high-speed access to the Internet and bridge the digital divide between east and west. The TASIM will link Eastern European countries, the former Soviet Union, Central Asia, Turkey, the Islamic Republic of Iran, Afghanistan, and Pakistan with an outlet to China and India. It is expected to reach more than half of the Eurasian population. In December 2009, the UN General Assembly endorsed the TASIM.

The TASIM will provide countries on its route with access to the Internet, telecommunication systems, and information resources. And most Eurasian countries will enjoy low rates for international traffic. The new network is expected to deliver substantial regional macroeconomic benefits by supporting regional economic connectivity and improving regional e-commerce.

The RCC characterizes the TASIM project as an interstate initiative. Unlike some existing trunk line networks, which are essentially a product of commercial cooperation, TASIM modernizes telecommunications, especially in segments where current networks fail to support actual or forecast traffic volume. The project also provides a technical basis for the RCC policy on enhancing the availability of a wide range of telecommunications services to the public (EDB 2010).

The Black Sea Interconnection Project

The Black Sea Interconnection project, launched in March 2008, was implemented under the Seventh Framework Program of the European Commission and the Istanbul-based Black Sea Economic Council. The project developed a high-speed backbone linking the national research and education networks of the South Caucasus countries and facilitated connectivity to the pan-European research network GEANT2. This flagship project—the largest of its kind in the region—will allow Caucasian research communities to participate effectively in joint research and educational activities with the rest of Europe.

Annex 3A

TABLE 3A.1

Air Carriers' Networks, 2000–11

Carrier	Hub	Spatial concentration, Freeman Index			Time concentration		Cities served	
		2011		2000	2011	2000	2011	2000
		Code-share	No code-share	No code-share	No code-share	No code-share	No code-share	No code-share
Aeroflot	Moscow	0.92	0.98	0.98	0.90	0.81	98	122
Transaero Airlines	Moscow	0.96	0.96	0.94	0.79	0.43	69	18
Uzbekistan Airways	Tashkent	0.96	0.96	0.97	0.78	0.67	54	48
Siberia Airlines-S7	Moscow	0.89	0.84	0.94	0.69	0.23	70	33
Rossiya Airlines	St. Petersburg	0.96	0.99	0.97[a]	0.77	0.57	57	54
Air Astana	Almaty[b]	0.70	0.70	0.52[c]	0.63	0.50	33	2
Aerosvit Airlines	Kiev	0.93	0.91	0.89	0.78	0.40	45	14
Ural Airlines	Yekat'burg	—	0.71	0.97	0.44	0	32	3
Vladivostok Air	Vladivostok	0.60	0.61	0.98	0.49	0.15	25	11
UTair	Moscow	0.77	0.77	0.59[c]	0.58	0.53	59	52
Turkmenistan Airlines	Ashgabat	—	0.99	1.00	0.69	0.33	18	13
Aircompany Yakutia	Yakutsk	0.38	0.40	—	0.32	—	31	—
Avianova	Moscow	—	0.95	—	0.25	—	16	—
VIM Airlines	Moscow	—	1.00	—	—	0.34	20	—
AZAL	Baku	0.99	0.94	0.71	0.41	0.06	20	14
Nordavia[d]	Arkhangelsk	0.72	0.73	0.90	0.37	0.31	24	8
Tajikair	Dushanbe	—	0.80	0.73[c]	0.39	0.06	19	12
Donavia	Rostov	—	0.88	0.82	0.39	0.24	19	22

Carrier	Hub	Spatial concentration, Freeman Index			Time concentration		Cities served	
		2011		2000	2011	2000	2011	2000
		Code-share	No code-share	No code-share	No code-share	No code-share	No code-share	No code-share
PLL Scat Aircompany	Shimkent	—	0.62	0.53[c]	0.41	0.40	27	21
Belavia	Minsk	1.00	1.00	0.94	0.69	0.41	29	22
Air Moldova	Chisinau	0.99	0.98	1.00	0.52	0.14	18	10
Aircompany Kyrg'tan	Bishkek	—	0.92	0.83[a]	0.35	0.20	10	9
Armavia	Yerevan	1.00	1.00	1.00[a]	0.43	0.11	25	25
Tatarstan Airlines	Kazan	0.91	0.91	0.91[a]	0.21	0.14	15	10
Avia Traffic Company	Bishkek	0.68	0.66	—	0.40	—	7	—
Georgian Airlines	Tbilisi	—	0.90	1.00	0.25	0.08	15	7
Somon Air	Dushanbe	—	0.68	—	0.19	—	16	—
Georgian International Airlines	Tbilisi	—	0.90	—	0.37	—	13	26

Source: Authors' calculations based on DIIO data.

Notes: The Freeman network centralization expresses the degree of inequality or variance in the network as a percentage of a perfect star network of the same size. This measure takes 1 for a star (pure HS configuration) and 0 for a complete graph (pure PP configuration). Time concentration is computed as the ratio between indirectly connected city-pairs (IC) through a specific airport, and the sum of IC and the number of direct connections from the same airport (see Nijkamp and others 2007). — = not available.

a. 2005 data.

b. Also operates from Astana.

c. 2008 data.

d. Also based in Sheremetyevo Airport.

TABLE 3A.2

Peripheralization of Eurasian Cities

percentage of cities in the air network

Airport size, tiers	Available connections at hubs	Change in number of destinations with direct services, 2002–10				Change in number of flight frequencies, 2002–10			
		Same	Increase	Decrease	Subtotal	Same	Increase	Decrease	Subtotal
Tier 2	Increase	0.6	13.3	7.0	20.9	—	20.3	0.6	20.9
	Increase	5.7	20.3	10.1	36.0	0.6	31.0	4.4	36.1
Tier 3	Decrease	0.6	—	0.6	1.2	0.6	—	0.6	1.3
	Subtotal	6.3	20.3	10.8	37.3	1.3	31.0	5.0	37.3
	Same	0.6	2.5	—	3.1	0.6	2.5	—	3.2
Tier 4 (smallest)	Increase	3.8	22.2	4.4	30.4	0.6	23.4	6.3	30.4
	Decrease	1.3	1.3	3.2	5.7	0.6	2.5	2.5	5.7
	Subtotal	6.3	25.9	7.6	39.3	1.9	28.5	8.9	39.4

Source: Authors, based on Burghouwt 2004.

Note: Tier 1 includes airports with more than 700 average daily connections, which include all main hubs in the region (Moscow, Kiev, St. Petersburg); tier 2 airports have between 50 and 700 connections (biggest capital cities and prominent regional centers: Almaty, Minsk, Astana, Baku, Rostov, Krasnoyarsk); tier 3 airports have between 5 and 50 connections (smaller capitals and cities having medium population density); and tier 4 airports are in the smallest cities with low population density and fewer than 5 connections. — = not available.

TABLE 3A.3
Onward Connectivity: Number of Available Indirectly Connected City Pairs, by Origin City, Hub, and Destination

Origin city	Dubai					Frankfurt					Istanbul					Moscow					All hubs
	Africa and Middle East	Americas	Asia and Pacific	Europe and Eurasia	Dubai total	Africa and Middle East	Americas	Asia and Pacific	Europe and Eurasia	Frankfurt total	Africa and Middle East	Americas	Asia and Pacific	Europe and Eurasia	Istanbul total	Africa and Middle East	Americas	Asia and Pacific	Europe and Eurasia	Moscow total	
Almaty	—	—	—	—	—	10	31	—	87	128	11	5	—	56	72	1	7	—	48	56	437
Ashgabat	28	—	22	6	56	6	31	—	62	99	6	7	—	60	73	—	5	1	37	43	321
Baku	24	4	34	—	62	3	23	—	47	73	10	2	3	55	70	—	7	11	69	87	412
Bishkek	22	1	4	3	30	—	—	—	—	—	6	7	—	57	70	1	9	—	62	72	231
Chisinau	—	—	—	—	—	9	37	7	53	106	33	5	10	43	91	1	5	5	49	60	335
Dushanbe	12	2	10	7	31	1	5	—	56	62	5	3	—	44	52	—	—	—	10	10	239
Minsk	—	—	—	—	—	4	10	12	55	81	20	2	4	22	48	7	5	7	37	56	415
Tashkent	18	—	1	3	22	7	20	—	54	81	9	7	—	64	80	—	6	—	30	36	477
Tbilisi	12	2	29	—	43	3	23	1	74	101	7	7	1	48	63	—	4	5	21	30	296
Yerevan	13	—	18	—	31	—	—	—	—	—	—	—	—	—	—	—	11	13	69	93	319

Source: World Bank data.

Note: — = not available.

TABLE 3A.4

"Hub" Connectivity: Number of Connected City-Pairs via Selected Airports

Airport	Relative stage-length									Total city-pairs
	Domestic-domestic	Regional-domestic	Domestic-regional	Int'l-domestic	Domestic-int'l	Regional-regional	Int'l-regional	Regional-int'l	Int'l-int'l	
All carriers										
Almaty	8	24	15	41	61	12	20	39	29	249
Ashkhabad	2	7	5	14	19	1	2	7	17	74
Baku	0	1	3	2	6	12	33	44	66	167
Bishkek	0	3	5	1	2	5	2	3	0	21
Chisinau	0	0	0	0	0	0	11	14	31	56
Dushanbe	0	7	8	4	5	15	10	12	5	66
Minsk	0	0	0	0	0	14	34	44	22	114
Moscow	1,229	435	484	1,675	2,460	131	434	782	1,581	9,211
Kiev	21	43	43	147	187	47	193	254	505	1,440
Tashkent	16	26	27	21	45	19	33	47	71	305
Tbilisi	0	0	0	1	0	9	15	15	17	57
Yerevan	0	0	0	0	0	4	12	14	14	44
Only hub carriers and alliance partners' online connections										
Almaty	3	11	6	16	19	1	6	12	10	84
Ashkhabad	2	5	5	10	19	0	0	5	13	59
Baku	0	0	0	0	2	2	5	3	26	38
Bishkek	0	3	4	0	0	0	0	0	0	7
Chisinau	0	0	0	0	0	0	5	5	15	25
Dushanbe	0	2	3	0	1	2	2	4	1	15
Minsk	0	0	0	0	0	14	24	36	5	79
Moscow	301	81	103	484	780	21	97	243	848	2,958
Kiev	15	3	1	19	20	14	64	80	190	406
Tashkent	16	14	18	15	38	4	18	36	61	220
Tbilisi	0	0	0	0	0	6	1	6	4	17
Yerevan	0	0	0	0	0	1	4	5	7	17

Source: World Bank data.
Note: Regional refers to Eurasian countries and international (int'l) refers to non-Eurasian countries. Belarus and Yerevan do not have scheduled domestic flights according to the March 2011 schedule.

TABLE 3A.5

Total Turnaround Costs for Selected Cities

dollars

City or airport	Take-off and landing charge	Charge for ensuring aviation safety	Charge for using the terminal building	Pax service charge	Other	Parking charges	Total turn-around costs
St. Petersburg	709.80	696.00	1,305.00			106.50	2,817.30
Domodedovo	819.00	730.80	974.40			81.90	2,524.20
Sheremetyevo	819.00	730.80	974.40			32.80	2,557.00
Kiev	819.00			1,972.00	Security charge 464.00		3,255.00
Almaty	1,385.00	Security charge 207.70		2,494.00	Marshalling charge 156.00		4,242.70
Tashkent	1,067.00	Transport security 106.70	2,505.60	DCS + Baggage (20 kg/pax) 1,236.10	Security charges 501.10		5,416.60
Dushanbe	780.00			1,044.00	78.00		1,902.00
Bishkek	1,067.10	160.10	780.00	797.20	Boarding bridge charge 146.60		2,951.00
Chisinau	943.50	33.70	Pax security charge 417.60	1,035.60	Modernization fee 1,503.40		3,933.80
Minsk	709.80			232.00	Security charge 142.00	156.20	1,083.80
Yerevan	651.50	Security charge 334.10		3,354.70	Pushback + Bridge + Bus 279.20		4,619.50
Tbilisi	585.00	Aircraft security charge 168.50	Pax security charge 618.00	2,552.00	Baggage. handling + SITA 336.40		4,259.90
Baku	1,010.90	300.70	1,123.20	3,340.80	Civil aviation tax 167.00		5,942.60
Ashgabat	858.00	85.80		2,900.00		214.50	3,843.80
Frankfurt	373.00	835.20		140.40			1,348.60
Istanbul	507.00	Safety charge 241.90		1,740.00	Loading bridge charge 146.90		2,635.80
Dubai	296.50			2,370.60	Aerobridge charge 204.40	53.20	2,871.40

Source: Authors based on ICAO 2010.

Note: DCS = departure control system; kg = kilogram.

Notes

1. According to Stalin, "The Soviet Union would be inconceivable as a state without first-class railway transport linking its many regions and areas into one whole" (Khachaturov 1945, 220).
2. Rosavtotrans is the Russian successor to what was called Soyuuvtotrans in the Soviet Union, with 260,000 trucks in operation.
3. SAS linked the Scandinavian capitals with Moscow, while Finnair operated between Helsinki and Moscow, KLM between Amsterdam and Moscow, Sabena between Brussels and Moscow, and Air France between Paris and Moscow.
4. For instance, using rank-degree analysis (Bagler 2008; Li and Cai 2004).
5. In mathematics, closeness is one of the basic concepts in a topological space. Intuitively we say two sets are close if they are arbitrarily near each other. The concept can be defined naturally in a metric space where a notion of distance between elements of the space is defined. In graph theory, closeness is a centrality measure of a vertex within a graph. Vertices that are "shallow" or "close" to other vertices—those that tend to have short geodesic distances to other vertices within the graph—have higher closeness.
6. This includes all cities in the region and all cities outside the region linked to them with a nonstop or direct flight. And the analysis of current aviation networks in Eurasia reveals that, compared with Aeroflot's flight schedule in the 1950s, a hierarchical hub structure is still prevalent. A hierarchical architecture implies that sparsely connected nodes are part of highly clustered areas, with communication between the different highly clustered neighborhoods being maintained by a few hubs (Barabási and Oltvai 2004). But changes in the configuration of airline operations in the region—and worldwide—have altered some of its structural features, the most important being the average shortest path. Accordingly, the expected number of flights to connect any two cities in the region has been reduced by half to little over a single connection (from 4.5 to 2.2 flights) in the last five decades.
7. For instance, this is the case with Arkhangelsk Airlines, acquired in 2004 by Aeroflot and renamed Aeroflot Nord.
8. Interline agreements allow ticketing and luggage checking at the departure airport for the entire journey. It is important for smaller capital cities that depend on interline connections (a continuing flight with another airline, usually from a different alliance, too). Although interline connections are increasingly less frequent, they are still important for cities without daily or regular services to every major hub—especially if they are underserved by the hub carrier itself (for example, low frequencies on the Dushanbe-Istanbul sector flown by Turkish Airlines), since they would depend also on the local carrier (Tajik Air) for the inbound flight, and thus on interline connections. Indeed, Tajik carriers do not have interline agreements with any other carriers. By contrast, the rest of the capitals with outbound nonstop services to Istanbul and Frankfurt have at least 70 percent of the flight frequencies covered by interline agreements.

9. Under a code-sharing agreement, the airline that operates the flight (the one providing the plane, the crew, and the ground handling services) is called the operating carrier. The company or companies that sell tickets for that flight but do not actually operate it are called marketing carriers or validating carriers. For connecting flights, this allows a customer to book travel from point A to point C through point B under one carrier's code, instead of a customer booking from point A to point B under one code, and from point B to point C under another code. Under this agreement, cooperating airlines also attempt to synchronize their schedules and coordinate luggage handling.

10. So far, most models used to measure the time dimension of connectivity are based on matching inbound and outbound flight schedules at a specific transfer point, within established minimum and maximum connecting times (Bootsma 1997). We followed Danesi (2006) for the methodology to compute indirect connections, which defines a minimum connecting time between flights of 45 minutes for outbound continental flights and 60 minutes for intercontinental departures. In turn, ideal connecting times are 90 and 120 minutes, respectively, and 120 and 180 minutes for maximum connecting times. A routing factor consisting of the ratio between the direct and indirect flight distance through the hub is calculated; all connections involving a routing factor higher than 1.25 are discarded to avoid "artificial" connections or excessive back-tracking (for example, London-Moscow-New York). Thus, a system of weights is set up for each connection, depending on the connection waiting time (quality of the connection) and distance, provided minimum and maximum connecting times are met. But the scarcity of demand information (real origin-destination counts) in international air transport poses a challenge to researchers, who have to rely on supply-side information (airline scheduling) to calculate the competitive position of hubs for connecting traffic.

11. See http://legacy.icao.int/icao/en/trivia/freedoms_air.htm for a description of the freedoms of the air.

12. The methodology is analogous to the one applied to onward connections in third-country hubs, but the unit of analysis when adding the number of connections is the city itself. See Nijkamp and others (2007) for an extensive discussion of the methodology replicated here.

13. See Dennis (1994, 1998) and Graham (1995) for a full description of the hub models.

14. Skyteam's Aeroflot at Sheremetyevo (Moscow) and Oneworld's Siberian Airlines at Domodedovo (Moscow).

15. Anecdotal evidence indicates that load factors in the Istanbul-Dushanbe-Istanbul, Istanbul-Ashgabat-Istanbul, and Istanbul-Almaty-Istanbul routes have exceeded 90 percent in past years.

16. For instance, up to 11 Uzbek airports are still managed by the national airline (Uzbekistan Airways), the only provider of scheduled domestic air services. Six of these airports are international, including Tashkent's (Yuzhny) Airport. Another example is Aeroflot's majority stake in OJSC Terminal (operates terminal D in Sheremetyevo). Other terminals within the Sheremetyevo territory are managed by the state-owned company International Airport Sheremetyevo (IAS).

17. For instance, the Russian government had a controlling stake in Aeroflot, full ownership in Rossiya Airlines and Pulkovo Aviation, and a minority stake in S7 Airlines as of July 2008.

18. For instance, the Armenian state has granted all traffic rights until 2013 to a single provider (Armavia), including "first refusal" rights to any new bilateral agreements signed by the government (ADB 2008; World Bank 2007).

19. According to FAS (Federal Antimonopoly Service), Russia's Antitrust Agency, No. 397 Resolution of the Government of the Russian Federation of 23.06.2007, "On Licensing carriage of passengers and goods by air, and on improving state regulation of air carriers," incorporates FAS Russia's proposals on abolishing the requirements that tie up licensees to a particular airport or route, which have long restrained competition of air carriers on the routes. The effective implementation of the resolution could not be verified independently.

20. According to the recent figures, Russia and the Commonwealth of Independent States countries had an accident rate of 7.15 hull losses per million sectors in 2010, which is almost three times the world rate.

21. For instance, more than 20 Kyrgyz and 30 Kazakh operators have been banned from the EU, only allowing western-built aircraft operations in the case of Air Astana, the Kazakh main carrier (http://ec.europa.eu /transport/air-ban/doc/list_en.pdf).

22. TRACECA. 2009. http://www.traceca-org.org/en/traceca/.

23. For example, Moscow's Pulkovo airport may charge up to €3700 per aircraft (based on Airbus 320's maximum takeoff weight), but Frankfurt would charge €1118 for the same aircraft.

24. Aeroflot actually launched competition in the fuel supply business in Sheremetyevo airport and now enjoys better pricing than most of its domestic and international competitors, saving around 37 million rubles on fuel last year as a result of competitive tenders among jet fuel suppliers.

25. We use an Airbus 320-200 with 70 percent load factor and 2 hours of daytime parking, based on the assumption that the flight is international. Fees include landing and parking fees, and security, passenger facility, and boarding bridge charges (or their equivalents). Other taxes and fees (like navigation services fees) are not included. Computed fees are expressed in current dollars and were extracted from ICAO's *Tariffs for Airports and Air Navigation Services* (2010).

26. While Ashgabat airport charges a fee of $25 per passenger, Dushanbe's published fee is only $9 per person. Other comparators are Dubai ($20.40), Istanbul (US$15), Tashkent ($27), Almaty ($21.50), Bishkek ($7), Yerevan ($32), Moscow Domodedovo ($13), and St. Petersburg ($11.25).

27. For instance, according to the Russian Federal Air Transport Agency, of the 329 operational airports in the country, only 62 percent have an artificial surface (runway), and 35 percent are not even equipped with lighting. Immediate reconstruction is required on 50 percent of the runways, and 18 percent of the runways with unpaved surfaces require major repairs.

28. See http://legacy.icao.int/icao/en/trivia/freedoms_air.htm.

29. International air travel is regulated by bilateral ASAs that govern the number of gateways served, the number and nationality of the carriers offering services, and the frequency, capacity, and even price (Condie 2005). Given their relevance for air transport flows, the effects of air services liberalization and bilateral agreements on air traffic have been the subject of many empirical studies, although little has been written from the perspective of connectivity. In this respect, an inherent problem with the country-level empirical work is the exclusion of airport-level provisions commonly found in bilateral agreements, with the use of scorecard approaches to estimate the restrictiveness of ASAs being favored. For further work on ASAs and their impact, see Hummels and Cristea (2011), Gönenç and Nicoletti (2000), Grosso (2008), Micco and Serebrisky (2004), WTO (2006), and Piermartini and Rousova (2008).

30. In general, negotiations on 5th freedom rights have often been very protracted, partly because they involve at least three parties or more, and also because potential grantor states have regarded 5th freedoms as encroachments upon their 3rd or 4th freedoms (Hanlon 2007).

31. But the prevalence of "orphan services" is still quite high, where up to 1,100 country pairs with direct air services do not have a corresponding codified ASA, representing up to 12 percent of worldwide passenger traffic (Carzaniga and Latrille 2010). In practice, traffic rights and capacity determination in bilateral agreements remain undisclosed and are only in the form of confidential memoranda. It should be noted that the ASA registration with ICAO is done on a voluntary basis by member countries. For an extensive discussion of the provisions and contents of the ASAs, see WTO (2006), and for the Air Liberalization Index see WTO's QUASAR database (http://www.wto.org/english/tratop_e/serv_e/transport_e/review2_e.htm#quasar).

32. We reviewed more than 50 bilateral agreements available at ICAO's WASA database, and national sources, especially Rosaviatsiya, the Russian Federal Air Transport Agency. Other forms of restrictions to the full liberalization of traffic still exist, such as the fees charged by Russia on the Trans-Siberian routes.

33. For instance, in Tajikistan a World Bank study found that restrictive provisions and limited competition resulted in an equivalent tax of 7 percent in the migrant workers' payroll, one of the world's poorest (World Bank 2005).

34. For example, Lufthansa's Frankfurt-Baku-Ashgabat beyond sector.

35. Eurasia-based airlines operating 5th freedom traffic rights between two extra-regional countries are rare, but examples exist, such as Uzbekistan Airways, operating the Riga-New York-Riga sector (from/to Tashkent).

36. By scheduling multiple stops, carriers increase capacity use "as they go" to mitigate the mismatch between inbound and outbound load factors. For instance, the imbalance of exported air cargo between Europe and China was 1:3.4 (for every ton exported, 3.4 were imported) in recent years, while that between Europe and the Middle East was 6.4:1. As a result, several European haulers established hubs and incorporated additional stops in the Middle East, Central Asia, or South Asia to increase capacity use on eastbound flights to Asia. Return legs, however, operate with higher load factors carrying mostly electronic products or

"economically perishable goods" such as garments and fashion items. Carriers with similar network design usually base their business model on the extensive use of 5th freedom rights. This is the case with Cargolux, which established its Caspian cargo operations in Baku, Azerbaijan. This hub serves two main purposes for the Luxembourg-based company: as a transshipment point for Caspian and South Asian destinations served by interline partners (Azal Cargo), and as a "5th freedom hub" with full traffic rights to East Asia and back. Some of the typical routes for the European carrier are Luxembourg-Baku-Shanghai-Baku-Luxembourg, and Luxembourg-Baku-Singapore-Kuala Lumpur-Madras-Baku-Luxembourg on B747Fs.

37. An example of such a strategy is Aeroflot, which serves a few destinations in Europe (Hahn, Helsinki) and East Asia (Tokyo; Seoul; Hong Kong SAR, China; Shanghai) by way of Moscow and Novosibirsk. Since great circle distances between European destinations and East Asia are in excess of 5,500 miles, cargo haulers operating along the Trans-Siberian route have typically scheduled technical stops in Russia (Krasnoyarsk, Sverdlovsk) or Kazakhstan (Almaty, Karaganda) given the range limitations of freighter aircraft when load factors are high. For Aeroflot, Novosibirsk is the entry point for eastbound operations to Tokyo, and in the return leg from Shanghai, which is probably operated at higher load factors. But return trips from Hong Kong SAR, China, and Seoul use Karaganda as an intermediate and commercial stop, which serves a number of different airlines.

   Another example is Airbridge Cargo (ABC), one of the largest providers of scheduled air cargo services in the region with bases in Moscow and Krasnoyarsk. Today, capacity is mostly allocated in European and Asian routes to Moscow (Amsterdam; Frankfurt; Hong Kong SAR, China; Shanghai) and in direct services between Europe and Asia. Given their current fleet composition, nonstop services between Europe and Shanghai or Hong Kong SAR, China are not attainable due to the maximum operational range of the B747-400F aircraft in use. Accordingly, technical stops are scheduled in Krasnoyarsk, where up to 95 percent of ABC's cargo throughput consists of goods in transit. Even so, a minor percentage of freight volumes are either local traffic or transshipments to interline partners and road feeder services.

38. Confidential Memorandum of Understanding between the Aeronautical Authorities of China and the Russian Federation, July 2011.

39. The term "broadband" has no generally accepted definition. According to the International Telecommunications Union definition, broadband refers to an Internet connection speed of 256 kilobits per second (kbps) or higher. But definitions based on data transfer speed do not consider the very fast evolution in technologies and uses. Is a bandwidth of 256 kbps a broadband connection? Or should the limit be set at 1 Mbps? There is no definitive answer, as the bandwidth required to run Internet applications is continuously increasing, and infrastructure standards are continuously improving to meet the growing demand. Such a definition can only be relative to a particular moment in time in a particular country (Fornefeld and others 2008).

40. The STM-4 (Synchronous Transport Module) is an SDH ITU-T fiber-optic network transmission standard. It has a bit rate of 622.08 Mbps. The STM-16 has a bit rate of 2,488.32 Mbps.

References

ADB (Asian Development Bank). 2008. *Armenia: Transport Sector Development Strategy*. Manila: ADB.

Akamai. 2010. *State of the Internet Report—3rd Quarter, 2010 Report*. Cambridge, MA: Akamai. http://www.akamai.com/stateoftheinternet/.

Arvis, Jean-François, Graham Smith, Robin Carruthers, and Christopher Willoughby, eds. 2011. *Connecting Landlocked Developing Countries to Markets*. Washington, DC: World Bank.

Bagler, Ganesh. 2008. "Analysis of the Airport Network of India as a Complex Weighted Network." *Physica A: Statistical Mechanics and its Applications* 387 (12): 2972–80.

Barabási, Albert-László, and Zoltán N. Oltvai. 2004. "Network Biology: Understanding the Cell's Functional Organization." *Nature Review Genetics* 5 (2): 101–13.

Berger, Lee F. 2001. "Proposed Legal Structure for the SilkSat Satellite Consortium: A Regional Intergovernmental Organization to Improve Telecommunications Infrastructure in Central Asia and the Trans-Caucasus Region." *Law and Policy in International Business* 33 (Fall): 99–143.

Boeing Commercial Airplanes. 2011. *Current Market Outlook*. Seattle, WA: Boeing.

Bootsma, Pieter D. 1997. "Airline Flight Schedule Development: Analysis and Design Tools for European Hinterland Hubs." Ph.D. thesis, University of Twente, Utrecht.

Bowen, John. 2002. "Network Change, Deregulation and Access in the Global Airline Industry." *Economic Geography* 78 (4): 425–39.

Burghouwt, Guillaume. 2004. *Airline Network Development in Europe and Its Implications for Airport Planning*. Hampshire, U.K.: Ashgate.

Buttkereit, Sören, Luis Enriquez, Ferry Grijpink, Suraj Moraje, Wim Torfs, and Tanja Vaheri-Delmulle. 2009. *Mobile Broadband for the Masses*. Louvain-la-Neuve, Belgium: McKinsey & Company.

Carzaniga, Antonia, and Pierre Latrille. 2010. "Fog in the Skies? Assessing the Openness of Aviation Policies." Presentation at World Trade Institute, Bern, Switzerland, November 3.

Condie, Stuart. 2005. "Airport Access—Review of Current Issues." In *Access Pricing, Investment and Efficient Use of Capacity in Network Industries—A Comparative Review of Charging Principles and Structure*, ed. Peter Vass, 99–112. Bath, U.K.: Centre for the Study of Regulated Industries, University of Bath.

Danesi, Antonio. 2006. "Measuring Airline Hub Timetable Co-Ordination and Connectivity: Definition of a New Index and Application to a Sample of European Hubs." *European Transport* (34): 54–74.

Dennis, Nigel P. 1994. "Airline Hub Operations in Europe." *Journal of Transport Geography* 2 (4): 219–33.

———. 1998. "Competition between Hub Airports in Europe and a Methodology for Forecasting Connecting Traffic." 8th World Conference on Transport Research, Antwerp, Belgium, July 12–17.

Derudder, Ben, Lomme Devriendt, and Frank Witlox. 2007. "Flying Where You Don't Want to Go: An Empirical Analysis of Hubs in the Global Airline Network." *Tijdschrift voor Economische en Sociale Geografie—2007* 98 (3): 307–24.

EDB (Eurasian Development Bank). 2010. *Integration Processes in CIS Telecommunications Sector.* Almaty, Kazakhstan: EDB.

Embraer Commercial Jets. 2009. *Market outlook 2011–2030.* Brazil: Embraer.

ESCAP (United Nations Economic and Social Commission for Asia and the Pacific). 2001. *Development of the Trans-Asian Railway: Trans-Asian Railway in the North-South Corridor—Northern Europe to the Persian Gulf.* Bangkok: ESCAP.

Evans, William N., and Ioannis N. Kessides. 1993. "Localized Market Power in the U.S. Airline Industry." *The Review of Economics and Statistics* 75 (1): 66–75.

Fidrmuc, Jan, and Jarko Fidrmuc. 2000. "Disintegration and Trade." CEPR Discussion Paper 2641, Centre for Economic and Policy Research, London.

Fornefeld, Martin, Gilles Delaunay, and Dieter Elixmann. 2008. *The Impact of Broadband on Growth and Productivity.* Study on behalf of the European Commission. Duesseldorf, Germany: MICUS Management Consulting.

Friedrich, Roman, Karim Sabbagh, Bahjat El-Darwiche, and Milind Singh. 2009. *Digital Highways: The Role of Government in 21st Century Infrastructure.* New York: Booz & Company.

GAO (U.S. General Accounting Office). 1997. *Airline Deregulation: Addressing the Air Service Problems of Some Communities.* Washington, DC: GAO.

Gönenç, Rauf, and Giuseppe Nicoletti. 2000. "Regulation, Market Structure and Performance in Air Passenger Transportation." Economics Department Working Papers 254, Organisation for Economic Co-operation and Development, Paris.

Graham, Brian J. 1995. *Geography and Air Transport.* Chichester, U.K.: John Wiley & Sons.

———. 1998. "Liberalization, Regional Economic Development and the Geography of Demand for Air Transport in the European Union." *Journal of Transport Geography* 6 (2): 87–104.

Grosso, Massimo G. 2008. "Liberalising Air Transport Services in APEC." GEM Working Paper, April 23, Groupe d'Economie Mondiale, Paris.

Gutierrez, Laurent, and Valérie Portefaix. 2005. "Network." *Urban China* 5 (December): 84.

Hanlon, Pat. 2007. *Global Airlines: Competition in a Transnational Industry.* Oxford, U.K.: Elsevier.

Heymann, Hans. 1958. "The Soviet Role in International Civil Aviation." *Journal of Air Law and Commerce* 25: 265.

Holloway, Stephen. 2007. *Straight and Level: Practical Airline Economics.* Hampshire, U.K.: Ashgate.

Hummels, David, and Anca Cristea. 2011. "Estimating the Gains from Liberalizing Services Trade: The Case of Passenger Aviation." Purdue University, West Lafayette, IL.

IATA (International Air Transport Association). 2011. "Strengthening Russian Aviation—IATA Celebrates 15 Years in Russia." Press release, June 20. www.iata.org/pressroom/pr/pages/2011-06-20-01.aspx.

ICAO (International Civil Aviation Organization). 2010. *Tariffs for Airports and Air Navigation Systems*. Montreal, Canada: ICAO.

ITU (International Telecommunications Union). 2009. *Information Society Statistical Profiles 2009*. Geneva: ITU.

Iyer, Seema D. 2003. "Increasing Unevenness in the Distribution of City Sizes in Post-Soviet Russia." *Eurasian Geography and Economics* 44 (5): 348–67.

Jenkins, Clive. 1963. "Aeroflot." *Flight Magazine,* January 11.

Kaminski, Bartlomiej, Matin Kholmatov, Saumya Mitra, and Gaël Raballand. 2010. "'Asiaregio': An Institutional Model to Deepen Integration in Central Asia's Border Regions." *Global Journal of Emerging Market Economies* 2 (3): 347–60.

Khachaturov, Tigran S. 1945. "Organization and Development of Railway Transport in the U.S.S.R." *International Affairs* 21 (2): 220–35.

Kish, George. 1958. "Soviet Air Transport." *Geographical Review* 48 (3): 309–20.

Klyueva, T., and E. Volkova. 2008. "Prospects of Kazakhstan's Telecommunications Transit Potential." *Informatsionnye Telekommunikatsionnye* 29–35.

Li, W., and X. Cai. 2004. "Statistical Analysis of Airport Network of China." *Physical Review E* 69 (4): 46106.

Lukyanov, Sergey, Elena Tissen, and Nadezda Kislyak. 2009. "The Russian Airline Industry: Contestable Market or...?" *Business and Economic Horizons* 2 (2): 30–33.

MacDonald, Hugh. 1975. *Aeroflot: Soviet Air Transport since 1923*. London: Putnam.

Micco, Alejandro, and Tomas Serebrisky. 2004. "Infrastructure, Competition Regimes, and Air Transport Costs: Cross-Country Evidence." Policy Research Working Paper 3355, World Bank, Washington, DC.

Nijkamp, Peter, Marco Alderighi, Alessandro Cento, and Piet Rietveld. 2007. "Assessment of New Hub-and-Spoke and Point-to-Point Airline Network Configurations." *Transport Reviews* 27 (5): 529–49.

Piermartini, Roberta, and Linda Rousova. 2008. "Liberalization of Air Transport Services and Passenger Traffic." WTO Staff Working Paper ERSD-2008-06, World Trade Organization, Geneva.

Pomfret, Richard. 2010. "Trade and Transport in Central Asia." *Global Journal of Emerging Market Economies* 2 (3): 237–56.

Porch, Harriet. 1964. "Aeroflot, The Soviet Airline—At Home and Abroad." *Journal of Air Law & Commerce* 193.

Raballand, Gaël. 2004. *Analyse économique de l'enclavement: Une application a l'Asie central post-sovietique*. Ph.D. thesis, Université Paris I-Pantheon, Sorbonne, Paris.

Reynolds-Feighan, Asling J. 1995. "European and American Approaches to Air Transport Liberalisation: Some Implications for Small Communities." *Transportation Research A: Policy and Practice* 29 (6): 467–83.

Sagers, Matthew J., and Thomas Maraffa. 1990. "Soviet Air-Passenger Transportation Network." *Geographical Review* 80 (3): 266–78.

Schlumberger, Charles E. 2010. *Open Skies for Africa: Implementing the Yamoussoukro Decision.* Washington, DC: World Bank.

Serebrisky, Tomas, 2003. "The Role of Advocacy in Competition Policy: The Case of the Argentine Gasoline Market." Policy Research Working Paper Series 3130, World Bank, Washington, DC.

Strong, John, John R. Meyer, Clell Harral, and Graham Smith. 1996. *Moving to Market: Restructuring Transport in the Former Soviet Union.* Cambridge, MA: Harvard Institute for International Development.

Taaffe, Robert N. 1962. "Transportation and Regional Specialization: The Example of Soviet Central Asia." *Annals of the Association of American Geographers* 52 (1): 80–98.

Ure, John. 2005. "ICT Sector Development in Five Central Asian Economies: A Policy Framework for Effective Investment Promotion and Facilitation." Paper presented at the International Conference on Strengthening Regional Cooperation for Managing Globalization, Moscow, September 28–30.

Wohl, Paul. 1945. "Transport in the Development of the Soviet Union." *Foreign Affairs* 24: 466–483.

World Bank. 1993. *Transport Strategies for the Russian Federation.* Washington, DC: World Bank.

———. 1998. *Russia: Priorities for Reform in the Transport Sector—Update of 1993 Study.* Washington, DC: World Bank.

———. 2005. *Review of the Air Transport Sector in Tajikistan.* Washington, DC: World Bank.

———. 2007. *Armenia: The Caucasian Tiger.* Washington, DC: World Bank, Poverty Reduction and Economic Management Unit, Europe and Central Asia Region.

———. 2009a. *World Development Indicators 2009.* Washington, DC: World Bank.

———. 2009b. *Confronting "Death on Wheels."* Washington, DC: World Bank, Europe and Central Asia Region.

———. 2011a. *Trade Expansion through Market Connection: The Central Asian Markets of Kazakhstan, Kyrgyz Republic, and Tajikistan.* World Bank Study Series 63435. Washington, DC: World Bank.

———. 2011b. *Aviation Sector Reforms in Tajikistan.* Washington, DC: World Bank.

WTO (World Trade Organization). 2006. *Council for Trade in Services—Second Review of the Air Transport Annex—Developments in the Air Transport.* Geneva: WTO.

CHAPTER 4

Greening Cities

Spotlight—Greening Kazan, the Russian Federation

Parasols, beach towels, and high spirits. Outdoor cafes and swimwear. We might be on Eurasia's glamorous Black Sea coast, but we are actually 1,000 kilometers inland, on the riverside "riviera" in the city of Kazan, the Russian Federation.

In the words of a participant in the 2010 G20 Summit, part of a city's success comes from being "a city that wives want to live in." This does not just mean showcase attractions—it also means incremental improvements in the many environmental aspects of a city that contribute to quality of life. Some of these aspects are mundane, but they help keep a city competitive. Efficient urban transport is one example. The "riviera" city, Kazan, has installed a new fleet of city buses, operated by private firms that bid for the right to operate on specific routes. It is also installing high-speed trams on major routes—like the large ring-road around the city and several trunk roads. This is similar to an indigenous version of Bus Rapid Transit technology, which has proved popular in cities around the world. These trams can run on the existing tramway infrastructure, but they have their own dedicated lanes amid a six-lane road. Average speeds have jumped from 16 kilometers an hour to around 26, and the trams can reach 80 kilometers an hour. One advantage the trams have over Bus Rapid Transit is that they run on electricity—not on combustion engines—and are thus more environmentally friendly.

This chapter examines issues concerning the side effects of urban growth and the need to maintain "green" cities.

Key Issues

- The Soviet era left a mixed environmental legacy—widespread industrial pollution, inefficient use of energy, and often poorly performing public services—but it also left compact cities, and efficient recycling, and high use of public transport.

- Since the transition, many inefficient, polluting industries have disappeared, and market mechanisms have slowly begun to encourage greater energy efficiency. At the same time, more market-oriented, consumerist economies have led to urban sprawl, a greater use of private cars, and a collapse of recycling systems.

- During the initial transition, urban governments rightfully focused on economic and social priorities—and dealt with many of them. Going forward, cities will need to tackle environmental issues more forcefully—not only to improve the welfare of today's residents, but also to be better able to compete for investments and for the skilled and knowledge workers who will drive tomorrow's economies.

The development of cities is shaped by more than people's needs and desires for food, water, shelter, or companionship. War, for example, has defined the development of cities through much of human history. The dense, compact design of medieval walled cities sprang from the need for protection against outside aggressors. In more recent history, industrialization and globalization have defined city development. With rapid urbanization and economic growth have come environmental challenges that many believe will define city development for generations to come.

These environmental challenges are both global (for example, climate change) and local (for example, soil and groundwater pollution). As cities develop, they generate positive and negative side effects, or *externalities*. Positive externalities, which include such benefits of agglomeration as a larger and more diverse customer and labor base, draw people and businesses into cities. Negative externalities—like pollution and congestion—push them out. The more a city develops, the more externalities it generates.

The challenge for local authorities is to enhance and encourage positive externalities while mitigating negative ones. For instance, the larger a city is, the more viable public transportation becomes. But growth can also congest the city with private vehicles. By encouraging dense development around the main transportation hubs, urban planners can mitigate congestion and air pollution from cars and make public transportation more efficient (through increased ridership).

Negative environmental externalities have economic costs that are hard to quantify but often significant. Direct impacts on human health reduce productivity and impose treatment costs. Local pollution and the loss of natural amenities make a city less attractive to high-skilled and high-knowledge workers, inhibiting potential economic transformation through industrial and specialized manufacturing and services. Emissions that contribute to long-term climate change require costly adaptation. Inefficient resource use—encouraged by price distortions—imposes other economic costs related to environmental quality.

In addition to being a drag on urban competitiveness, climate change and pollution are two of the world's most pressing environmental challenges. Cities are central to combating both. To improve the global environment, all cities must become better environmental performers. No mechanism can force global actors to move in a common direction, however. And many developing countries and transition economies feel entitled to pollute on their way to higher growth, just as developed countries did for more than a century.

Without a global effort to reduce pollution and greenhouse gas emissions, everyone will eventually be worse off—the classic "tragedy of the commons" situation. The challenge for Eurasian cities is thus to encourage economic growth while minimizing negative environmental externalities. Mitigating climate change and reducing pollution can make cities both better global environmental stewards and more competitive in their quest for talent and investment.

The Soviet Past: Institutions Without Markets

The Soviet Union failed to combat environmental challenges adequately because—despite having strong (albeit unequally strong) institutions—it had no functioning markets to ensure the efficiency and sustainability of various measures, including the provision of quality public transportation and district heating as populations were increasing and cities were expanding.

In much of the developed world, strong institutions are crucial in reducing market inefficiencies. The Soviet Union had strong institutions, and it did a good job of reducing many of these inefficiencies, such as the poor's lack of access to housing. Yet, environmental institutions did not rank high in that hierarchy. Environmental concerns rarely played a pivotal role in development decisions; Soviet planners tended to take an anthropocentric view of the world, in which natural resources were to meet human needs, particularly through industrialization. Industrial plants went up at breakneck speed, and urban areas were created from scratch. Unprecedented levels of pollution followed, most of it generated in cities, particularly industrial cities.

Central planning—not market principles—guided industrial development, so that industrial facilities were often oversized and overclustered. Industrial managers chose such development patterns because clustering allowed economies of scale and vertical integration reduced transaction and transportation costs. And large plants, more visible and impressive than small ones, gave a greater sense of Soviet "might." They facilitated the allocation and disbursement of funds—it is easier to allocate funds to one large company than to several small ones—and they streamlined the management of an increasingly complex system.

Industrial concentration made economic sense, but it generated an unprecedented amount of pollution in a compact area. Toward the end of the 1980s, Eurasian cities had become some of the world's most polluted places. The Russian city of Norilsk, for example, emitted more sulfur dioxide than all of Italy. A 1989 air quality study in 534 Soviet cities found that virtually all of them exceeded established norms in the concentration of suspended particulate matter. Because their air pollution was so severe, 130 of those cities were put on a black list for further government investigation (Peterson 1993). Although transport contributed a large share of urban air emissions—despite a fairly low car ownership rate—most pollution came from stationary sources, such as industry and power plants (table 4.1).

Industrial pollution was exacerbated by the propensity of managers to overuse resources and allow plants to fall into decay. Because there were no price mechanisms to guide trade and investment (all prices were artificially set at the center) and the state's focus was on production and measurable outcomes, managers had no incentives to run their plants efficiently. It was more profitable—and looked better on paper—to invest in more production capacity than to retrofit and upgrade existing technology, as modernizing existing facilities meant halting production and thus risking the possibility of not meeting production quotas. By contrast, building a new facility won praise, and it came at a derisory cost in an economy in which 1,000 kilograms of steel could be bought for the price of 20 kilograms of apples, and a barrel of oil could be bought for the price of a liter of vodka.

As the state was both the polluter and the regulator, there was no checks and balances mechanism to monitor pollution and enforce pollution standards. Environmental plans set lofty goals, but few managers considered them. Most preferred to pay repeated environmental sanctions—when they were enforced at all—than to stop production and install pollution-abatement technologies.

A lack of decentralization made for poor environmental monitoring in most cities. Sometimes, local governments issued sanctions against particularly bad polluters, but powerful central ministries protected most polluters, so that little came of official efforts. In most cases, local authorities did not meddle with the activity of the industrial plants (they had nothing to gain from doing so and everything to lose), apart from monitoring whether they met their production quotas.

Pollution went largely unabated in most cities, and few environmental improvements were made. Change usually came only when a high-ranking official became aware of environmental degradation. In 1960, for example, Nikita Khrushchev was entertaining a foreign delegation in Moscow when a cloud of toxic air blew over from a nearby paint and dye factory. Caught in the moment, he ordered that the factory be converted to plastics production and that 83 of the most polluting plants be moved outside the city (Colton 1995). But such measures were the exception, not the norm.

Soviet planners remained oblivious—or rather immune—to the environmental and social impacts of rapid urbanization and industrialization.[1] Championing the environment brought no gains. Instead, it risked igniting the wrath of central leaders. And, as the system was

TABLE 4.1

Atmospheric Pollution Emissions in Selected Cities, 1987

City, country	Population, thousands	Level of emissions		Source of emission, percent	
		Metric tons, thousands	Metric tons per capita	Transport	Stationary
Former Soviet Union					
Norilsk, Russian Federation	175	2,426	13.89	1	99
Krivoi Rog, Ukraine	713	1,369	1.92	6	94
Moscow, Russian Federation	8,769	1,211	0.14	70	30
Temirtau, Kazakhstan	214	1,018	4.76	2	98
Novokuznetsk, Russian Federation	600	949	1.58	6	94
Magnitogorsk, Russian Federation	440	900	2.04	3	97
Baku, Azerbaijan	1,022	788	0.77	38	62
Nizhnii Tagil, Russian Federation	439	712	1.62	4	96
St. Petersburg, Russian Federation	4,461	626	0.14	59	41
Chelyabinsk, Russian Federation	1,144	534	0.47	16	84
Angarsk, Russian Federation	266	482	1.81	3	97
Ufa, Russian Federation	1,082	475	0.44	27	73
Dnepropetrovsk, Ukraine	1,178	444	0.38	28	72
Krasnoyarsk, Russian Federation	913	400	0.44	27	73
Volgograd, Russian Federation	999	396	0.40	29	71
Tashkent, Uzbekistan	1,780	362	0.20	86	14
Donetsk, Ukraine	1,109	328	0.30	41	59

City, country	Population, thousands	Level of emissions		Source of emission, percent	
		Metric tons, thousands	Metric tons per capita	Transport	Stationary
Kiev, Ukraine	2,588	327	0.13	71	29
Tbilisi, Georgia	1,243	312	0.25	87	13
Yerevan, Armenia	1,199	248	0.21	71	29
Minsk, Belarus	1,276	235	0.18	53	47
Almaty, Kazakhstan	1,072	213	0.20	77	23
Sterlitamak, Russian Federation	247	201	0.81	9	91
Bishkek, Kyrgyz Republic	627	163	0.26	46	54
Irkutsk, Russian Federation	626	152	0.24	41	59
Chisinau, Moldova	665	133	0.20	68	32
Arkhangelsk, Russian Federation	416	116	0.28	28	72
Dushanbe, Tajikistan	604	114	0.19	67	33
Ashkhabad, Turkmenistan	402	46	0.11	87	13
Cities outside the region					
Mexico City, Mexico	8,300	5,027	0.61	80	20
Los Angeles, United States (1982)	3,300	3,391	1.03	87	13
São Paolo, Brazil	9,200	2,110	0.23	86	14
London, United Kingdom (1978)	6,500	1,200	0.18	86	14
Athens, Greece (1976)	772	394	0.51	59	41
Munich, Germany (1974/75)	1,185	213	0.18	27	73

Source: Peterson 1993, authors' calculations.
Note: Figures for all cities are for 1987, except where otherwise indicated in parentheses.

highly centralized and tightly controlled, local governments had no incentives to make their cities more environmentally friendly.

In the west, citizens had a voice and many demanded change. They also could vote. And if the status quo remained, many voted with their feet—by moving elsewhere. Soviet citizens had none of these options.

With all their faults, however, Eurasian cities did do some things that would be considered "green" today. They provided broad access to public transportation, had high rates of access to water and sanitation, operated recycling programs, used district heating, and combined heat and power systems. But with no markets, there were no viable price mechanisms to promote efficiency.

Inefficient Use of Energy

Eurasia urbanized very quickly, generating multiple environmental externalities that are typical of cities and urban growth. As millions of people moved from rural areas to electrified urban apartments, thousands of industrial and power chimneys went up to accommodate them. People moved to urban, often colder areas on an unprecedented scale.

The Soviet Union had the world's largest absolute number of people living in areas with low temperatures (see table 4A.1). Of the world's 25 coldest cities with more than 500,000 people in 2001, 23 were in Russia (and home to 19 million people). The population rises substantially when including smaller cities and towns (Hill and Gaddy 2003).

Maintaining people in frigid climates placed a huge demand on Eurasia's energy production, as cities had to be heated. The Soviet Union's power production, rising rapidly, kept up with Western Europe's (figure 4.1). But Western Europe enjoyed higher and more consistent economic growth.

Soviet planners did not consider the temperature when building cities in colder areas. Buildings and infrastructure were seldom adapted to atmospheric conditions. Whether in Ashgabat in the Central Asian desert or in Norilsk above the Arctic Circle, apartment blocks were all designed the same, forcing northern residents to brave Arctic winters with thin walls and large windows.

Energy efficiency was not exactly a staple of Soviet building design. Concrete is six times more thermally conductive than brick, and seven times more conductive than wood (the material traditionally used for buildings in Siberia). Concrete also ages faster than does brick or wood. To make matters worse, people were oblivious to the

FIGURE 4.1

Electricity Production in Western Europe and the Soviet Union, 1950–80

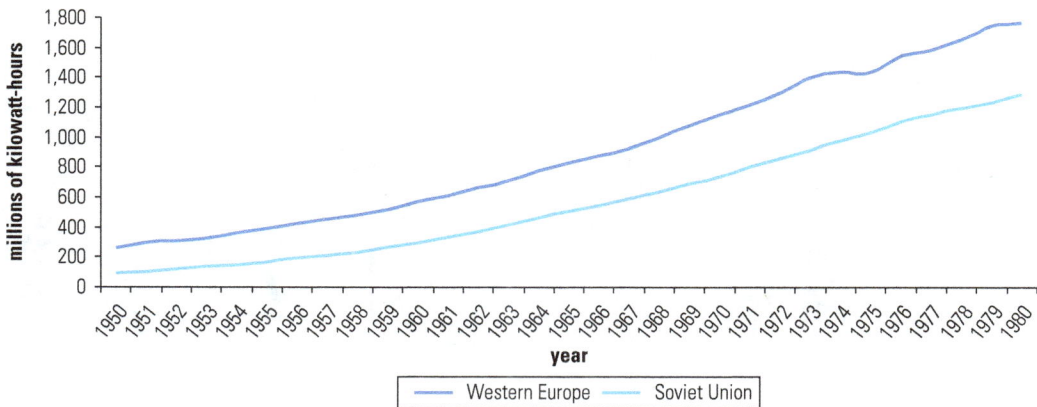

Source: UN 1980.

true cost of heating an apartment in a cold area. And fossil fuels were delivered to power plants and district heating units at artificial prices.

To meet these high energy demands, Soviet planners relied initially on cheaper, dirtier energy sources, such as thermal electric plants that burned coal, oil, and gas. But so did Western countries at the time (see figure 4.2). As technologies improved, many countries shifted toward cleaner energy sources. The switch from coal was much more pronounced in Eurasia than in the rest of the world, and reflected the region's discovery of abundant sources of oil and gas. Indeed, when the 1973 oil crisis hit, the Soviet Union responded by increasing domestic supply rather than increasing energy efficiency. The Soviet Union's vast fossil fuel reserves made it energy independent, but they also discouraged investing in cleaner, more efficient technologies.

Fairly Efficient Public Transportation

To move people in ever-growing cities, Soviet planners built extensive public transportation systems. This was one thing Soviet cities did markedly better than many other cities in the world. However, like most public transportation systems, the Soviet systems relied on subsidies, and no legitimate attempts were made to increase cost-recovery. On the contrary, Moscow and Tashkent, for example, built their metro systems with lavish designs and ornaments to impress and please the average citizen. Beautifying these facilities is commendable, but the maintenance costs were often substantial.

FIGURE 4.2

Production of Primary Energy in the Soviet Union and Elsewhere, 1950s–80s

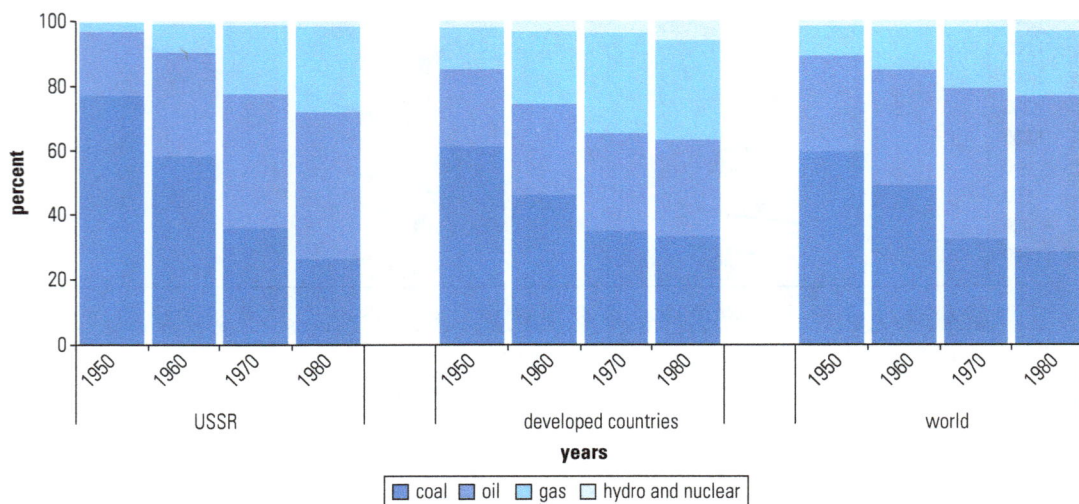

Source: UN 1980.

Car ownership and use were much lower than in Western cities, as people had more public transportation options and less purchasing power. In addition, the state controlled the formal vehicle market—there were virtually no car imports—and second-hand markets were usually word-of-mouth affairs that relied on friendships and social networks. The transport sector was nevertheless a substantial source of air pollution in most Soviet cities. In 1988, despite having just a tenth of the United States's car fleet and only half of its truck freight, Soviet transport generated two-thirds as much atmospheric pollution (Feshbach and Friendly 1992). In 1960, the Soviet Union produced a small fraction of the number of cars produced in the United States, France, the United Kingdom, or the Federal Republic of Germany—but produced only slightly fewer than Japan (table 4.2). By 1986, Soviet production had risen above the United Kingdom's but was only a seventh of Japan's.

Because of an "artificial" market for trucks and buses (that is, competition among state-owned industries and organizations), more were produced. Indeed, until the early 1970s, the Soviet Union produced more buses and trucks than passenger cars. In 1986, the Soviet Union produced more buses and trucks than France, the United Kingdom, and the Federal Republic of Germany combined, though just a small fraction of those countries' combined passenger vehicle output.

TABLE 4.2

Vehicle Production in the Soviet Union and Selected Countries, 1960–86

1,000 units

Country	1960		1970		1980		1986	
	Passenger cars	Buses and trucks	Passenger cars	Buses and trucks	Passenger cars	Buses and trucks	Passenger cars	Buses and trucks
Soviet Union	139	385	344	572	1,327	872	1,326	918
Federal Republic of Germany	1,817	238	3,528	318	3,512	380	4,273	179
France	1,136	234	2,458	292	3,487	505	2,732	462
Japan	165	595	3,179	2,126	7,038	4,006	7,811	4,458
United Kingdom	1,353	458	1,641	458	924	389	1,019	229
United States	6,675	1,194	6,547	1,692	6,400	1,667	7,516	3,393

Source: Pollard 1990.

With more cars on the road came more car pollution. Most wealthier cities (particularly Eurasian capitals) had more cars per capita and higher pollution from transport (see table 4.1). Most of the cities with the highest share of pollution from transport are historic, clustered around the western and southern borders of the Soviet Union (exhibit 4.1). This geographic pattern had several causes. First, historic cities were already fairly well developed by the time of the aggressive industrialization wave and thus did not always accommodate large industrial plants. Second, with World War II, the Soviets developed more industrial capabilities inland, away from the borders and potential enemy attack. Third, most industrial development went to areas with solid Russian or pro-Russian majorities. Moldova's capital, for example, had virtually no major industry by the time the Soviet Union collapsed. The same was true of other capitals in the Caucasus and Central Asia.

Rudimentary Waste Management

The Soviet Union was not a consumerist society; it generated much less waste than did Western countries. Its lack of markets translated into a lack of diversity in goods and packaging. Cities surrounded by active rural communities often relied on regional produce for their daily food needs. People in these cities bought local meat from the butcher (or cut the meat themselves, if they had relatives in the countryside) instead of buying prepackaged cuts from the supermarket; received milk delivery in returnable glass bottles, not in cartons

EXHIBIT 4.1

Air Pollution from Transport in the Soviet Union, 1988

Transport pollution in 1988,
percentage of all pollution

- 1.1 – 50.0
- 50.1 – 75.0
- 75.1 – 100.0

Source: Feshbach and Friendly 1992.

or plastic bottles; and bought most of their vegetables at the local market. Soviet households generated less waste than did Western households.[2] In addition, most cities had recycling networks for paper, glass, and metal.

Many newer cities and those in cold regions relied too much on food shipments from other areas of the Soviet Union, however. These shipments were not only taxing on the environment—a tomato transported from the Caucasus to Irkutsk leaves a fairly large environmental footprint—but also heavily subsidized. In addition, industrial soil pollution went unchecked in most industrial cities. Heavy metals, construction materials, pharmaceuticals, and exhausted fuels and oils were often just dumped on site or in dumps in wild areas on the outskirts of cities.

Environmental regulations were poorly enforced, and even when they were enforced, the fines to encourage better behavior were minimal. Almost 90 percent of the waste generated by industries was not safely disposed of (table 4.3).

The situation was little better when waste was discarded in state-operated landfills, which were usually nothing more than open pits in periurban areas. Many smaller cities and towns did not even have access to solid waste infrastructure, dumping their trash in makeshift dumpsites. Most operating landfills had no provisions to protect

TABLE 4.3
Generation and Disposal of Toxic Waste in the Soviet Union, by Sector, 1990

Sector	Volume generated, 1,000 metric tons	Recovered and safely disposed of, percent
Ferrous and nonferrous metals	241,500	9.8
Construction materials	11,100	4.5
Fertilizer	7,200	9.5
Chemicals and petrochemicals	5,900	32.3
Energy	5,300	33.5
Automobiles and farm equipment	3,800	17.2
Lathes and instruments	1,600	7.3
Electronics	400	3.8
Pharmaceuticals	400	25.0
Coal	300	30.0
Heavy machinery	200	20.0
Other	22,583	26.5
Total	302,083	11.85

Source: Peterson 1993.

against waste leachates into the soil and groundwater, and methane emissions from decomposing organic waste were not captured. As disposing waste was fairly cheap, smaller cities and towns had no incentive to upgrade facilities.

Western countries were not much better in their solid waste management. For example, the Federal Republic of Germany, one of the countries most innovative in solid waste management, did not take a proactive stance on it until the mid-1960s, when the economic and consumption boom led to a waste avalanche. Up to that point, it discarded much of its waste in some 50,000 open garbage dumps. There were only 130 sanitary landfills, 16 composting plants, and 30 incinerators. After the country passed its Waste Disposal Act in 1972, most open dumps closed, and national solid waste management consolidated around fewer large sanitary landfills and incinerators. By 1984, 385 sanitary landfills were handling about 70 percent of the country's municipal waste (Bilitewski, Härdtle, and Marek 1997).

Good Utilities Coverage, Inefficient Delivery

Access to water and sanitation in Soviet urban areas was generally good, with larger cities usually having full coverage. Some cities were underserviced (especially in the Caucasus and Central Asia), but overall the Soviet Union provided services at a level higher than even some developed Western countries.

In 1988, 87 percent of cities and 53 percent of towns were served by some form of sewerage system (Peterson 1993). The quality of wastewater treatment technology in the Soviet Union—which several Western cities, such as Milan, lacked entirely—was fairly high. But a lack of incentives for workers and managers often translated into poorly constructed, badly maintained, and loosely monitored systems. In addition, the need to meet plan and production quotas (measured, for example, in tons of effluent treated) was a strong disincentive for interrupting operations for repairs, improvements, or upgrades.

Just 25 percent of the Soviet Union's wastewater was treated in compliance with norms, and 24 percent went untreated altogether (table 4.4). There were, however, high performers, such as Belarus and the Kyrgyz Republic, the latter of which was responsible for the

TABLE 4.4

Performance of Water and Wastewater Sector in the Former Soviet Union, 1989

percent, except where otherwise indicated

Republic	Requiring treatment, millions of cubic meters	Treated in compliance with norm	Treated but not in compliance with norm	Untreated	Chemical indicators	Bacteriological indicators
	Wastewater				Noncompliance with drinking water standards in municipal water supply systems	
Armenia	557	55	1	44	5.3	10.9
Azerbaijan	597	51	12	37	31.4	21.8
Belarus	994	93	7	0	29.5	9.0
Georgia	626	49	9	42	7.9	14.7
Kazakhstan	591	43	48	9	12.7	7.4
Kyrgyz Republic	180	78	17	6	3.7	14.1
Moldova	298	37	48	39	14.5	8.6
Russian Federation	30,633	11	61	28	20.5	11.7
Tajikistan	286	62	35	3	21.5	21.7
Turkmenistan	—	—	—	—	27.5	23.4
Ukraine	6,706	57	36	7	13.1	9.9
Uzbekistan	762	65	8	27	25.9	14.7
Soviet Union	43,564	25	51	24	18.5	11.3

Source: Peterson 1993.
Note: — = not available.

quality of water in much of Central Asia, as the region's two major rivers pass through it.

The quality of drinking water suffered because of industrial discharge and seepage from sewer lines. Chemical indicators were particularly high in the water systems of Azerbaijan, Belarus, and Turkmenistan. Households often had brown tap water, especially after service shutdowns. Groundwater sources in Central Asian cities were also heavily contaminated, as fertilizers were used heavily in mass agriculture.

Industrial plants were especially bad water managers, using huge quantities and returning it to the system full of toxins and contaminants. Households also consumed excessive amounts of water. As a result, the processing capacity of water and wastewater systems had to be continually adjusted upward (ADB 1998).

As water and wastewater systems expanded, few paid attention to the systems as they were. Indeed, the focus was on producing more, not on maintaining what was already there. Not surprisingly, most water and wastewater systems leaked, wasting a precious resource and raising the energy requirement for delivery, processing, and disposal.

Many Green Areas, but Decaying

Soviet planners made good provisions for urban green space. Central planners usually made ample space for green infrastructure in their city designs. Exhibit 4.2 shows what early planners had in mind for Moscow in the 1930s and how much green space is left now. As cities expanded, green space gave way to new neighborhoods and factories.

Although the number of urban green spaces was impressive, the quality was not. Green spaces were not tended with sound landscape principles. Nor were they designed to enhance the visitor experience. They were instead simply put there to be there. And for all their green, Soviet cities had one color that sprang to visitors' minds—gray. Trees, buildings, and infrastructure were covered with a blanket of soot, the result of air pollution, lack of maintenance, and the neutralization of the carbon-sink capacity of urban forests in some high-emission cities.

Most cities had a shortage of trees and parks that could act as urban lungs. Most of Moscow's green space, for example, was beyond the city's outer rings. Thus, people in Moscow had 29 percent less green space per capita than the Soviet norm, and the deficit in the city center was almost 80 percent (Feshbach and Friendly 1992).

EXHIBIT 4.2
Moscow Green Areas

a. Moscow reconstruction plan in the 1930s	b. Moscow, 2011
Roads, railroads, and borders based on situation 2011	

Land use
- urban core
- resident
- industry
- nature
- other

Land use
- administration/public
- resident
- industry
- nature
- other

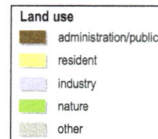

Source: Adapted from Colton (1995) and Moscow Masterplan.

The Transitional Present: Weak Institutions and Weak Markets

The dissolution of institutions and the continued absence of markets plagued the first half of the transition. This first half created some environmental dividends, as many industries folded or scaled down, but it also led to the widespread disintegration of the environmental infrastructure. The second half of the transition saw the emergence of markets but a slower recovery of institutional support.

The transition affected Eurasian countries at varying levels of both development and environmental degradation. On the whole, resource-rich, industrialized countries (Belarus, Kazakhstan, Russia, and Ukraine) were poorer environmental performers than were smaller, less developed countries. There were, however, at least five idiosyncratic challenges that all countries shared: inefficient and wasteful industries, a large environmental infrastructure that was falling apart and expensive to operate, a culture of centralized environmental management with inactive local governments and a weak civil society, poorly enforced regulations, and a general lack of political interest in the environment. The Soviets built extensive public services infrastructure—more than did other countries at their development level—but they did not have the mechanisms in place (such as a proper tariff structure) to ensure the sustainability of the infrastructure. Without the subsidies from the central government that they had enjoyed before, much of this infrastructure fell into disrepair.

With the economic downturn of the 1990s came a drop in pollution from industrial facilities and power plants. And with the fall of the Communist system, many industrial facilities were producing without real markets to serve. These facilities had relied on artificial pricing for fuel, energy, and raw material purchases, "employing" people who just stood around and did nothing. When the system fell, it fell with all its might, and so did pollution. It was not a call to arms for the environment but an adjustment to "real" production and pollution levels.

Before 1991, an oversized industry produced an oversized amount of pollution. But after 1991, production contracted and pollution fell dramatically. Every Eurasian country emitted less carbon dioxide after the Soviet Union broke up—and shortly before (figure 4.3).

In the industrial giants, the adjustment was huge. But even the smaller, less developed countries saw an environmental dividend from deindustrialization. Three heavy hitters—Kazakhstan, Russia, and Ukraine—each belched more carbon dioxide per capita in the heyday of Communism than did the average high-income country in the Organisation for Economic Co-operation and Development (OECD). The other Eurasian countries, except for Armenia, the Kyrgyz Republic, and Turkmenistan, generated more carbon dioxide per capita than the world average.

The transition saw the world's pollution levels stay in step with those of the OECD, but it marked a large downward adjustment for Eurasian countries. As Eurasian economies began adjusting to markets, pollution began growing again. But the growth has been much less pronounced than the initial downward trend, and except for Kazakhstan—which greatly expanded its resource exploitation—no Eurasian country has risen above the OECD average. Azerbaijan, Moldova, Tajikistan, and Uzbekistan dropped their carbon dioxide emissions below the world average and kept them there.

FIGURE 4.3

Carbon Dioxide Emissions in Selected Countries, 1989–2007

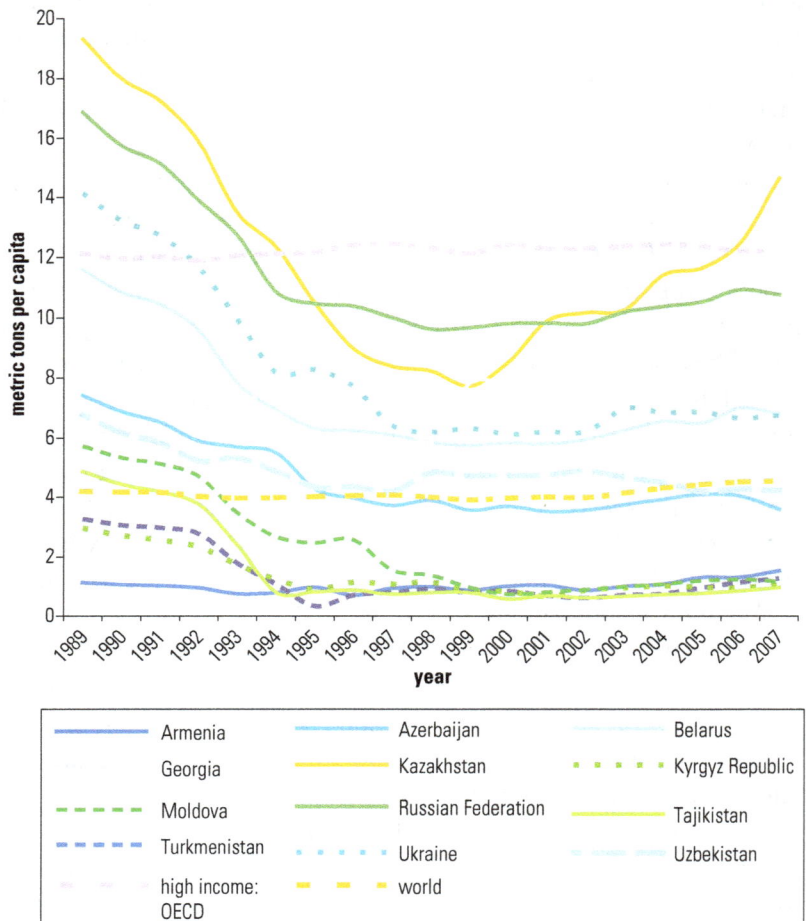

Source: World Bank 2011.
Note: OECD = Organisation for Economic Co-operation and Development.

This decline in atmospheric pollution is clearly good for both the global climate and the quality of life in cities in the former Soviet Union. However, normalizing carbon dioxide emissions for GDP output reveals that, despite polluting less, Eurasian countries are still big polluters (figure 4.4).

Eurasian factories thus polluted less but still averaged more pollution per unit of output than did the world and the OECD. In 1990, almost all Eurasian countries polluted more per unit of output than did the average OECD country. Uzbekistan polluted six times as much, and Kazakhstan five times as much. Still, Eurasian countries were among a select group that reduced greenhouse gas emissions in the 1990s and 2000s while increasing economic growth.

FIGURE 4.4

Carbon Dioxide Emissions in Selected Countries, 1990 and 2007

2005 PPP

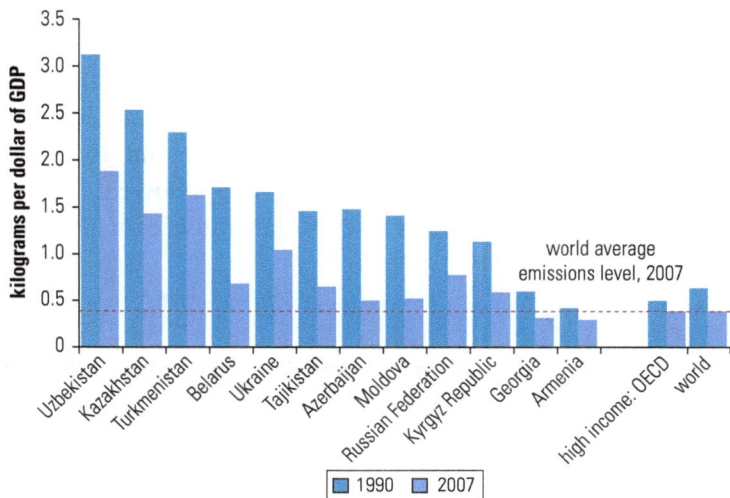

Source: World Bank 2011.

Note: GDP = gross domestic product; OECD = Organisation for Economic Co-operation and Development; PPP = purchasing power parity.

On the flip side, lower budgets, weakened institutions, a lack of price mechanisms and efficient markets, and few environmental priorities led to the deterioration of the environmental infrastructure. Problems included leaking and underperforming water and wastewater networks, overwhelmed landfills, collapsed recycling networks, poor transportation systems, and green areas under attack from new developments.

Eurasian countries came out of Communism with an environmental infrastructure that was, in many respects, beyond their level of development. Many Eurasian cities have thus failed to maintain and operate their infrastructure properly. Higher tariffs and better collection rates were needed to finance the repairs and upgrades, but achieving these changes proved difficult because of low household incomes and poorly managed utilities companies.

Civil society continued to play a marginal role in a system that was shaken by the collapse of Communism but that was still unwilling to cede power and decentralize. Most Eurasian countries continued to garner bad civil society ratings well into 2010 (Mootz 2010). Although the situation improved dramatically in Hungary, Poland, and Romania, many Eurasian countries neither allowed a functional market system to develop nor provided institutions strong enough to tackle the worst market inefficiencies. Even when the strong institutions were there, the political will was often missing.

Energy Consumption

With many outdated, inefficient industrial facilities folding during the transition, energy demand declined in most of Eurasia. A declining population also contributed to this fall in demand, though only modestly. Energy consumption patterns followed economic performance (figure 4.5). Less energy demand meant less energy

FIGURE 4.5

Electric Power Consumption in Selected Countries, 1990–2007

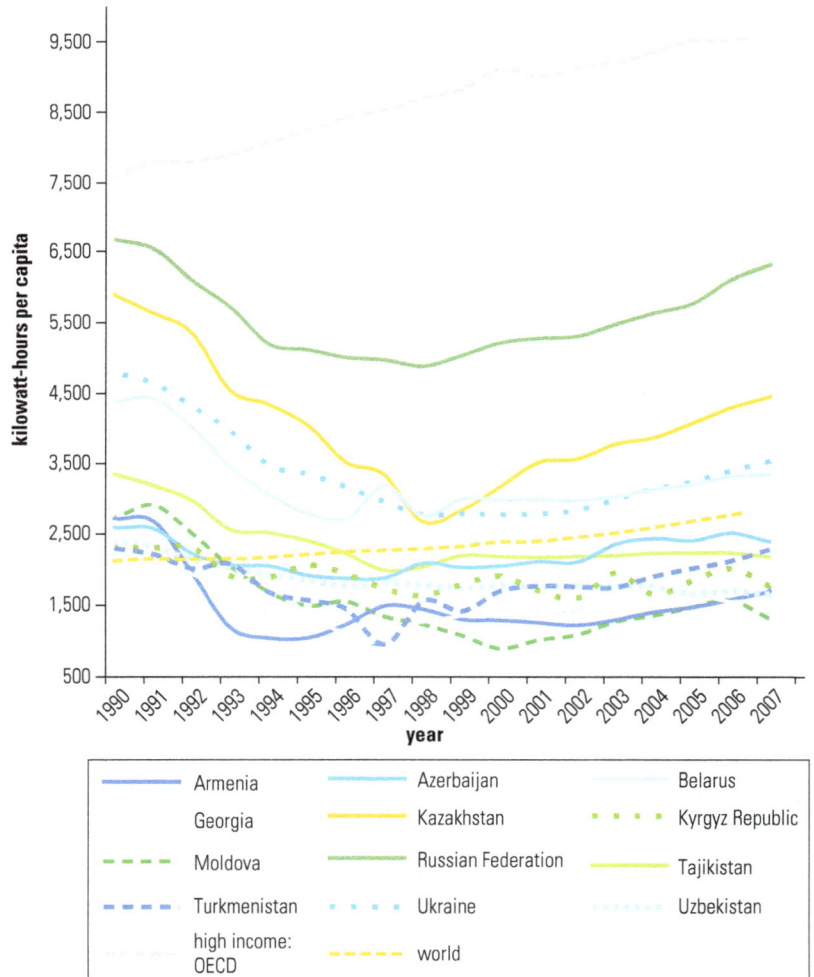

Source: World Bank 2011.
Note: OECD = Organisation for Economic Co-operation and Development.

production, and less energy production translated into less pollution from thermal power plants—the chief emitter of greenhouse gases.

As the economy began to recover, so did energy production. But by 2007, no Eurasian country had returned to its 1990 level. All the Eurasian countries consumed less energy per capita than the OECD countries, and eight (the smaller, less industrialized countries in Eurasia) fell below world averages at the onset of the transition and stayed there.

All in all, Eurasian countries has performed rather well environmentally. And even better, very few of them rely substantially on energy generated from coal—only Kazakhstan is above the world average in coal-generated energy—and several rely substantially on low-emission sources like hydroelectricity and nuclear power. Some countries' large fluctuations from 1990 to 2007 (figure 4.6) can be explained by their reliance on energy imports—Moldova, for example, imports almost all its energy—and on the discovery of new and more cheaply exploitable energy sources (such as natural gas in Azerbaijan).

Still, Europe and Central Asia is the world's least energy-efficient region, accounting for 10 percent of global energy demand but generating only 5 percent of global gross domestic product (GDP) (World Bank 2010). The low GDP per unit of energy use in Eurasian countries can be attributed to old, poorly maintained energy facilities (80 percent were installed before 1980). In addition, energy tariffs and prices are below production costs, leading to a skewed economic structure and inefficient energy use. Some countries, like Turkmenistan and Uzbekistan, consume less energy per

FIGURE 4.6

Composition of Energy Sources in Selected Countries, 1990 and 2007

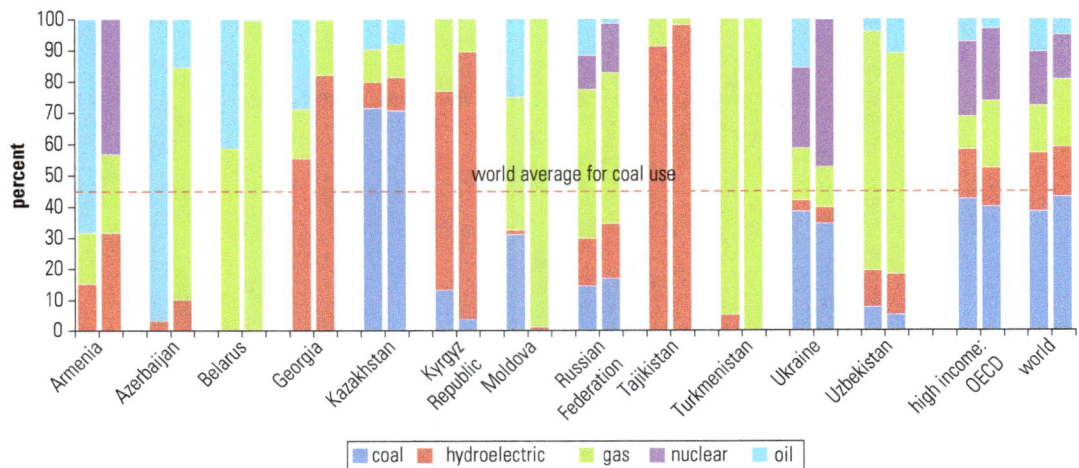

Source: World Bank 2011.
Note: OECD = Organisation for Economic Co-operation and Development.

capita than the global average, but they still manage to emit more energy-related carbon dioxide (Zoi Environment Network 2009).

Most Eurasian cities do not control energy production directly, so they cannot play a direct role in reducing energy emissions from the source. This task is for national and regional stakeholders. Eurasian cities can, however, play a big role in increasing local energy efficiency—for example, by offering incentives for the thermal insulation of buildings and educating citizens to turn off appliances when they are not in use. Eurasian cities can also strive for greater energy independence.

Even without local government intervention—and most local Eurasian authorities have not been tackling environmental issues proactively—urban greenhouse gas emissions and pollution fell during the transition, thanks largely to declining industrial output. Air pollution dropped in nearly every major Russian city between 1992 and 2009, and in several cities, pollution fell more than 75 percent (exhibit 4.3).

EXHIBIT 4.3

Air Pollution from Stationary Sources in Cities in the Russian Federation, 1992 and 2009

a. Air pollution from stationary sources in 1992, tons per capita

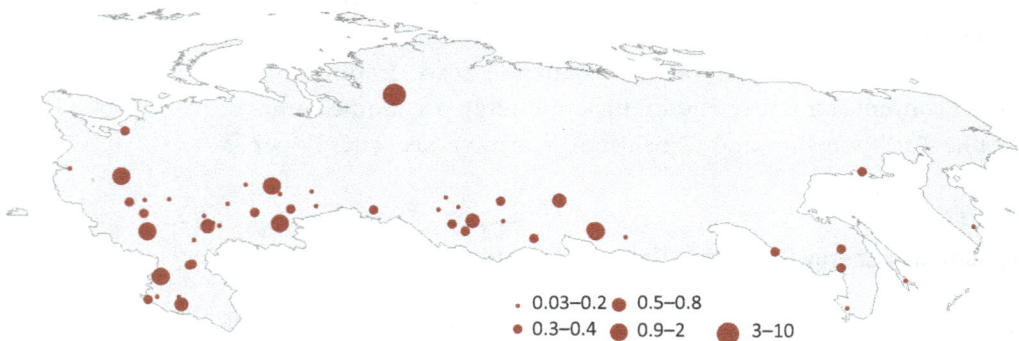

. 0.03–0.2   ● 0.5–0.8
● 0.3–0.4   ● 0.9–2   ● 3–10

b. Changes in stationary air pollution levels from 1992 to 2009, percent

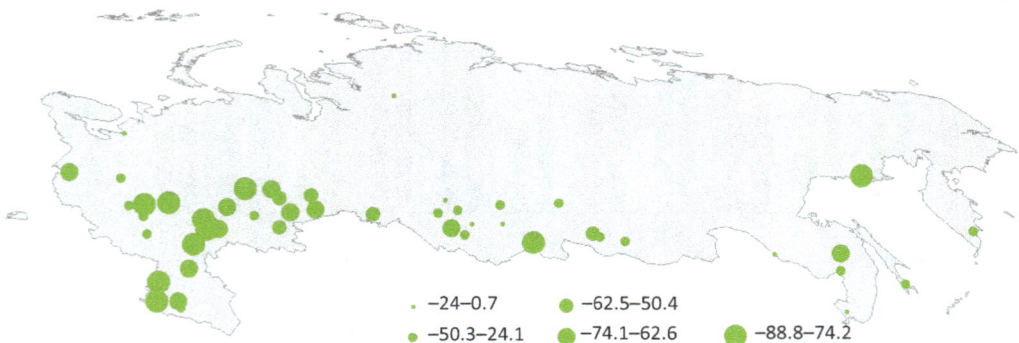

. −24–0.7   ● −62.5–50.4
● −50.3–24.1   ● −74.1–62.6   ● −88.8–74.2

Source: Rosstat 2010.

The situation is similar in other Eurasian countries. In Belarus, pollution from stationary sources fell in all major cities, though some (such as Minsk and Mogilev) continue to be big polluters (Belarus National Statistics Committee 2009). In Ukraine, air pollution from stationary sources fell 63 percent from 1985 to 2000. It has increased since 2000, however, and many of the country's big industrial centers—Donetsk, Kryviy Rih, Luhansk, Mariupol, and Zaporizhzhya—continue to be big polluters (Ukraine State Statistics Committee 2001, 2009).

High concentrations of pollutants still threaten more than 30 million urban dwellers in Russia. And similar problems persist in other Eurasian countries. High levels of pollution are found in Almaty, Kazakhstan (formaldehyde); Ashgabat, Turkmenistan (formaldehyde and particulates); Bishkek, Kyrgyz Republic (carbon monoxide, nitrogen oxides, and particulates); Chisinau, Moldova (nitrogen oxides); Dushanbe, Tajikistan (sulfur dioxide and particulates); Kiev, Ukraine (nitrogen oxides); Tbilisi, Georgia (sulfur dioxide and particulates); and Yerevan, Armenia (nitrogen oxides, sulfur oxides, carbon monoxide, and particulates) (ADB 1998; OECD 2005).

Rapid Increase of Private Cars

Eurasia's economy took more than a decade to adjust to new market realities, but its use of private vehicles rose almost instantly. Every year brought more cars to city streets, generating more pollution and greenhouse gas emissions (OECD 2005). A large share of new cars did not have a catalytic converter to curtail emissions, and many were old, second-hand cars with even poorer environmental performance, exacerbating the already-high transport emissions.

Gasoline consumption rose in most Eurasian countries, more than doubling between 2000 and 2008 in Azerbaijan, the Kyrgyz Republic, and Moldova (figure 4.7). Over the same period, world consumption leveled off, actually falling in OECD countries. Nonetheless, most Eurasian countries consume less motor gasoline per capita than the world average, and the countries that consume more are oil rich and have substantial motor oil subsidies (particularly Turkmenistan). OECD countries consumed more gasoline than did Eurasia, though with cleaner-burning cars.

In 2008, France, Germany, Italy, and Sweden had two to three times more registered vehicles per 1,000 people than did countries in the former Soviet Union. And the United States had more than four times as many registered vehicles per 1,000 people than did every Eurasian country except Russia and Belarus (World Health Organization [WHO]

FIGURE 4.7

Motor Gasoline Consumption in Selected Countries, 2000 and 2008

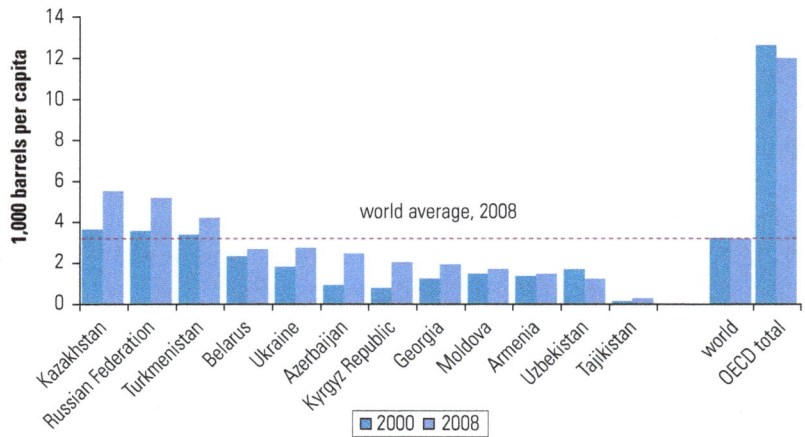

Source: IEA 2010a, 2010b.
Note: OECD = Organisation for Economic Co-operation and Development.

online database). This discrepancy shows that Eurasian countries have the potential for better environmental performance in transport, but if they are not careful, their emissions could reach OECD levels.

This onslaught of private vehicles has increased congestion in Eurasian cities in recent years, and public transportation networks have had a hard time keeping up. In many situations, an institutional vacuum and a lack of market pricing have led to a continued deterioration of transit lines (exhibit 4.4). In addition, urban sprawl and increasing disposable incomes have increased people's reliance on and appetite for private vehicles. Extensions of public transportation have not kept up with extensions of the urban mass, and some cities (such as in Dushanbe, L'viv, and Tashkent) have abandoned dedicated transit lines, particularly tram lines. A lack of investment in rolling stock and in upkeep of public transport infrastructure has made public transportation less reliable, less comfortable, and slower than private cars.

Nonetheless, people in Eurasian cities rely much more on environmentally friendly modes of commuting than do people in more developed cities. Eurasian city dwellers overwhelmingly take trains, trams, or buses, and many, especially in smaller cities, walk or bike. Former Communist cities in other countries— like Katowice, Poznań, and Prague—have quickly become dependent on private vehicles (table 4.5). These cities offer a glimpse of what might happen in cities in the former Soviet Union if public transit networks are not properly maintained and supported.

EXHIBIT 4.4

Developments in Public Transport in Selected Eurasian Cities

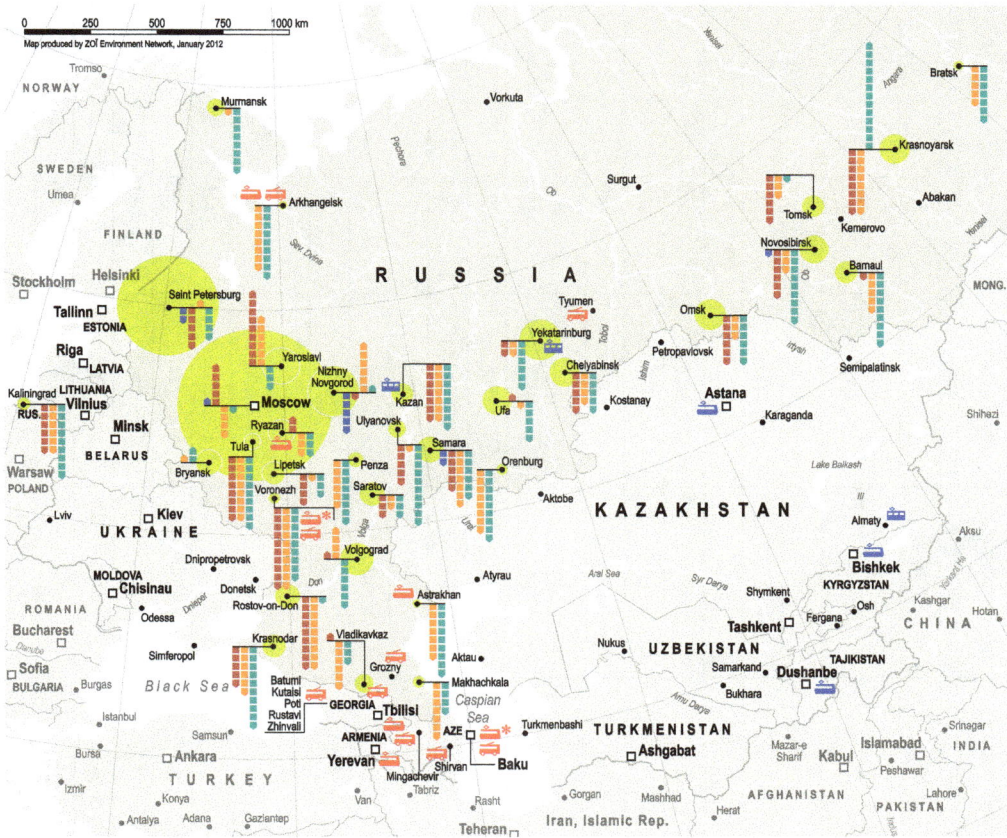

Map produced by ZOÏ Environment Network, January 2012

Public transportation

Developments in public transportation

- Metro: recently opened or planned (Kazan 2007, Almaty 2011)
- Tram: planned new service
- Tram: service terminated
- Tram: service terminated, to be revitalized *
- Trolleybus: service terminated

Passengers 2005, millions; Metro, Tram, Trolleybus, Citybus

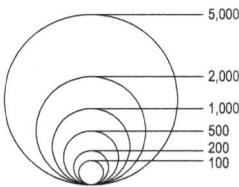

- 5,000
- 2,000
- 1,000
- 500
- 200
- 100

Change in public transportation usage between 1990 and 2005, in percent*

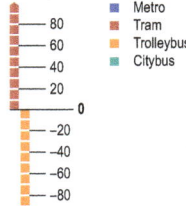

- 80
- 60
- 40
- 20
- 0
- −20
- −40
- −60
- −80

- Metro
- Tram
- Trolleybus
- Citybus

* Bratsk: change of citybus usage between 1999 and 2005; Ekaterinburg: change of metro usage between 1995 and 2005;
Krasnoyarsk: change of citybus usage between 1999 and 2005; Moscow: change of citybus usage between 2003 and 2005;
Saint Petersburg: change of citybus usage between 2003 and 2005

TABLE 4.5
Commuter Statistics in Selected Cities, 1998

City	Country	Population, thousands	Travel time per work-trip, minutes	Private motorized, percent	Train or tram, percent	Bus or minibus, percent	Bicycle, walking, or other, percent
Moscow	Russian Federation	8,537.8	62	15.00	63.70	21.00	0.30
Nizhny Novgorod	Russian Federation	1,326.9	35	17.00	37.30	41.70	4.00
Yerevan	Armenia	1,250.0	30	2.00	11.50	72.50	14.00
Omsk	Russian Federation	1,158.4	43	9.50	16.50	69.00	5.00
Bishkek	Kyrgyz Republic	762.3	35	5.00	35.36	59.61	0.03
Chisinau	Moldova	664.2	23	15.00	0	80.00	5.00
Astrakhan	Russian Federation	484.7	35	16.00	31.00	35.00	18.00
Astana	Kazakhstan	318.2	27	30.00	28.00	34.00	8.00
Kostroma	Russian Federation	288.5	20	5.00	19.50	48.00	27.50
Surgut	Russian Federation	277.8	57	1.50	0	81.00	17.50
Veliky Novgorod	Russian Federation	230.9	30	9.50	0	75.00	15.50
Novomoscovsk	Russian Federation	139.7	25	5.00	22.50	38.90	33.60
Pushkin	Russian Federation	92.2	15	6.00	0	60.20	33.80
Singapore	Singapore	3,163.5	30	25.10	14.50	38.70	21.70
Prague	Czech Republic	1,193.0	22	33.00	0	54.50	12.50
Birmingham	United Kingdom	1,013.0	20	73.90	1.40	9.10	15.60
Stockholm	Sweden	736.0	28	35.10	34.50	13.80	16.60
Poznań	Poland	579.3	25	33.00	30.00	21.00	16.00
Gdansk	Poland	459.0	20	43.00	32.90	23.42	0.68
Edinburgh	United Kingdom	450.0	20	69.90	2.40	13.00	14.70
Manchester	United Kingdom	430.0	19	71.80	1.90	8.10	18.00
Cardiff	United Kingdom	321.0	20	81.00	0.30	5.70	13.00
Katowice	Poland	308.7	36	46.15	9.35	19.90	24.60

Source: UN-Habitat Global Urban Indicators Database.

In another worrisome sign, the share of people in large Eurasian cities who walk and bike has fallen. Indeed, both walking and biking have fallen out of fashion. Car ownership is a status symbol, a way of showing off wealth. As household incomes grow, so will people's desire for private cars, and local authorities will have to counter with effective policies, incentives, and investments in environmentally friendly transport options. A lack of walking and biking translates into more urban pollution—even public transportation emits some toxins—and leads to adverse health conditions such as obesity, the incidence of which has increased throughout Eurasia (WHO online database).

New Mountains of Waste

Over 1991–2008, consumption rose in most Eurasian countries, as people's thirst to buy "stuff" grew faster than their actual incomes (figure 4.8). And as incomes increased, so did people's predisposition to buy throwaway goods, such as plastic cups, plates, and bags, as well as goods with throwaway packaging. What once was milk in returnable glass bottles is now milk in cartons. What once was meat from the butcher or family farm is now prepackaged and vacuum sealed. And what once were reusable seltzer bottles are now plastic bottles of juice and water. The Communist queues for the most basic consumer goods have been replaced by supermarkets.

Consumption is one way that people define themselves. In many countries, it has also become a form of recreation. Unfortunately, more consumption translates into more waste, and more waste has to be disposed of. The Soviet Union's landfills were not designed to handle the surge in waste after its dissolution in 1991.

There are no uniform data tracking how much waste individual cities generate. Methodologies, when they exist, vary widely across countries, and many landfills lack the technology to accurately measure the amount of waste hauled in. It is known, however, that more than 90 percent of waste is landfilled—usually improperly (table 4.6). Because dumping sites were not designed for such a surge in municipal waste, and owing also to a lack of institutional oversight, many disposal sites are overloaded, improperly operated and maintained, and in violation of environmental and human health regulations (OECD 2005). Most municipalities cannot afford to invest in sustainable solid waste management facilities, and they lack levers for pooling resources and cooperating across jurisdiction lines (for example, to establish regional landfills).

FIGURE 4.8

Household Consumption per Capita in the Former Soviet Union, by Country, 1991–2008

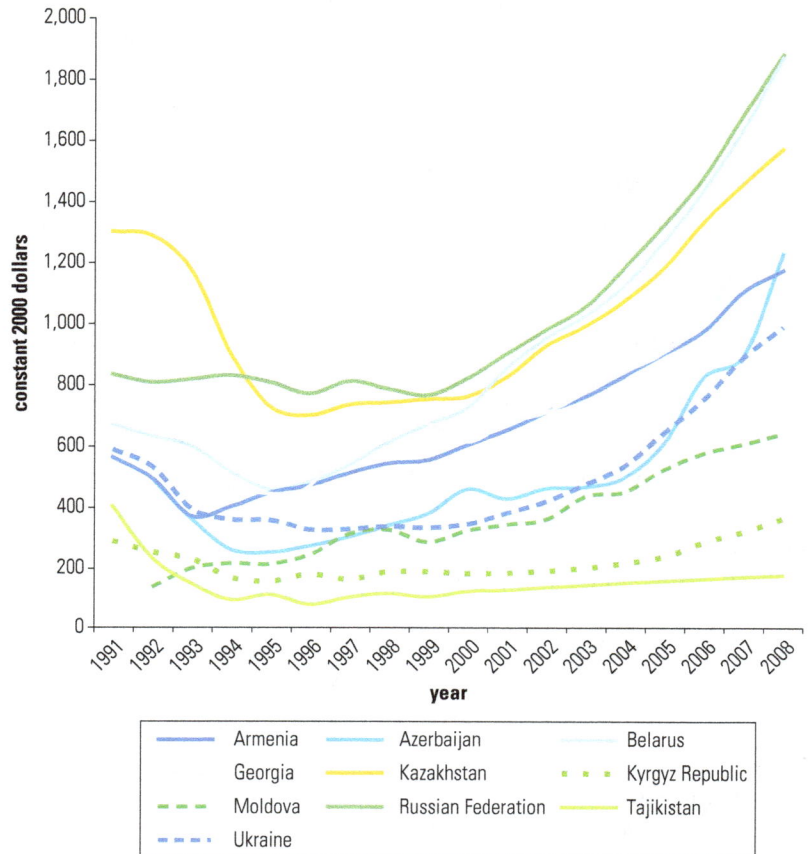

Source: World Bank 2011.
Note: No continuous data series are available for Turkmenistan and Uzbekistan.

Most waste generated in Eurasian cities is disposed of in their many open dumps, from which leachates often contaminate soil and groundwater and methane emissions spew freely into the air. Little waste is recycled. The recycling networks that were operational in most Eurasian cities disappeared as quickly as consumption rose—there were no funds to keep them going, no adequate pricing to make recycling economical, and no institutional oversight or proper management to ensure the functioning of the system. Some small recycling initiatives still operate, taking advantage of the old recycling infrastructure put in place during the Soviet years. In Tashkent, for example, a plant collects paper and recycles

TABLE 4.6

Waste Disposal Methods in Selected Cities, 1998

percent, except where otherwise indicated

City	Population, thousands	Sanitary landfill	Incinerated	Open dump	Recycled	Burned openly
Former Soviet Union						
Astrakhan, Russian Federation	484.7	0	0	86.4	13.6	0
Bishkek, Kyrgyz Republic	762.3	0	0	100.0	0	0
Minsk, Belarus	1,728.9	100.0	0	0	0	0
Moscow, Russian Federation	8,537.8	66.2	1.2	24.0	8.0	0.6
Nizhny Novgorod, Russian Federation	1,326.9	0	0	90.2	9.8	0
Omsk, Russian Federation	1,158.4	0	0	100.0	0	0
Pushkin, Russian Federation	92.2	0	0	90.0	10.0	0
Surgut, Russian Federation	277.8	0	0	100.0	0	0
Veliky Novgorod, Russian Federation	230.9	2.0	0	97.0	1.0	0
Yerevan, Armenia	1,250.0	0	0	35.0	0	65.0
Western Europe						
Amal, Sweden	13.0	71.0	0	0	29.0	0
Basel, Switzerland	169.0	27.0	58.0	0	15.0	0
Birmingham, United Kingdom	1,013.0	43.0	53.0	0	4.0	0
Cardiff, United Kingdom	321.0	95.0	0	0	5.0	0
London, United Kingdom	7,187.0	72.0	23.0	0	5.0	0
Manchester, United Kingdom	430.0	92.0	0	0	3.0	0
Pamplona, Spain	262.5	82.0	1.8	0	16.2	0
Singapore	3,163.5	33.7	66.3	0	0	0
Stockholm, Sweden	736.0	1.0	74.0	0	25.0	0
Umea, Sweden	103.5	1.0	78.0	0	21.0	0

Source: UN-Habitat Global Urban Indicators Database.

it in return for household goods, such as soap and shampoo. Two other city plants recycle glass and aluminum. These efforts are marginal, however.

Although urban dwellers in Eurasian cities as a whole generate less waste per capita than do their Western counterparts, Belarus, the Kyrgyz Republic, Ukraine, and Uzbekistan generate much more hazardous waste per capita than many Western countries (UNEP 2004). A legacy of industrial pollution in cities is present, with many polluted brownfield sites. Virtually every industrial city in Eurasia has some sort of soil pollution issue. For example, Shymkent and Ust-Kamenogorsk in Kazakhstan have registered soil concentrations of contaminants (lead, copper, cadmium, zinc, and other components of heavy and nonferrous metals) well in excess of legal levels. In the Kyrgyz Republic, more than 28.5 million cubic meters of industrial waste polluted the soil in and around production facilities (ADB 1998).

Most industrial facilities dispose of their own waste, often on site, with few considerations for their potential pollution. Local and national environmental authorities are weak. Disposal practices are poorly monitored, and environmental regulations are poorly enforced. A lack of civic engagement leads to households littering and dumping construction rubble in random places.

Crumbling Utilities Networks

Most Eurasian urban dwellers have access to water services and sanitation—to a greater extent than world averages. However, a lack of institutional oversight, heavily subsidized tariffs, and a lack of clear accountability to end-consumers have led to the deterioration of many utilities networks.

Pipes are leaking, service is poor, and increasingly poor quality water has led to a higher incidence of waterborne diseases. Many utilities networks are too large for their cities' level of development. They were not designed for effective cost-recovery, and many of their customers cannot afford the higher tariffs needed to support the networks. Urban shrinkage has forced some utilities networks to operate under capacity. Others are old and obsolete and have a hard time meeting demand.

Worldwide, about 70 percent of used freshwater goes to irrigation, 22 percent goes to industry, and only 8 percent goes to municipal use (UNESCO WWAP). On the whole, Eurasian countries use proportionally less municipal water than some developed countries. Central Asian countries use a large share of the water they draw for agriculture, especially irrigation. Heavily industrialized countries like Belarus, Russia, and Ukraine use huge quantities of water in industrial processes (figure 4.9).

What is striking in looking at municipal water use is that Eurasian countries' consumption appears to be comparable to that of developed countries (figure 4.10). This has to do with both the way water is priced and poor efficiency. Much of the water pumped in Eurasian cities gets lost along the way. A lack of funds for maintenance and improvements leaves many urban water systems running at suboptimal levels.

Poor utilities networks have led to a higher incidence of waterborne diseases. Many Eurasian cities have waste treatment plants,

FIGURE 4.9

Water Use in Selected Countries, by Sector and Year

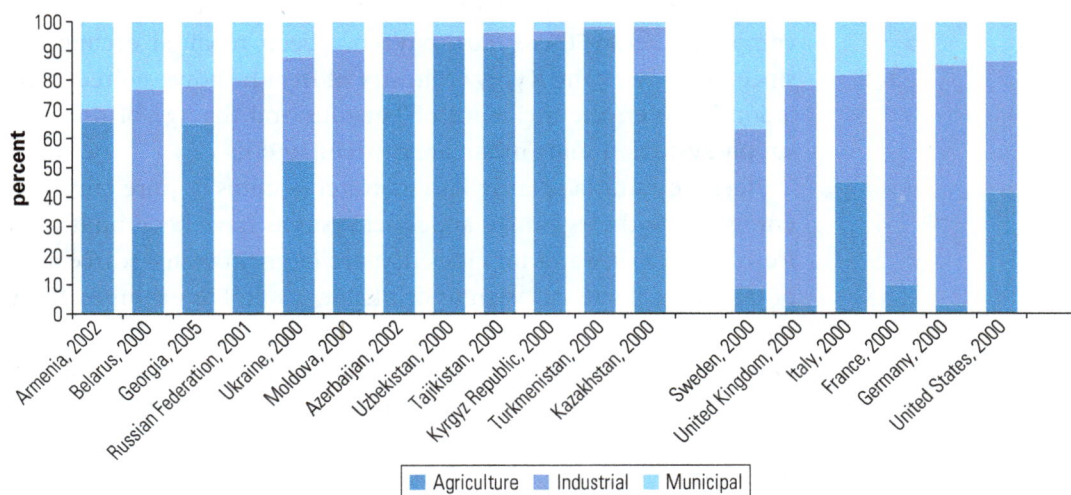

Source: FAO Aquastat.

FIGURE 4.10

Municipal Water Withdrawal in Selected Countries, 2002

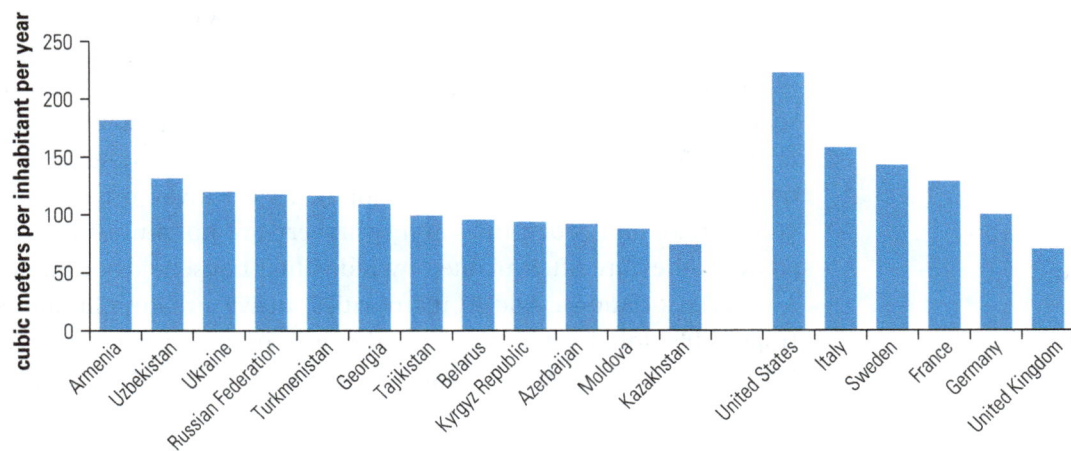

Source: FAO Aquastat.
Note: Data for Georgia are for 2007.

but many of these plants suffer from a lack of investment and are either obsolete or ineffective. Eurasian cities have made very few investments in constructing new wastewater plants or modernizing those already in place. In Tajikistan, Turkmenistan, and Uzbekistan, microbiological pollution of the water and wastewater systems pose serious health concerns. In more industrialized countries, like Belarus, Russia, and Ukraine, water pollution by industrial toxins and chemical substances is a more pressing problem (ADB 1998).

Throughout Eurasia, the discharge of untreated sewage and the suboptimal operation of sewage treatment installations contaminate drinking water. Most urban water and wastewater systems, many completed before the 1980s, have not been repaired or upgraded since. A study by the Kyrgyz Ministry of Health shows a direct correlation between the incidence of hepatitis and the age of the water supply system in some urban areas (ADB 1998).

Because Eurasia is fairly flat, its water systems require fairly little energy. Nonetheless, huge aqueduct systems have been built to tap fresh sources of water for cities that are large, in water-scarce areas, or on polluted streams with undrinkable water. For example, Nukus (Uzbekistan), a city of 260,000 that sits at the mouth of a river, draws its drinking water from 100 kilometers away. It cannot draw water from the Amu Darya River because the water is polluted from agricultural and industrial use upstream and is not fit even for irrigation.

Disappearing Urban Green Space

In many Eurasian cities, green areas have fallen victim to rapacious urban development. Since the Soviet Union dissolved, more urban green land has probably been lost than created.

No uniform database tracks city-level changes in urban green space. Such data are hard to collect, because city boundaries often change (for instance, to incorporate new jurisdictions and potentially new green areas); new developments eat away unprotected green areas; and added trees and shrubbery are not always easy to track, as they are often planted by individual households or homeowners associations. And in many cities, heavy urban pollution is responsible for a large share of the loss of urban green space. Norilsk's soil, for example, is so contaminated with chemicals that trees can spontaneously ignite. Trees well adapted to the harsh winter cold and permafrost conditions have not been able to withstand human pollution.

Green areas are crucial for the ecology of cities because they act as carbon sinks, mitigating local pollution. They are also important drivers of the quality of life, offering recreational opportunities and helping reduce the incidence of respiratory diseases, which is usually associated with air pollution in Eurasian countries and is about as high as in some developed countries (figure 4.11).[3]

As cities compete for human capital in the global economy, a good quality of life becomes even more important. A successful city is a city where people want to be.

FIGURE 4.11

Respiratory Diseases per 1,000 People in Selected Countries, 2004

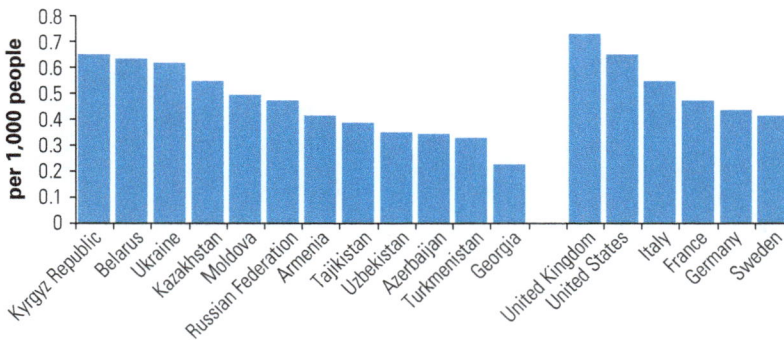

Source: WHO.

A Sustainable Future: Strong Institutions and Strong Markets

Greening cities will become more important as they become wealthier and citizens begin to demand a better environment after other needs are satisfied. Environmental quality will become more and more important for attracting knowledge-intensive businesses and highly qualified people. Eurasia will also feel the effects of global warming and have to play its part in adaptation and mitigation efforts (figure 4.12).

Eurasian cities need a healthy balance between strong institutions and strong markets. They should preserve their positive features, such as compact design and extensive public transportation networks, and combat the rise in private vehicle use and ownership. Regulations should be more strictly enforced, and new measures should be created for handling negative environmental externalities and enhancing the efficiency of environmental networks.

Eurasian cities should be open to learning from the best practices around the world while staying attuned to their own idiosyncrasies. What works in one place does not necessarily work in another. Sustainable development offers plenty of low-hanging fruit, but local authorities must be careful not to pick lemons. The range of options for tackling similar environmental challenges should be considered carefully for each country and each city.

First and foremost, Eurasian cities must have strong markets in place. Often, though not always, strong markets help solve a broad range of problems. When dealing with negative environmental externalities, public institutions think about how to mitigate them most efficiently. But far too often they ignore the indirect distortional

FIGURE 4.12

Indexes of Exposure to Climate Change and Adaptive Capacity to Climate Change in the Former Soviet Union, by Country

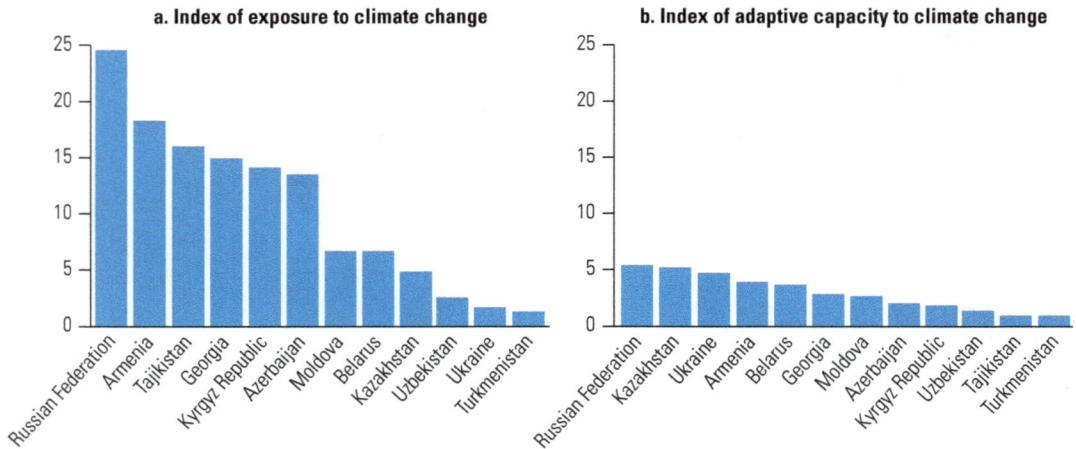

a. Index of exposure to climate change

b. Index of adaptive capacity to climate change

Source: Fay, Block, and Ebinger 2010.

effects these measures may have, such as a loss of business revenue, bankruptcy, loss of investment, and so on. Nobel Prize winner Ronald Coase cautions:

> The usual treatment of [externality] problems … proceeds in terms of a comparison between a state of laissez faire and some kind of ideal world. … A better approach would seem to be to start our analysis with a situation about that which actually exists, to examine the effects of proposed policy change and to attempt to decide whether the new situation would be, in total, better or worse than the original one. In this way, conclusions for policy would have some relevance to the actual situation. (Coase 1960, p. 43)

Coase argues that when property rights are well defined and protected (for example, when people can easily seek justice if someone infringes on their property rights, say, by polluting their land); when transaction costs are low (such as when not too many parties are involved in a dispute); and when information is symmetrical (as when all involved parties know what the costs of an externality are), the market can usually find better solutions than the public sector.

Strong markets can help green Eurasian cities by properly pricing delivered goods and services to include adaptation and mitigation costs, by encouraging voluntary actions, and by taking advantage of bargaining mechanisms (for example, a polluting industrial plant could compensate the people affected by the pollution rather than be subjected to a more costly pollution tax or regulation).

Mixed market-government solutions to negative environmental externalities stem from the tradition of Alfred Pigou (Pigou 1920). This type of solution involves the pricing of externalities by the public sector and is usually sought when transaction costs are high (for example, when too many parties are involved, which would make bargaining to reach a mutually agreeable solution difficult) and information is symmetrical. They can include taxing and pricing (carbon taxes and congestion charges), tradable points systems (cap and trade), incentives (subsidies to the private sector), and public-private partnership investments (brownfield redevelopment with public and private participation).

Pure government solutions are usually sought when transaction costs are high, when information is asymmetrical (for example, many people might not be aware of the effect air pollution has on them), and when market imperfections discourage the private sector or households from taking action on their own. The public sector has an arsenal of measures at its disposal, including information (publicly revealing the worst polluters in a city), disclosure (requiring private firms to disclose what goes into their products), standards (capping how much carbon dioxide a factory can emit), public investments (developing public parks), and regulation (requiring that all cars have catalytic converters).

The optimal solution—the solution most efficient in mitigating the negative externality and that creates the weakest distortional effects—will depend on local circumstances (city size, level of decentralization, market strength, and so on). As a rule, pure market solutions are the least distortional (because they are self-serving). Pure government solutions by contrast, are the most distortional (because they affect a wide range of actors; box 4.1).

The following sections identify ways to tackle some of the challenges highlighted in this chapter. Local authorities in Eurasian cities should be mindful that not all of these solutions will have universal application—some may work in one place and fail in another. These solutions can help Eurasian cities identify goals they would like to achieve, each of which can be met with the measures that best fit the local context.

Improving the Environmental Performance of Energy Use

Eurasian cities have two main avenues to improve the environmental performance of the energy sector: increasing energy efficiency from current sources and becoming more energy independent through alternative sources (for example, solar panels on buildings).

BOX 4.1

What Is the Best Way to Reduce Emissions from a Taxi Fleet?

A local authority looking to reduce emissions from a city's taxi fleet could do one or several of the following:

- Directly discuss with taxi companies the possibility of having their fleets equipped with catalytic converters and encourage them to buy and install them.

- Introduce a tax on taxis not equipped with catalytic converters.

- Create a tradable points system that allows polluting taxis to drive a certain number of kilometers, after which they can buy "polluting rights" from taxis that drive less or are equipped with catalytic converters.

- Offer subsidies to taxi drivers to equip their cars with pollution-reducing devices.

- Establish, with private participation, designated and reserved parking spaces for environmentally friendly taxicabs in key spots, such as airports, railway stations, and major hotels.

- Publicize the names of the taxi companies with the worst-polluting fleets, so that environmentally conscious people can avoid riding with them.

- Cap how many kilometers polluting taxis can drive or how polluting a car can be.

- Enact a local regulation that requires all taxis to run with catalytic converters.

Energy efficiency—which can be dealt with on both the demand side and the supply side—should be the highest priority because of its double dividend: cost and carbon savings. Developing alternative energy sources requires large initial investments, but doing so can yield important cost savings down the road, often very quickly.

Increasing Energy Efficiency

Markets and institutions should complement each other in making cities better energy performers. Table 4.7 summarizes some possible solutions.

Local efforts can be particularly effective in three areas: buildings, appliances, and street lighting. Buildings are among the most important energy users in cities. Indeed, 30–40 percent of carbon dioxide emissions worldwide come from heating, cooling, and lighting buildings. Street lighting has been identified as a target for one of

TABLE 4.7

Market, Mixed, and Government Solutions to Increasing Energy Efficiency

Energy user	Market	Mixed	Government
Buildings	• Price electricity at market prices. • Raise the price of energy during peak daytime hours and reduce it at night. • Pass on cost savings to individual households and private enterprises by making more buildings more energy-efficient. • Draw in a larger clientele that is environmentally conscious by advertising the energy performance of buildings.	• Apply progressive block tariffs (lower tariffs for consumers who consume below a certain threshold). • Reduce local taxes on energy-efficient buildings. • Provide incentives for the thermal insulation of buildings.	• Make public buildings more energy-efficient (for example, through thermal insulation, thermopane windows, and modernized central heating systems). • Use zoning to encourage dense development. • Inform the public about private companies and household associations that are efficient energy users. • Use public systems to monitor energy use in public buildings (for example, by using ambient orbs that turn red when energy use is high and green when energy use is low). • Establish greenhouse gas and pollution inventories of the worst-performing buildings. • Use energy-efficiency certification systems (for example, the LEED system in the United States) to encourage private companies to be better environmental stewards. • Use building construction standards that favor energy efficiency. • Convert district heating plants to heat-and-power plants and use cleaner heating fuels.
Appliances	• Price electricity at market prices. • Provide marketing incentives (selling appliances that will save people money). • Take advantage of better and more environmentally friendly technologies. • Solicit voluntary commitments to environmental stewardship (for example, General Electric has committed to producing more energy-efficient appliances). • Offer cash and price incentives to clients that turn in old appliances and buy new, more energy-efficient ones (an appliance chain in Romania has implemented this measure with great success).	• Offer incentives for switching to energy-efficient appliances (such as cash-for-clunker programs). • Offer local tax breaks for companies that invest in energy-saving equipment (for example, combined heat and power units, more efficient lighting and refrigeration).	• Switch to energy-efficient appliances in public buildings (for example, lights and cooling units that shut off when no one is in the room). • Inform and educate citizens on their energy use. • Use energy-efficiency certification systems (such as EnergyStar in the United States).
Street lighting			• Invest in energy-efficient LED light bulbs.

Note: LED = light-emitting diode; LEED = Leadership in Energy and Environmental Design.

the quickest wins for local governments, producing a return on investment almost immediately (WB-IEG 2010).

To reduce the negative externalities associated with overconsumption, local authorities could track the consumption patterns of all public users and encourage them to reduce their energy use. Ambient orbs (a ball that glows red when energy use is high and green when energy use is modest) could be placed outside all public buildings, so that the public could track use patterns. Such a system would increase incentives for public institutions to present themselves to their citizens as users of sustainable practices. And equipping all public offices with a card system that allows employees to turn light and air conditioning on and off and that provides them access their offices could strengthen this measure.

The private sector can encourage energy savings, as documented by Howarth, Haddad, and Paton (2000). Green Lights, an information program started by the Environmental Protection Agency (EPA), follows a voluntary memorandum of understanding with private enterprises and nonprofit organizations (for example, hospitals, universities, and state and local governments) throughout the United States. The program sought to reduce pollution from industrial and commercial lighting, which accounts for 13 percent of U.S. electricity demand. Participating organizations agreed to survey their energy consumption and systematically adopt energy-saving lighting improvements. In exchange, the EPA offered information, software, and technical assistance. The program's six-year run was recognized as a great success, saving participants more than $440 million and reducing harmful emissions (carbon dioxide and nitrogen oxides) and pollution from energy production.

Developing Alternative Energy Sources

Cities rarely generate their own electricity, but many realize substantial benefits from having some degree of energy independence. After the Soviet Union dissolved, several Eurasian countries found themselves part of electricity grids they could not control—and thus without any capacity to generate energy (figure 4.13).

Energy independence has become an imperative. Russia's and Ukraine's recent energy crises prompted them to think strongly about how they could generate more of their own energy.

As Eurasian countries move toward greater energy independence, they should think about how they can tap renewable resources (sun, water, wind, geothermal) rather than create a power grid that depends on fossil fuels. Relying less on fossil fuels can also protect countries against price fluctuations and global shortages (figure 4.14).

FIGURE 4.13

Net Energy Imports in the Former Soviet Union, by Country, 2007

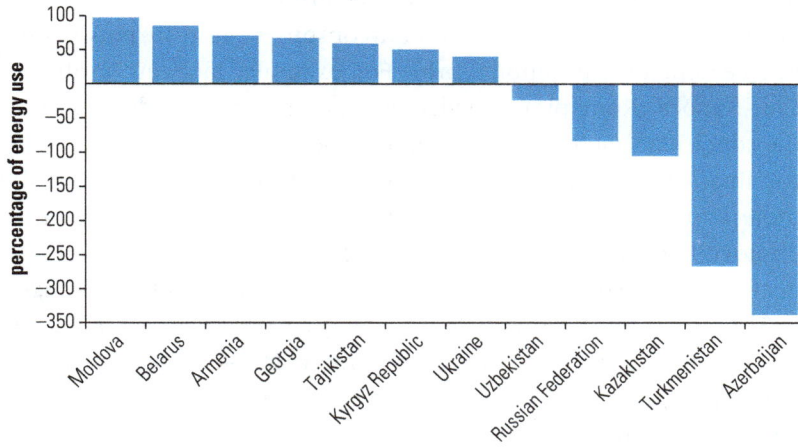

Source: Authors.

FIGURE 4.14

Real Prices of Coal, Gas, and Oil on World Market, 1991–2008

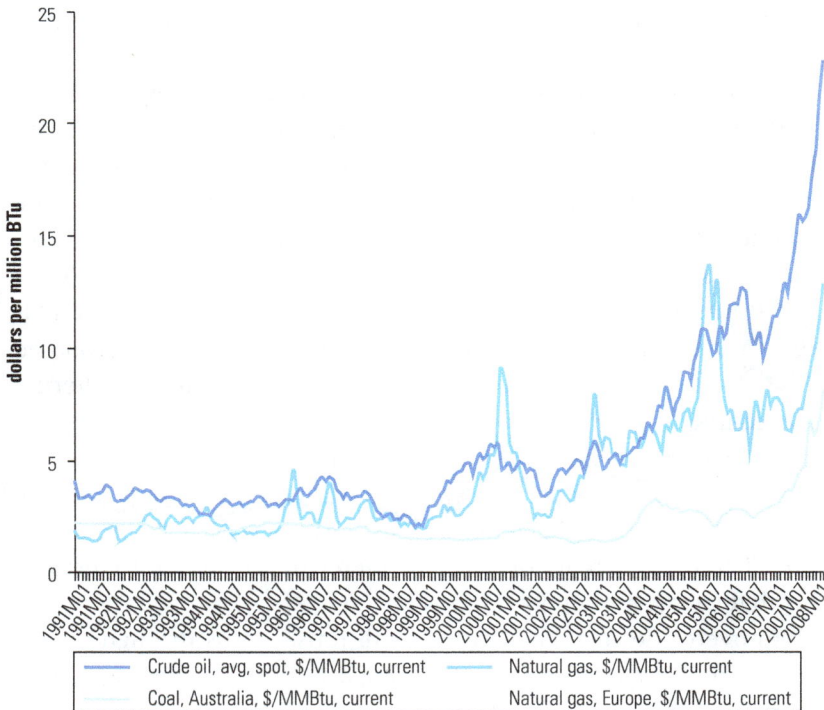

Source: World Bank Global Economic Monitor 2009.
Note: BTu = British thermal unit; MMBTu = million British thermal unit; Mo = month.

Cities can play a crucial role in the quest for energy independence, as they do not require a national electricity grid and can eliminate burdensome distribution and intermediary costs. Local energy producers can sell directly to local end-consumers, and surplus energy can be sent to the national grid. For example, local authorities in Cluj-Napoca (Romania) provided city land to a private developer on the condition that it build a certain number of affordable units. When the financial crisis hit, the developer could no longer complete the project and make a profit. So it decided instead to turn the site into a photovoltaic farm. In exchange for use of the city's land, the developer offered to cover 30 percent of energy needs in public buildings.

The use of building roofs to capture solar power is a popular and efficient way of using photovoltaic energy. In Germany and Japan, buildings equipped with photovoltaic roofing material have two-way meters. The building owners sell energy to the grid when they produce more than they need and buy from the grid when solar cells are not enough.

The new energy economy is already shifting from centralized systems to decentralized small-scale power sources. Photovoltaic plants and wind farms require less downtime than coal plants, and they are much more flexible. When an individual wind or solar device is not working properly, only a small fraction of the energy produced is affected. When a coal plant goes offline, it severely affects energy generation.

A big challenge for alternative energy sources, however, is intermittency. The sun does not always shine, and wind does not always blow in a given location. But mixing in more reliable and steady sources of alternative energy, such as hydro and geothermal, is one way to solve the problem. Geothermal energy is everywhere, representing the world's annual energy use 280,000 times over (Gore 2009). It can be tapped by individual buildings and groups of buildings for heating and cooling. Researchers in California have proposed a scheme for generating all of California's energy needs from alternative sources (figure 4.15).

Cities that depend on private energy providers for electricity can work together to demand cleaner, more efficient energy. Service delivery can be cumbersome and expensive, especially in smaller jurisdictions, which are often at the mercy of private service providers that charge monopoly prices.

To overcome such challenges, small jurisdictions throughout the southern United States formed compacts—legally binding agreements without a lot of bite—that allow them to achieve economies of scale and drive down service delivery prices. Electricity co-ops, for

FIGURE 4.15

Proposed Clean Energy Mix for California

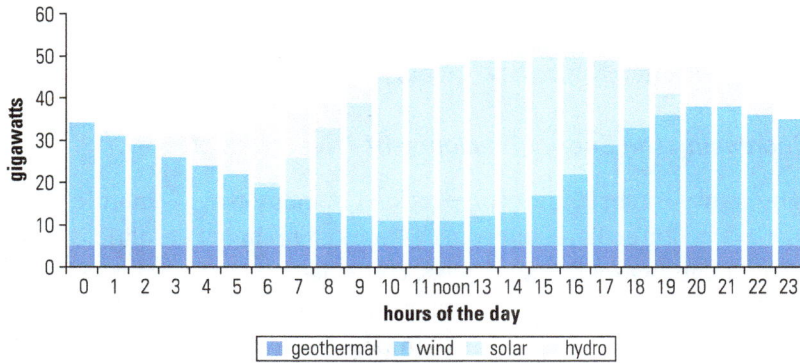

Source: Jacobson and Delucchi 2009.

example—which afford groups of jurisdictions more leverage in their bargaining with regional electricity monopolies—take their business elsewhere if their demands are not met.

Cities could also retrofit their thermal power plants and district heating systems into combined heat and power plants. Russia is a leader in the use of combined heat and power. Many Russian cities have district heat systems that receive water from power plants, and more than 30 percent of the country's power is generated by combined heat and power systems (Gore 2009).

Eurasian cities cannot shift to alternative energy sources overnight. The costs can be prohibitive, so many planners will wait until cheaper, more advanced technologies arrive. Also, many Eurasian countries—Russia and Azerbaijan, for example—have access to vast fossil fuel reserves and so are unlikely to invest in alternative energy for the time being. Similarly, Kazakhstan taps its coal and oil reserves to generate energy and has done little to exploit its great potential for wind and geothermal energy (ADB 1998).

Cities can find creative ways to finance sustainable development projects. For example, they could allow builders to add floors to highrises, using the money generated from the extra units to finance building retrofits (thermal insulation, solar panels, more efficient boilers, and so on).

More Walking, Biking, and Public Transportation

Greening the transport sector is one of the main challenges facing Eurasian cities. Action is critical—particularly as pollution from transport is likely to get worse before it gets better in most countries.

Eurasian cities still have fewer cars than Western cities, and millions of people in Eurasia want the independence a private vehicle offers. To reduce emissions and pollution from transport, local authorities must simultaneously promote a more efficient vehicle fleet and encourage environmentally friendly modes of transport.

Increasing the Energy Efficiency of Private Vehicles

The transport challenge can be tackled in many ways—and the benefits can be immediate. Introducing market pricing of gasoline is a first step. Taxing gasoline, how most countries price the environmental and social costs of transport pollution, is the next. Eurasian cities will not have the executive levers to impose such measures, but they can pressure policy makers to do so, as most of the negative externalities of transport are felt in urban areas.

All Eurasian countries are rather good performers on the transport front (figure 4.16). Except for Turkmenistan, which has very high subsidies for oil, all Eurasian countries charge more per liter of gasoline than the United States. Uzbekistan and Belarus charge more for gasoline than Spain, which has the lowest gasoline prices in Europe.

Besides taxing gasoline, many countries have used cash-for-clunkers programs—another mixed market-government solution—to renew their vehicle fleets. People who trade in their old cars when buying a new, environmentally friendly car (for example, a hybrid, electric car, or one equipped with a catalytic converter) receive a premium (€2,500 in Germany). Cash-for-clunkers programs aim to put more fuel-efficient cars on the road and to swap energy-inefficient cars (in which 80 percent of the energy generated by burning gasoline is wasted as heat) for energy-efficient ones

FIGURE 4.16

Retail Prices for Gasoline in Selected Countries, 2008

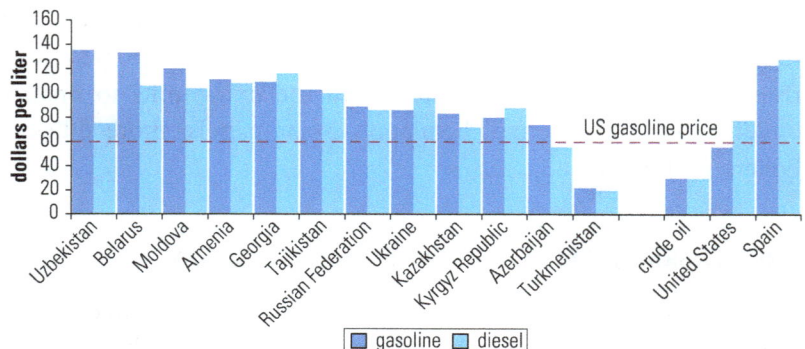

Source: GTZ 2009.

(just 15 percent of energy is wasted as heat in an electric car; Jacobson and Delucchi 2009).

Local governments have tools to reduce emissions from private vehicles, such as congestion charges—a mixed market-government solution—and restrictions on parking in city centers—a pure government solution. Congestion charges were successfully introduced in London and have been adopted by cities the world over. Before the congestion charge, a car's average speed in London's city center was no faster than that of a horse-drawn carriage a century earlier (Brown 2001). But after the congestion charge was introduced, the number of vehicles coming into the city center dropped 34 percent, the number of buses fell 21 percent, and the number of bicycles fell 28 percent. With the proceeds from the congestion charge, local governments can finance improvements to the public transportation system.

Using Alternative Modes of Transport

Local authorities can also encourage people to use their cars less. Eurasian cities have an advantage in this respect, as they are more compact and have strong public transportation infrastructure. However, their infrastructure is slowly falling apart. As public transport suffers from a lack of investment, cities invest more and more in building new roads to fight congestion. More roads are costly, and building them often leads to even more cars in the city, further increasing urban congestion and pollution.

Instead of allocating money for new roads, Eurasian cities should think about how these funds could be used to encourage people to use alternative modes of transportation more often—in particular, walking, biking, and public transit. In some European cities, transport investments are almost exclusively sustainable development projects. Copenhagen, for example, plans to increase its share of commuters who bike to work to 50 percent. To that end, it has invested earnestly in its bicycle network and introduced a system (the "green wave") that times green lights at intersections so that bicyclists can have more seamless rides.

Walking and biking paths should be connected to public transportation routes, and local authorities should make it easier for bicyclists and pedestrians to connect to public transit hubs (for example, by having secure parking lots for bicycles). If walking or biking is unfeasible, as in exurbs areas, public transit stations should have adequate parking for people who commute to work—to reduce driving times and decongest the city center.

Proper care and investment can encourage a virtuous cycle in public transportation. A good transportation system encourages dense urban development, especially around the transit hubs. Dense urban development means more customers for the transit network, more customers equal higher revenues, higher revenues can be used to continually improve the system and keep it performing at a high level, and a well-performing public transit system attracts even more people around transit hubs. The cycle then starts over. Both the public and private sector can support this virtuous cycle. See chapter 2 for ways that local authorities can encourage dense development patterns.

In addition, local banks can reward buyers or renovators of buildings close to transportation hubs with "location-efficient" mortgages (for example, by providing loan guarantees that allow them access to larger loans). Investments in the maintenance and extension of the existing system should be accompanied by investments in new transit infrastructure, where warranted. Bus Rapid Transit systems, with dedicated lanes separated from the rest of the traffic, have proven effective in cities across the world. They make bus traffic faster, more fluid, and more efficient. Mexico City's new Bus Rapid Transit system has had an 81 percent economic return and has helped reduce greenhouse gas emissions by 10 kilograms for every $1 spent (WB-IEG 2010).

Reduce-Reuse-Recycle

To reduce negative environmental externalities from solid waste management, local authorities should encourage reduce-reuse-recycle programs, limit the amount of waste, and improve disposal systems.

Reducing the Amount of Disposed Waste

Recycling requires upfront investments and an efficient infrastructure (collection points, distribution systems, and processing plants). Eurasia had this infrastructure, but it quickly fell apart during the transition. Even if cities had the resources to establish collection points for recyclables, they would need regional processing centers to turn recyclables into valuable material. Cities could spearhead a national recycling pledge to get the system running.

Until such systems are revived or put in place, however, Eurasian cities can reduce their amount of waste. Education and information programs are efficient if they are part of school curricula or have media support. Information campaigns can be run fairly cheaply if they piggyback on existing programs. The virtues of recycling can be stressed in environmental classes or embedded in newspaper articles or television shows, too (Jensen and Oster 2009).

The disclosure of information can also be used to curtail pollution by private enterprises. The U.S. Environmental Protection Agency set up its Toxic Release Inventory—a public database that gathers information on the environment (concerning, for example, chemical releases and waste management activities) from industries and federal facilities and reports it annually. This name-and-shame technique is highly effective, as negative media coverage and public pressure ease enforcement (Fung and O'Rourke 2000).

Indonesia has a similar initiative. Environmental authorities developed an effective disclosure program to improve the environmental performance of large enterprises. Companies were color-coded based on a series of national and world standards, and the color codes were displayed outside the firm for everyone to see. The resulting peer pressure and social stigma helped improve sustainability practices among Indonesian companies (Zinnes 2009).

Improving Waste Disposal

A good first step in improving waste disposal is to establish close cooperation between neighboring municipalities—to create regional solid waste management systems (with, for example, conforming landfills close to large urban centers and transfer stations around smaller cities and towns). Such an arrangement can ensure economies of scale, allowing private operators to earn a profit while keeping service charges low.

A second important step is to close old landfills (especially dumpsites in wild areas) and build larger, better ones—landfills equipped with capture devices that keep methane from seeping into the soil. Sanitary landfills need to be carefully engineered and constructed. Environmental safeguards should minimize seepage of contaminants into the ground and methane emissions into the air.[4] Wealthier cities can also consider establishing waste-to-energy incinerator facilities.

Efficient and Safe Utilities

To improve the environmental performance of their utilities networks, Eurasian cities should encourage end-consumers to use less water while improving water delivery and wastewater treatment technologies. Such measures should target both consumers and service providers.

Many of the solutions aimed at reducing water use can be derived from the recommendations above. For example, local authorities can offer incentives to encourage households to buy showerheads, toilets, and water faucets that use less water. Most public toilets in Europe have two flush buttons—one that releases less water (to flush urine) and one that releases more water (for feces). Requiring such toilets in Eurasian countries could save substantial amounts of water. But Eurasian countries can save even more by fixing broken toilets. A broken toilet that allows water to run continuously can waste up to a liter of water per minute. This translates into nearly 1,500 liters a day, or a staggering 500,000 liters per year—the equivalent of 25 swimming pools or a small lake.

Local authorities can also provide incentives for "blackwater" and "graywater" systems. Blackwater systems capture and treat sanitary wastewater from buildings and recycle it for nonpotable use. Graywater systems capture used water from washing machines, showers, and dishwashers and recycle it as toilet water or water for other nonpotable uses. Buildings that have such systems in place could reduce their water and sewerage bills.

Changes at the source would involve better upkeep of distribution systems (for example, fixing leaking piping), improving wastewater treatment plants, and adjusting systems to the changing urban layout (for example, by installing larger pipes in high-density neighborhoods and smaller pipes in low-density neighborhoods). Water should be sourced locally when possible but not by exhausting groundwater reserves. Freshwater sources should be protected by limiting pollution. Wastewater plants should be properly maintained and upgraded, and new ones should be created where they are missing.

In Copenhagen, the wastewater treatment system is so good that discharged water is safe enough to swim in. In fact, the city's inner harbor is opened up for public swimming in the summer. Of course, such measures come at a price: Copenhagen has the highest water and wastewater tariffs in the world—three times the amount charged in Moscow and nine times that in Kiev (Global Water Intelligence 2009).

To avoid a "tragedy of the commons" situations—in which everyone pollutes a shared resource because others are doing so—and to better manage resources, municipalities situated on the same water body should cooperate for better resource exploitation.

Greener Cities

In *Eco-Economy,* Lester Brown points out that the ratio of parks to parking lots may be the best indicator of a city's livability. He argues that urban greenery has a positive effect on the psyche of a city's citizens. Brown (2001) shows that hospital patients who stayed in rooms with a "green" view recovered much more rapidly than patients whose rooms overlooked a parking lot. Protecting the stock of urban green and extending and enhancing it are some of the best investments Eurasian cities can make. An impressive body of research shows that urban greenery is an asset to a city's economic, social, and environmental health. Green spaces conserve energy and reduce summer air temperatures, storm water runoff, greenhouse gas emissions, and air pollution. They are one of the most effective carbon sinks. They also add tremendously to citizens' quality of life.

People in Eurasian cities are generally fond of green spaces, and investments in urban greenery are usually not capital-intensive; they can often be done with the participation of civil society and nongovernmental organizations through, for example, tree-planting days. Local authorities should thus consider increasing the amount of green space wherever possible. One way would be to create a zoning regulation that requires all new parking lots to have a certain number of trees—to absorb storm water runoff (parking lots tend to be large impervious urban spaces) and to beautify these urban deserts.

Green cities are more livable, and they are a primary way that voters assess the industriousness and quality of their local governments. Recognizing this, Copenhagen plans to make parks or beaches accessible to all residents within a 15-minute walk. In Stockholm, 90 percent of people live less than 300 meters from a park, natural reserve, or body of water. With a little ingenuity, all Eurasian cities can ensure that their citizens have access to adequate green space.

Annex 4A

TABLE 4A.1
The 25 Coldest Cities in the Russian Federation and North America with about 500,000 People, 2001

Rank by temperature	City	Country	Mean January temperature, degree Celsius	2001 population, thousands
1	Khabarovsk	Russian Federation	−22.0	604
2	Irkutsk	Russian Federation	−21.0	587
3	Novosibirsk[a]	Russian Federation	−19.0	1,393
4	Omsk[a]	Russian Federation	−19.0	1,138
5	Tomsk	Russian Federation	−19.0	483
6	Winnipeg	Canada	−18.6	686

continued

TABLE 4A.1

Continued

Rank by temperature	City	Country	Mean January temperature, degree Celsius	2001 population, thousands
7	Barnaul	Russian Federation	−18.0	573
8	Novokuznetsk	Russian Federation	−18.0	565
9	Kemerovo	Russian Federation	−18.0	487
10	Krasnoyarsk	Russian Federation	−17.0	876
11	Yekaterinburg[a]	Russian Federation	−16.0	1,257
12	Tyumen	Russian Federation	−16.0	500
13	Edmonton	Canada	−15.3	967
14	Chelyabinsk[a]	Russian Federation	−15.0	1,081
15	Perm[a]	Russian Federation	−15.0	1,005
16	Orenburg	Russian Federation	−15.0	517
17	Samara[a]	Russian Federation	−14.0	1,146
18	Ufa[a]	Russian Federation	−14.0	1,089
19	Tolyati	Russian Federation	−14.0	724
20	Ulyanovsk	Russian Federation	−14.0	662
21	Izhevsk	Russian Federation	−14.0	650
22	Vladivostok	Russian Federation	−14.0	599
23	Naberezhnyye Chelny	Russian Federation	−14.0	518
24	Kazan[a]	Russian Federation	−13.0	1,090
25	Nizhniy Novgorod[a]	Russian Federation	−12.0	1,343

Source: Hill and Gaddy 2003.

a. Among the world's coldest 10 cities with more than 1 million people.

Notes

1. In December 1952, smog from industrial pollution and soot from more than 1 million coal-heated households rolled over London and immersed the city in a toxic blanket for five days straight. Some 12,000 people died, and the city's citizens were outraged. In 1956, the British Parliament introduced the Clean Air Act, outlawing the burning of coal in open-hearth fires and establishing incentives for switching from coal in energy production.

2. In the 1980s, the Soviet Union produced an average of about 195 kilograms of waste per capita, much less than the 655 kilograms per capita generated over the same period in the United States (Peterson 1993).

3. The Russian Statistical Office finds that respiratory diseases are among the most common diseases in Russia. See Rosstat, *Statistical Yearbooks of the Russian Federation: 1991–2009.*

4. Even the most sophisticated multibarrier landfill systems cannot be guaranteed to prevent contamination fully. For example, the Georgswerder sanitary landfill in Hamburg, Germany, closed in 1979, and soil

contamination was discovered as early as 1983. Removing the discovered leachate from the soil required hundreds of millions of dollars (Bilitewski, Härdtle, and Marek 1997).

References

ADB (African Development Bank). 1998. *Central Asian Environments in Transition.* Tunis: ADB.

Belarus National Statistics Committee. 2009. *Statistical Yearbook.* Minsk: Belarus National Statistics Committee.

Bilitewski, Bernd, Georg Härdtle, and Klaus Marek. 1997. *Waste Management.* New York: Springer.

Brown, Lester R. 2001. *Eco-Economy: Building an Economy for the Earth.* New York: W.W. Norton & Company.

Coase, Ronald. 1960. "The Problem of Social Cost." *Journal of Law and Economics* 3: 1–44.

Colton, Timothy J. 1995. *Moscow: Governing the Socialist Metropolis.* Cambridge, MA: The Belknap Press of Harvard University Press.

Fay, Marianne, Rachel I. Block, and Jane Ebinger. 2010. *Adapting to Climate Change in Eastern Europe and Central Asia.* Washington, DC: World Bank.

Feshbach, Murray, and Alfred Friendly Jr. 1992. *Ecocide in the USSR: Health and Nature under Siege.* New York: Basic Books.

Fung, Archon, and Dara O'Rourke. 2000. "Reinventing Environmental Regulation from the Grassroots Up: Explaining and Expanding the Success of the Toxic Release Inventory." *Environmental Management* 25 (2): 115–27.

Gore, Albert. 2009. *Our Choice: A Plan to Solve the Climate Crisis.* Emmaus, PA: Rodale Press.

GTZ (German Society for International Cooperation). 2009. *International Fuel Prices 2009.* 6th ed. Bonn, Germany: GTZ.

Hill, Fiona, and Clifford G. Gaddy. 2003. *The Siberian Curse: How Communist Planners Left Russia Out in the Cold.* Washington, DC: Brookings Institution Press.

Howarth, Rob W., Brent M. Haddad, and Bruce Paton. 2000. "The Economics of Energy Efficiency: Insights from Voluntary Participation Programs." *Energy Policy* 28 (6–7): 477–486.

IEA (International Energy Agency). 2010a. "World Energy Balances (IEA World Energy Statistics and Balances database)." Paris. doi: 10.1787/data-00512-en.

———. 2010b. *The Scope of Fossil-Fuel Subsidies in 2009 and a Roadmap for Phasing Out Fossil-Fuel Subsidies.* Paris: IEA.

Jacobson, Mark Z., and Mark A. Delucchi. 2009. "A Path to Sustainable Energy by 2030." *Scientific American*, November.

Jensen, Robert, and Emily Oster. 2009. "The Power of TV: Cable Television and Women's Status in India." *Quarterly Journal of Economics* 124 (3): 1057.

Mootz, Lisa. 2010. *Nations in Transit: Democratization from Central Europe to Eurasia.* Washington, DC: Freedom House.

OECD (Organisation for Economic Co-operation and Development). 2005. *Environmental Management in Eastern Europe, Caucasus and Central Asia.* Paris: OECD.

Peterson, D.J. 1993. *Troubled Lands: The Legacy of Soviet Environmental Destruction.* Boulder, CO: Westview.

Pigou, Alfred C. 1920. *The Economics of Welfare.* New York: Macmillan.

Pollard, Alan P. 1990. *USSR: Facts and Figures Annual.* Gulf Breeze, FL: Academic International Press.

Ukraine State Statistics Committee. 2001. *Statistical Yearbook 2000.* Kiev: Ukraine State Statistics Committee.

———. 2009. *Ukraine in Figures 2008.* Kiev: Ukraine State Statistics Committee.

UN (United Nations). 1980. *World Energy Supplies: 1950–1974.* New York: UN.

UNEP (United Nations Environment Programme). 2004. *Vital Waste Graphics.* Nairobi: UNEP.

WB-IEG (World Bank Independent Evaluation Group). 2010. *Climate Change and the World Bank Group. Phase II: The Challenge of Low-Carbon Development.* Washington, DC: WB-IEG.

World Bank. 2010. "The Management of Brownfields Redevelopment: A Guidance Note." World Bank, Washington, DC.

———. 2011. *World Development Indicators.* World Bank: Washington, DC.

Zinnes, Clifford F. 2009. *Tournament Approaches to Policy Reform: Making Development Assistance More Effective.* Washington, DC: Brookings Institution Press.

Zoi Environment Network. 2009. *Climate Change in Central Asia: A Visual Synthesis.* Geneva: Zoi Environment Network.

Statistical Websites

Armenia—National Statistical Service of the Republic of Armenia: http://www.armstat.am/.

Azerbaijan—State Statistical Committee of the Azerbaijan Republic: http://www.azstat.org/indexen.php.

Belarus—National Statistical Committee of the Republic of Belarus: http://www.belstat.gov.by/homep/en/main.html.

Georgia—State Department for Statistics for Georgia: http://www.statistics.ge/index_eng.htm.

Kazakhstan—Agency for Statistics of the Republic of Kazakhstan: http://www.stat.kz/.

Kyrgyz Republic—National Statistical Committee of the Kyrgyz Republic: http://stat-gvc.bishkek.su/English/.

Moldova—Department of Statistical and Sociological Analysis: http://www
.statistica.md/index.php?lang=en.

Russia—Goskomstat (State Committee for Statistics): http://www.gks.ru/
eng. Federal State Statistics Service (Rosstat): http://www.rosstat.ru.

Turkmenistan—Turkmenistan Statistics: http://www.turkmenistan.gov.tm/
ekonom/ek&stat_eng.htm.

Ukraine—State Committee of Statistics of Ukraine: http://www.ukrstat.gov
.ua/.

Uzbekistan—State Committee of the Republic of Uzbekistan on Statistics:
http://www.stat.uz.

Regional Sources

Interstate Statistical Committee of the Commonwealth of Independent States
(CIS STAT): http://www.cisstat.com/.

Global Sources

FAO–Aquastat: http://www.fao.org/nr/water/aquastat/dbase/index.stm.

Global Water Intelligence: http://www.globalwaterintel.com/.

International Energy Agency (IEA) data services: http://data.iea.org/
IEASTORE/DEFAULT.ASP.

UNESCO World Water Assessment Programme: http://www.unesco.org/
water/new/en/natural-services/environment/water/wwap.

UN-Habitat Global Urban Indicators Database: http://ww2.unhabitat.org/
programmes/guo/guo_indicators.asp.

UNSD Statistical Databases: http://unstats.un.org/unsd/databases.htm.

Water System Analysis Group: http://wwdrii.sr.unh.edu/download.html.

World Bank Data: http://data.worldbank.org/.

World Health Organization: http://www.who.int/gho/en/.

CHAPTER 5

Financing Cities

Spotlight—Financing Uzgen, the Kyrgyz Republic

"I could not sleep all night, so impressed I was with what I saw." That was the reaction of the head of a municipality in the Kyrgyz Republic, after watching an educational film on municipal land auctions.[1] His reaction was provoked by the power of land auctions to generate large revenues from dormant assets. In Uzgen, for example, a town of 50,000 between Osh and Jalal-Abad, a vacant site of 1.3 square kilometers sold for almost five times the estimated market value—more than $26,000. In Jalal-Abad, Kara-Balta, and Karakol land auction sale prices exceeded starting prices by between 32 and 84 percent. Comparing another method of selling municipal assets—"direct land sales" with prices determined by professional appraisers—Osh found that revenues were on average two to three times lower than the prices obtained through land auctions, even though the sites for direct sales were in better areas than the auctioned sites.

These auctions succeeded due to a careful methodology and advertising campaign. Land was "packaged" with documents that minimized contractual uncertainties for investors. Limitations on land use were removed. A clear bidding process was established. And the auction was well advertised. For the Uzgen auction, for example, billboards about the site and auction were placed in the eight most populated areas across the city. Notices in three languages were broadcast on mass media and placed in the central marketplace and neighborhood community centers. At the time of this writing, a mixed-use building (a supermarket and hotel) had almost been completed.

Key Issues

- Eurasia is moving toward modern subnational finance, with transparent systems of revenue sharing, and equalization transfers—though some countries are moving faster than others.

- Increased spending on urban services could be financed through increases in local taxes (particularly the local share of the personal income tax) and in housing maintenance fees and charges for water, heating, and public transport.

- Efforts to do so are hampered by central government regulations and local administrative constraints.

The previous chapters of this book have discussed the ways Eurasian cities can adapt to the market-oriented economies that they find themselves in—ways they can become engines of economic growth as well as more livable and environmentally sustainable. Many of these changes involve policy decisions, such as international agreements on cross-border trade and improvements in land use and housing policies. But others involve public expenditure. The recent increases in intercity traffic have generated pressure to expand and rehabilitate the highway network. Growing metropolitan areas require investments in public transit. Collapsing or inefficient public utilities require rehabilitation or replacement. Major investments in pollution control are needed to bring Eurasian cities up to international environmental standards.

Consumers can bear, to an extent, the costs of these investments. As noted in earlier chapters, there is a strong economic case for financing many infrastructure services through user charges. Raising tariffs to reflect the economic costs of services can ration demand to efficient levels. But tariffs are not the only answer. Direct cost-recovery in some sectors, such as road maintenance, is often impractical. Government subsidies may be needed to reflect the positive externalities some services, such as public transit, generate—or to achieve social objectives, such as lifeline subsidies for public utilities. And government intervention may also be needed to ensure the timely construction of large, long-lived infrastructure. Few Eurasian countries have large, well-regulated private capital markets. Fewer still have an encouraging record of subnational borrowing. Until such market mechanisms are in place, central government financing will be needed to ensure that projects with high economic rates of return are built promptly.

The system for financing cities has undergone substantial transformation since the breakup of the Soviet Union.[2] With rising competition from highway-based transport, some state railroads are struggling to cover costs through operating revenues. Changes have also occurred in the systems to finance infrastructure services within cities, including the urban road network, the water supply, sewerage, district heating, housing maintenance, and public transport—services usually the responsibility of subnational governments. Under the Soviet system, they tended to be heavily subsidized. Recurrent costs, as well as costs of capital investments, were typically financed through a complex system of tax sharing and intergovernmental transfers, which was adjusted often because of intraparty negotiations.

The system for financing subnational tiers of government has changed, however. During the Soviet era, the resources allocated to subnational governments were based largely on plan targets and closed-door intraparty negotiations. Utility services were subsidized as a matter of policy. Since the breakup, the successor governments have moved toward more transparent and mechanical systems for financing the lowest tier of government. They have also raised tariffs for infrastructure services. But not all Eurasian countries have advanced equally along this path. And even those that have now find themselves without the tools to fully exploit their growing tax bases.

Intergovernmental Financing in the Soviet Union

The Soviet Union had a complex, hierarchical structure of government. Each of the 15 nominally sovereign republics was divided into several subordinate tiers of administration. The larger republics—including the Russian Federation and Ukraine—had three such tiers (table 5.1).[3] In Russia, the largest of the top-tier units of subnational administration was divided into districts (rayons), which were divided into settlements. In urban areas, the tiers of subnational administration were consolidated. Major regional cities—"Cities of Oblast Subordination"—performed the functions of rayons and settlements. The two largest cities (Moscow and Leningrad) performed the roles of all three tiers of subnational government.

The lowest tier of administration (cities and settlements) normally provided primary health care and primary and secondary education. Enterprises attached to key urban infrastructure services normally provided water supply, heating, and public transport. These services were, to varying degrees, financed by tariffs, deliberately kept far below cost-recovery levels. Thus, water, heating, and transport companies typically depended on financial support from their municipal owners both to subsidize operating costs and to finance capital investment. Subnational governments' ability to finance these companies, in turn, depended on the resources allocated to them through the budget process.

The budget process comprised a complex system of negotiations among party officials representing different tiers of government and the various economic enterprises attached to them (box 5.1). The negotiations revolved around the projected expenditure needs and revenues of each governmental unit. Expenditure needs were based on norms for various services (there was, for example, a norm for the number of maternity hospital beds per 1,000 women living in a jurisdiction). The revenue sources that negotiations focused on comprised shares of various taxes administered by the state, with the most important being taxes on the profits of state enterprises, a turnover tax (on consumer goods, foods, and some extractive and light industries), and the personal income tax. In principle, if a jurisdiction's revenues were projected to fall short of its projected expenditures, it was allowed to retain a larger percentage of shared

TABLE 5.1

Structure of Subnational Government in the Soviet Union

Tier	Unit		
First	Cities of Republican Subordination	Oblasts	
Second		Cities of Oblast Subordination	Rayons
Third			Settlements

Source: Authors.

BOX 5.1

The Communist Party and the Soviet Political Structure

The Soviet political structure had some of the trappings of Western democracies. At the republic level, legislative bodies (congresses of people's deputies) were elected by universal adult suffrage. As these congresses met infrequently, each republic also had a smaller standing legislature, whose chair functioned as head of state and oversaw the council of ministers, which acted as the government's executive branch.

A parallel structure existed at each subnational level. Each unit had its own council, elected by universal suffrage. Like their counterparts at the republic level, these councils met infrequently. Between sessions, each council delegated its authority to an executive committee, whose chair acted as chief executive and oversaw the functioning of the various administrative departments.

Actual political power was wielded by the Communist Party, which had branches at each level of subnational administration. In theory, the leadership of a local branch of the Party was chosen by local Party members. In practice, the Party leadership designated the people who would be put on the ballot to elect it. In the classic characterization, the Party set policy, and the government implemented it.

The relationship between the Party and the government was, in practice, more intimate. The Party determined which candidates would be on the ballot for local councils and appointed the key officials of the administration. Management controls reflected the spirit of democratic centralism, with sector managers at the local level subordinate to both their local executive and their sector counterpart at the central level.

Source: Authors.

taxes, and if necessary, a subsidy would also be provided. If a jurisdiction's revenues were projected to exceed its expenditures needs, its portion of shared taxes could be reduced.

Despite the appearance of objectivity, the process was subject to strategic behavior by all parts of government: subordinate units exaggerated expenditure needs and understated potential revenue yields, and officials responsible for setting shares and allocating subsidies understated expenditures and exaggerated revenues. In the final analysis, the resources available to a given jurisdiction were largely determined by the previous year's budget, though they could rise or fall depending on whether a local Party secretary remained on good terms with the Party bosses at higher levels and with the managers of state farms or factories.

Intergovernmental Financing during the Transition

Two fundamental changes followed the breakup of the Soviet Union: first, the end of the Communist Party's monopoly on political power, and second, the privatization of the economy.

The Move to Multiparty Democracy

In 1989, President Gorbachev allowed other political associations (de facto political parties) to coexist with the Communist Party. The first nominally multiparty elections (for the Congress of People's Deputies) were held in 1989. In February 1990, the Central Committee of the Communist Party of the Soviet Union formally agreed to give up its constitutional mandate as the "leading and guiding force" of Soviet society.

After the breakup, some form of multiparty democracy was enshrined in most of the constitutions of the successor republics. Many also adopted systems of nominally independent local governments with separately elected local officials. But the extent that the former monolithic political decision-making process has disappeared varies. A single dominant party remains in control in most Eurasian countries—in some cases headed by a long-standing executive from the Soviet era.

A Wide Range of Multiparty Democracy

Four Eurasian countries are characteristic of the wide range of multiparty democracy: Georgia, Russia, Tajikistan, and Ukraine. They will be used throughout this chapter to illustrate variations in intergovernmental finance.

Georgia has the constitutional attributes of a multiparty, multitier democracy. Its constitution defines the country as a democratic republic and affirms "the commitment of the Georgian people to a democratic social order and the right of citizens to form and join political parties." According to the constitution, both the parliament and the president are to be elected through secret ballots through universal, equal, and direct suffrage. Since the Rose Revolution of late 2003, however, the United National Movement party has dominated politics both nationally and locally, garnering 79 percent of the 150 seats in the May 2008 elections, ensuring its ability to pass legislation.

Russia's 1993 constitution declares the country to be a democratic, federative state. During the initial transition years, de facto power was highly dispersed, with the federal government forced to sign "bilateral pacts" with resource-rich regions to fend off demands for secession (or at least to persuade them to contribute tax revenues to the federal treasury). The subsequent years have seen a strong executive emerge at the federal level. A single political party—United Russia—has established political hegemony throughout the country, winning 70 percent of the votes in the 2008 presidential elections, though the results of the 2011 legislative election indicate an erosion of the party's dominance.

Tajikistan is dominated not only by a single party, but also by a single individual. The country's postindependence (1994) constitution declares the country to be a democratic state and guarantees all adult citizens the right to vote through universal, direct, and secret suffrage. But after the 1992–97 civil war, Tajikistan emerged as a centralized unitary state with the president exercising strong control. The constitution names the president head of state and government, supreme commander, and head of the security council. The president appoints members of the upper house of parliament, and most members of the lower house belong to his party.

Ukraine is one of the few Eurasian countries where partisan political competition at the central level occurs in the manner it does in Western European countries. Its constitution—adopted in 1996, amended in 2004 and 2006, and returned to its 1996 form in 2010—stipulates a de facto semipresidential system granting parliament the power to initiate legislation and consent to the person the president appoints as prime minister. The constitution leaves the president with strong executive powers, such as appointing cabinet ministers. Since independence in 1991, Ukraine has held five presidential elections and five parliamentary elections, with power shifting from one party to another, often with one party holding the presidency while another controls the parliament. But Ukraine is an outlier. The Russian model of single party dominance of a nominally multiparty, multitiered democracy is more characteristic of Eurasian countries.

Local multiparty politics exists de jure, if not de facto, at the lowest tier of subnational government in most Eurasian countries. While central governments continue to appoint the executives of the top-tier subnational governments, local democracy—through constituents, directly or indirectly, electing executives—is typical at the lowest tier of subnational government. In Russia, local democracy extends to the second and third tiers of subnational government.[4] And in Ukraine, the two upper tiers of subnational government (oblasts and rayons) are headed by executives that the government appoints. Provisions for local elections apply only to the lowest tier: the village, settlement, and city. Opposition candidates can and do win local elections. For example, the mayor of Kiev won reelection in 2008 despite the opposition of both government parties. In Georgia, local executives are elected, albeit indirectly. The mayors (*gamgebeli*) of the cities and districts are elected by local councils (*sakrebulo*), which in turn are directly elected by the voters.[5] By contrast, in Tajikistan executive power at all levels of local government is exercised by political appointees of the president. Chairs of oblasts, rayons, and towns serve at the pleasure of the president, who may dismiss them at any time or reappoint them for unlimited terms. Each level of local government has its own legislative branch, but local legislatures exert little control over the executive.[6]

The increasing power of regional interests, combined with the end of the Communist Party's political monopoly, forced a change in the arrangements for allocating public resources. The old methods of allocating resources—through top-down, closed-door intraparty meetings—proved unworkable. With competing political powers—both nationally and subnationally—more transparent and mechanical methods of dividing resources became necessary.

Privatization of the Economy

Privatization of the economy occurred at different speeds across the region. Shortly after the breakup, Russia implemented the largest and fastest privatization program ever. Quantitatively, the results of the program, launched in mid-1992, were impressive—within 2 years, most state-owned firms were transferred to private ownership. Thus, by September 1994 there were 100,000 privatized firms in Russia (outside of agriculture), accounting for more than 80 percent of the industrial workforce. Most small enterprises had been privatized, and of the 24,000 medium and large enterprises, most had been corporatized and more than 15,000 privatized by the end of 1994.

Privatization then lost momentum to some extent, continuing much more slowly in subsequent years. After 1996, privatization was increasingly on a case-by-case basis, with most transactions prepared with a known buyer in mind. Even so, by the end of the decade the main goal of separating the business sector from the state had at least formally been achieved (Hare and Muravyev 2003).

In Georgia and Tajikistan, privatization proceeded more rapidly with smaller enterprises than with larger ones. Nevertheless, by the end of the transition's second decade most firms in the manufacturing, services, and agricultural sectors were in private hands.

The pace of privatization was considerably slower in Ukraine. Although the state had privatized more than 80 percent of all enterprises (accounting for more than 60 percent of output) by early 1999, controlling shares in many privatized enterprises remained in government hands. Privatization intensified in 2003–04, but it was marred by controversy, particularly over the terms that large enterprises were sold on.

Privatization had two important implications for subnational government finance. First, it eliminated an important auxiliary provider of public services. Under the Soviet system, state enterprises had built and supported hospitals, constructed and maintained housing, built and run kindergartens and preschools, and made donations toward public transportation. With privatization, this role was curtailed.

Second, privatization drastically altered taxation, as profits from government-owned enterprises ceased to be a major revenue source. As central governments revised their tax structures to capture revenues from the growing private sector, the basis for intergovernmental tax sharing had to be altered.

Democratization and privatization affected some Eurasian countries more than others. Change has been most radical in the Baltic countries and, arguably, Georgia. It has been less pronounced in the Central Asian countries. Whatever the pace of change, all countries in the region operate differently from the way they did before the breakup.

Intergovernmental Financing Today

With few exceptions, the structure of subnational government in Eurasian countries has not changed much since the Soviet era. But the distribution of functions among the various tiers has shifted.

What Do Different Government Levels Do?

The responsibility for urban infrastructure generally remains at the lowest tier of subnational government, but the responsibility for social spending has been centralized, either to higher tiers of subnational government or to the central government.

Georgia

Georgia has centralized all social services (social assistance, education, and health). Before the 2006 consolidation, subnational governments at both the first and the second tiers were the main providers of primary education. They also played an important role in health care and social assistance. The central government now performs these functions, including paying salaries, operating costs, and facilities maintenance expenses. The responsibilities of subnational governments consist principally of providing urban public utilities (water supply and district heating) and public transportation and maintaining housing and intrasettlement roads.

Russia

The responsibility for service provision in Russia is divided among the three tiers of subnational government. First-tier subnational governments are the main providers of social services. They directly pay child allowances, social assistance for poor people, and medical insurance for the unemployed. They finance preprimary, primary, and secondary education. And they build and maintain regional roads and intercity transportation.

Second-tier subnational governments are responsible for delivering education and health services. They provide preprimary, primary, and secondary education and most hospital care. Funding for education is provided by the first tier of subnational government; funding for hospital care is provided partly by regional health insurance funds and partly from each jurisdiction's own revenues. Second-tier subnational governments are also responsible for building and maintaining intrasettlement roads. The lowest tier (settlements) is responsible for maintaining housing and providing urban public utilities and public transport.

Larger cities subsume the roles of multiple tiers of subnational government. Thus, Cities of Oblast Subordination are responsible for the functions assigned to both the second and third tiers of subnational government. And Cities of Republican Subordination (Moscow and St. Petersburg) are responsible for these functions and those of first-tier subnational governments.

Tajikistan

The Law on Local Self-Management (1991, amended in 1992 and 1993) assigns a broad range of responsibilities to subnational governments in Tajikistan (rayons, Cities of Oblast Subordination, and Dushanbe). The responsibilities include education, health, and social assistance (the local role in pensions is limited to helping unpaid pensioners contact the appropriate government authorities). Second-tier subnational governments are responsible for preschools and schools

covering grades 1–11 (the Ministry of Education is directly responsible for specialized secondary schools and universities). Except for
some specialized hospitals in Dushanbe and policlinics operated by
large factories and enterprises, local administrations manage almost
all public health care and finance it through their budgets. Oblasts
perform a largely administrative and supervisory role.

Responsibility for urban utilities and housing in Tajikistan remains
centralized. Although subnational governments bear nominal responsibility for these functions, in most urban areas they are performed
by units of the State Unitary Enterprise-Kojagii Naziliyu Kommunali, a large undertaking that operates 32 water supply and sewerage enterprises, five heating enterprises, and various companies
responsible for building maintenance. In eight cities (including
Dushanbe, Khujand, and Tursunzade) and two rayons (Varzob and
Shahrinav), communal service enterprises subordinate to their
local governments provide these functions (Kudosova 2007; Urban
Institute 2007).

Ukraine

The responsibility for social services is more decentralized in Ukraine.
Following major reforms in 2001, the responsibilities of first-tier subnational governments have been limited largely to administering the
national system of social assistance to low-income families. Second-
tier subnational governments are responsible for paying child allowances, benefits to war veterans, and various consumption subsidies
(for rent, utility, public transport, and so forth). The lowest tier of
subnational government is responsible for financing and operating
schools and health care facilities. The 2001 budget law specifically
requires third-tier subnational governments to provide preschool
education, primary and secondary education, primary medical and
sanitary aid, and outpatient and inpatient medical care (through district hospitals, ambulatory centers, first-aid and obstetrics centers,
and first-aid stations).[7]

Who Finances What—and How?

During the transition, most Eurasian countries moved from a reliance on intraparty negotiations toward a more stable division of
taxing powers and a transparent system of intergovernmental
transfers (except Tajikistan, which still has a Soviet-style model).
Eurasian countries devised various mechanisms to finance their
expenditures.

Georgia

Georgia spent much of the 1990s making marginal adjustments to the structure of subnational financing it inherited from the Soviet Union. Early on, the government abolished the system based on negotiated shares of central government taxes, replacing it with a system in which local governments were assigned all of the revenue from the centrally administered personal income tax, as well as a centrally administered property tax. At the time, there were two tiers of subnational government but no fixed rules governing the relationship between the two. In late 2005, Georgia abolished the lower tier of subnational government and centralized education and health (box 5.2). The 2009 budget code reassigned the personal income tax exclusively to the central government, leaving local governments to rely on a newly created equalization transfer, along with the property tax, fees, charges, and income from the rent, lease, or sale of their own real estate.

Georgia's equalization transfer has gone through several major modifications. Under the Law on the Budgets of Local Self-Government Units (which took effect January 1, 2007), the transfer

---

BOX 5.2

Territorial Reform in Georgia

Georgia is one of the few former Soviet republics (excluding the Baltics, which are outside this book's scope) that fundamentally changed the structure of its subnational governments following the collapse of the Soviet Union. Before reform, Georgia's territory was divided into 60 districts (rayons), which in turn were divided into about 1,100 second-tier subnational governments, consisting of towns, settlements, and villages. Four cities, as well as Tbilisi, were directly subordinate to the central government. The division of functions between the first and second tiers of subnational governments was poorly defined. Neither level had a stable source of revenues, instead deriving revenues from annually negotiated shares of nationally administered taxes.

The new organic law of December 2005 eliminated the second tier of subnational governments, consolidating them into their respective rayons. Cities that were directly subordinate to the central government were given the same status as the former rayons—and thus remain directly subordinate to the central government. The reform reduced the number of local governments from 1,105 to 65. Municipal elections were successfully conducted based on the new territorial arrangements in October 2006. And new municipal councils were in place by January 1, 2007.

Source: Authors.

would have provided funding to first-tier subnational governments with per capita revenues below the national average. (At the time, subnational revenues included both the personal income tax and the property tax.) Specifically, the equalization transfer compensated each local government for 70 percent of the difference between what it was expected to raise from the personal income tax, the property tax, and other local revenues—and what it would have raised if its revenues from these sources were equal to the national average per capita. (Tbilisi was excluded from the calculation of the national averages.)

With the centralization of the personal income tax and of the responsibility for education and health, the formula has been radically revised, and thus considerably more complicated. Under the new system, every year the Ministry of Finance determines the total amount of the transfer in advance.[8] The distribution of the transfer is based on the difference between each jurisdiction's expenditure needs and projected revenues.[9] Expenditure needs are based on each jurisdiction's total population, as well as the number of children and adolescents, the number of people below the poverty level, its land area, the length of its local roads, its status (town versus municipality), and certain unspecified "equalization coefficients." Revenues exclude grants and thus largely reflect property tax revenues.

Russia

The breakup of the Soviet Union was followed by economic decline throughout its former republics, as the once close connections among their economies were severed. Russia's gross domestic product (GDP) shrank by nearly half between 1989 and 1998, with tax revenues and state enterprise profits declining accordingly (figure 5.1). At the same time, the weakened authority of the central government prompted resource-rich regions to refuse to remit the central government's portion of shared taxes. The central government was thus forced to sign bilateral agreements with these regions.

Attempts to create order from chaos began in the mid-1990s, when a series of tax reforms was enacted to permit the government to capture revenues from the growing private sector. A value added tax (VAT) was introduced in 1992. In 2001, the personal and corporate income tax systems were simplified (exemptions were reduced, rates made uniform). The turnover tax was abolished in 2003.

These measures accompanied efforts to put the financial relationship between the federal government and subnational governments

FIGURE 5.1

GDP in the Russian Federation, 1989–2009

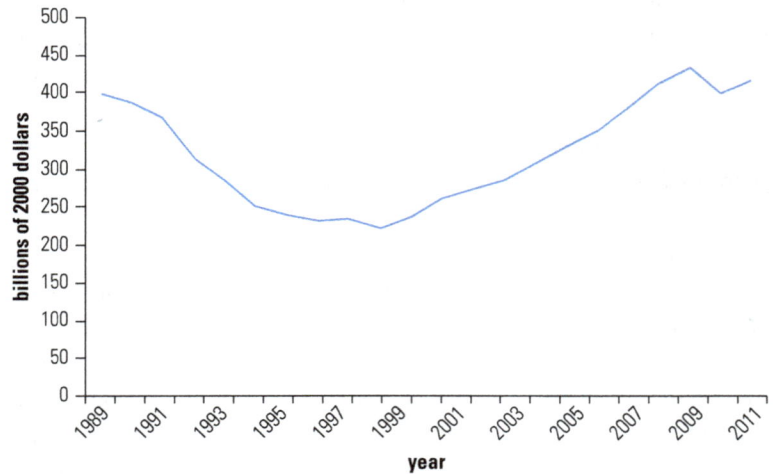

Source: World Bank 2012.

on a regular footing. In 1994, the rates for federal shared taxes were made uniform (previously, they had varied from year to year and place to place). After that, shortfalls between revenues and expenditures were to be met through a new Federal Fund for the Financial Support of Regions (FFFSR). As in the previous system based on varying tax shares, the allocation of FFFSR funds was intended to reflect variations in expenditure needs and revenue potential. But unlike the previous system, allocations were to be based on a formula rather than case-by-case negotiations. The formula was further refined in 2001 (though parliament retained the power to change the formula annually). In 2005, federal legislation called for the formula-based allocation system to be extended to second- and third-tier subnational governments.[10]

The general budgets of all three tiers of subnational government are now financed from taxes (assigned in whole or in part to each tier), intergovernmental transfers, and various fees and service charges. Taxes are the largest single source (table 5.2 lists the taxes assigned to each subnational tier, along with the share of each tax that each tier is allowed to retain).[11] The central government administers all subnational taxes through the federal tax service, and taxes are paid into branches of the federal treasury. The federal government sets all tax rates, except for minor regional and local taxes and the regional share of the enterprise profit tax.

TABLE 5.2

Distribution of Tax Instruments across Subnational Tiers of Government in the Russian Federation, 2009

Tax	Share retained by each tier			
	Federal	Regional	Rayon	Settlement
Federally controlled taxes				
Enterprise profit tax	27	73	0	0
Personal income tax	0	70	20	10
Excise on alcohol	50	50	0	0
Excise on gasoline	40	60	0	0
Special tax on imputed income	10	0	90	0
Special tax on small businesses	10	90	0	0
Special agriculture enterprises tax	10	30	30	30
Regionally controlled taxes				
Taxes on transport, gambling, and enterprise assets	0	100	0	0
Locally controlled taxes				
Individual property and land taxes	0	0	0	100

Source: Government of Russia 2010.
Note: The federal government defines the bases and administers all taxes. Regional governments set the regionally controlled taxes, and local governments set the locally controlled taxes.

In 2009, subnational governments derived about two-thirds of their income from taxes. The personal income tax was the single largest source of revenue, accounting for 28 percent of total revenues. The corporate income tax contributed 18 percent, the property tax 10 percent (nearly all of it from enterprises), and excise taxes and various "simplified" taxes 7 percent. Of total revenues, 27 percent were derived from intergovernmental transfers. And much of the remaining 10 percent came from charges for services and the use of property, enterprise income, and the sale of assets (Government of Russia 2010).

The principal transfer from the federal government to first-tier subnational government remains a gap-filling equalization grant, to reduce disparities in per capita tax revenues. All first-tier subnational governments that collect less than 60 percent of the national per capita average (a calculation that excludes the richest and poorest 10 percent) receive a transfer covering 85 percent of the gap. (The taxes to be equalized include the personal income tax, the corporate income tax, taxes on imputed income, property taxes, excise taxes, and taxes on mineral extraction.) Over time, the formula has been modified to reflect regional variations in the costs of providing public

services. The 2010 formula includes factors reflecting federally determined variations in wage rates, indicators of remoteness, and variations in living costs. It also includes a bonus subsidy for regional
governments that reduces their arrears.

In principle, the total amount of the equalization transfer is determined endogenously: the federal government is required to contribute whatever sum is needed to meet the equalization target. But
under the system of multiyear budgeting, the amount is fixed 3 years
in advance. In addition to the equalization grant, transfers compensate for federal mandates such as rent subsidies for veterans and the
costs of operating civil registration offices, capital transfers, and some
cofinancing for social expenditures.

The system of transfers from first-tier subnational governments to
their subordinate tiers varies across jurisdictions, though it is subject
to general guidelines specified in the federal budget code. The code
authorizes first-tier subnational governments to use two instruments
to provide general budget support (as opposed to earmarked funding
for such functions as education) to subordinate tiers. First, they may
assign fixed shares of their own taxes (for example, transport, gam-
bling, and enterprise property taxes). These shares must be uniform
for all jurisdictions. Second, they may establish formula-based equalization transfers. The code envisions that these transfers will be allocated based on tax capacity and cost drivers (say, the climate and the
socioeconomic status and age profile of the population). It also allows
for negative transfers. If a subordinate jurisdiction's per capita revenues are more than twice the region's average, the regional government is permitted to take up to 50 percent of the excess and reallocate
it to poorer jurisdictions.

So, the revenues available to a third-tier subnational government
in Russia are the product of cascading events and decisions at higher
levels of government, beginning with the level of personal income
tax and corporate income tax revenues collected and retained by its
oblast, and its oblast's share of federal equalization transfers. Oblasts
pool these revenues, allocate some to finance their own expenditures, and transfer some to their rayons. Rayons then pool these revenues with their own shares of the personal income tax, along with
receipts from the agriculture tax and smaller taxes; allocate some to
finance their own expenditures; and transfer some to their settlements. The resources available to a settlement are the sum of these
transfers, its own share of the personal income tax, and receipts from
property taxes and other local fees and charges. Some of this revenue
is used to finance the settlement's own expenditures, and some goes
toward recurrent subsidies or capital investments undertaken by
their enterprises.

Tajikistan

Unlike Georgia, Russia, or Ukraine, Tajikistan still adheres to the Soviet model of subnational government finance, based on negotiated calculations of expenditure gaps at each tier of government. The formal process of estimating expenditures begins with the Ministry of Finance's distribution of budget directives. Expenditure estimates are, in theory, based on centrally determined expenditure norms that specify "expenditure drivers" in various sectors (say, the number of schools, teachers, and students at various education levels).[12] These estimates are then multiplied by expenditure norms to estimate expenditures for the year to come.

There is evidence that the norm-based approach is no longer observed—if it ever was. Spending per pupil on primary and secondary education varies widely across jurisdictions, in a manner that the official norms cannot entirely explain. Expenditure estimates appear to be based on each rayon's budget for the previous year, modified to consider expected changes in major cost items (caused by inflation or changes in the budget parameters the central government controls, such as wage rates for various civil service grades, allowable staffing levels across grades, and tariffs for certain public utilities and communal services).

While the rayons develop the expenditure side of the local budgets, local representatives of the national tax committee work with local finance departments to project tax revenues. Article 41 of the Law on Local Self-Management assigns two categories of taxes to local administrations. The larger category—"regulated taxes"—includes a large share of the VAT (on domestic transactions) and the corporate and personal income taxes. In addition, local governments are permitted to impose some "nonregulated" taxes. According to the tax code, local governments may impose a retail sales tax and a tax on immovable property owned by individuals (table 5.3). These taxes are imposed at governmental fixed rates.

With this estimate of expenditures and revenues, the negotiating process begins. The chair of the rayon or town first presents the expenditure estimate to the oblast governor (or directly to the Ministry of Finance, for Dushanbe and Rayons of Republican Subordination). Negotiations between the oblast governor and individual rayon chairs then ensue. These talks may reduce some spending proposals or add other items, for which the oblast executive is expected to contribute supplementary funding. After completing similar budget negotiations with departments and enterprises of the oblast itself, the oblast chair packages a consolidated budget and submits it to the Ministry of Finance, which reconciles the spending proposals of all

TABLE 5.3

Distribution of Shared Taxes in Tajikistan, 2009

percent

Type of tax	Republic	Subnational
Shared taxes[a]		
Domestic value added tax	55	45
Corporate income tax	40	60
Personal income tax	25	75
Local taxes		
Retail sales tax	0	100
Property tax	0	100

Source: Dillinger 2011.
a. Shares vary across subnational jurisdictions.

first-tier subnational administrations with the overall availability of resources and the demands of the other government ministries and agencies. An ad hoc budget commission—typically consisting of the minister and deputy minister of finance, the tax committee, the statistical office, the customs service, and other sectoral ministries, as required—advises the Ministry of Finance.

Once the aggregate level of subnational funding is determined, the Ministry of Finance determines the budget ceiling for each first-tier subnational administration. A second round of budget negotiations then ensues, in which the oblast governor (or the Ministry of Finance, for Dushanbe and the Rayons of Republican Subordination) negotiates a substantially reduced budget ceiling with the city and rayon executive in his jurisdiction. The budget law precludes cuts to a specific set of "protected items," including wages, pensions, stipends, and utility payments. Cuts to local spending are thus concentrated in areas such as capital investment, purchases of supplies, and low-priority items such as travel. Once the local government receives the disaggregated "control figures" from the oblast, the funding reflected in those figures is not subject to change. The local council must officially approve the budget, but its approval is largely a formality.

Ukraine

Ukraine's system of subnational finance is similar to Russia's, with the main difference being that its systems achieve greater functional decentralization.

Like Russia, Ukraine suffered an economic disaster after the breakup of the Soviet Union. And it also attempted feebly to reorganize its system of subnational finance during the 1990s. In 1996, it made an initial effort to define the division of functions among tiers of government and the structure of intergovernmental fiscal relations. A 1997 law on local self-government set out minimum spending standards (based on per capita norms) for various local government functions and the basic principles of an equalization mechanism. The equalization mechanism called for subsidies to jurisdictions lacking enough revenue to meet the spending norms and for "negative transfers" from jurisdictions with surpluses.[13] In practice, the calculation of the expenditure needs of each jurisdiction continued to be based on the costs of maintaining the facilities assigned to it rather than its legally assigned functions. The level of transfers was based largely on case-by-case negotiations conducted during budget preparations. In the course of these negotiations, the list of taxes assigned to subnational governments and their respective shares varied from year to year (Reminga and others 2003).

Ukraine's system of subnational finance is the result of a major rewrite of the budget code in 2001. As in Russia, the budgets of all three tiers of subnational government are now financed from a combination of centrally controlled taxes (with shares assigned to each tier), intergovernmental transfers, and various minor taxes and fees that subnational governments exercise some control over. Only two taxes are subject to sharing: the personal income tax and the land tax (table 5.4). Shares of the personal income tax are divided among oblasts, rayons, and villages on a 25/50/25 basis. The land tax is divided on a 25/15/60 basis. As in Russia, cities are entitled to the revenues of multiple tiers of subnational government. Cities of Oblast Subordination receive 75 percent of the personal income tax and the land tax. Kiev and Sevastopol receive all of both.

Ukraine's system of tax sharing is simpler than Russia's, but its system of equalization transfers is far more complicated. As defined in the 2001 budget code, transfers from the central government to first-tier subnational governments are based on expenditure gaps

TABLE 5.4

Distribution of Shared Taxes in Ukraine, 2009

Government level	Personal income tax	Land tax
Oblast	25	25
Rayon	50	15
Village and City of Rayon Subordination	25	60
City of Oblast Subordination	75	75
Kiev and Sevastopol	100	100

Source: Government of Ukraine 2004.

(the difference between each jurisdiction's expenditure needs and its revenue potential). For this purpose, expenditure needs are calculated for six functions: administration, health, education, culture, sports, and social protection. At the time the system was formulated, it was expected that a single indicator would be used for each function (a standard per capita amount for public administration, health care, culture, and social programs; a standard per student amount for education; and a standard per eligible recipient amount for social protection). The budget code does not define the formula, however. Rather, it states that the calculation of expenditure needs to consider "budget sufficiency, population, numbers of recipients, and other factors."

Dozens of factors have been added since the 2001 reform, undermining transparency and encouraging local governments to lobby for including factors favorable to their own situations. As of 2007, the number of factors and adjustment coefficients used to determine the nominal spending needs of rayons was 32 in education and 23 in the health sector; 12–15 factors were used for oblasts (Order No. 33 Ministry of Health). As discussed in box 5.3, even this abundance of coefficients fails to compensate local governments for the cost of centrally imposed norms.

BOX 5.3

Norms, Inefficiencies, and Unfunded Mandates in Ukraine

In preparing their budgets, subnational governments are still required to follow norms that come from the Soviet system. These norms dictate staffing levels and other cost-drivers based on facilities. For example, rayon hospitals are required to employ one obstetrician per 20 beds; health facilities must employ one cook per 30 beds. In both education and health, more staff members are employed than are actually needed. But local governments are not allowed to shrink staffs or facilities to match demand, and Article 49 of the Constitution forbids any level of government from closing hospitals.

Who pays for this inefficiency? If the calculation of expenditure needs used in the equalization transfer were based literally on these norms, the central government would have to finance expenditures. But if the calculation of expenditure needs was based on demand indicators (numbers of students or patients), local governments would have to. In practice, responsibility lies somewhere in between. Although the equalization formula has an adjustment coefficient for jurisdictions with high wage bills, it does not literally compensate local governments for the costs imposed by the norms. As a result, local governments, not the central government, are forced to finance the inefficiencies imposed by the norms.

Source: Saavedra 2008.

The system for determining the revenue potential of each jurisdiction is more straightforward. In 1998, 1999, and the first 10 months of 2000, the amounts were based on actual revenues from shared taxes in each jurisdiction. Since then, revenue potential has been based on actual collections the preceding 3 years.

The total amount of the transfer to each first-tier subnational government is, in principle, equal to its expenditure gap—the difference between its estimated expenditure needs (including the needs of its subordinate jurisdictions) and its historical revenues (including the revenues of its subordinate jurisdictions). For a first-tier subnational government whose revenues exceed its estimated expenditure needs, the law requires a negative transfer—such jurisdictions are required to transfer 80–100 percent of the surplus to the central budget. The 2001 law suggests, but does not require, that transfers from first-tier subnational governments to second-tier subnational governments use the same methodology.

As in Russia, the law also authorizes various other transfers from the central government, including transfers to finance functions performed on behalf of the state (such as education and health care) and funds to finance subsidies for electric power, natural gas, and housing and communal services. The extent of local taxing powers is limited. Subnational governments are permitted to retain the corporate profits tax from their own enterprises.

Mobilizing Additional Finance for Cities

The rules governing the assignment of functions and revenues to subnational governments apply to all subnational jurisdictions—urban and rural, large and small. But the structure of subnational governments allows for distinctions among large cities, smaller cities, and rural settlements. Major regional cities—generally called Cities of Oblast Subordination—perform the functions and receive the revenues of both second- and third-tier subnational governments.

Big Versus Small Cities

The largest cities—generally called Cities of Republic Subordination—perform the functions and receive the revenues of all three tiers. This distinction has two important implications.

First, it means that larger cities enjoy considerably greater access to local tax bases than do smaller jurisdictions. In Russia, Moscow and St. Petersburg are entitled to all of the personal income taxes and property taxes collected within their boundaries, 73 percent of the corporate income tax, and roughly half of the excise taxes on alcohol and fuels. By contrast, Cities of Oblast Subordination are entitled to just 20 percent of personal income tax and none of the enterprise profit or excise taxes collected. In Ukraine, Kiev and Sevastopol retain all of the personal income and land taxes, while Cities of Oblast Subordination are entitled to only 75 percent of the two taxes, and Cities of Rayon Subordination to only 25 percent of the personal income tax and 60 percent of the land tax.

Second, it means that larger cities have considerably broader expenditure responsibilities than do smaller jurisdictions. Moscow and St. Petersburg are responsible not only for a wide array of infrastructure services, but also for financing primary and secondary education and health services.

These distinctions have an important implication for the financing of urban infrastructure services: although big cities are rich, most of their money goes elsewhere, because the tax advantage big cities enjoy is offset considerably by equalization transfers and other intergovernmental grants that favor smaller jurisdictions.

The results are evident in St. Petersburg's budget, which derives nearly 70 percent of its revenues from taxes. The personal and corporate income tax each contribute just under 30 percent of total revenues, rents and other income from the use of municipal property 9 percent, property taxes about 8 percent, receipts from business activities (which includes reimbursements from the regional health insurance funds as well as income from municipal enterprises and proceeds from the sale of their assets) about 8 percent, and excise taxes about 4 percent (figure 5.2).[14] Intergovernmental transfers contribute 10 percent, but most of this consists of federal cofinancing of capital works, with the rest including compensation for various federally mandated programs, such as utility subsidies, unemployment benefits, and social housing for World War II veterans.[15]

Spending on social services—education, health, and social assistance—consumed roughly half of St. Petersburg's budget in 2010 (figure 5.3). Spending on infrastructure services (largely transportation and energy) consumed less than 20 percent, with spending on housing (including water supply) consuming another 17 percent.[16]

More detailed data on the sectoral composition of the city's recent expenditures are not available. A detailed breakdown of the city's future spending in key infrastructure sectors is provided, however, by the 2010 budget's breakdown of expenditures by organizational unit. According to the 2010 budget, spending on road construction and maintenance (including traffic management) was

FIGURE 5.2
Revenue Composition in St. Petersburg, 2005–09
millions of 2005 Rub

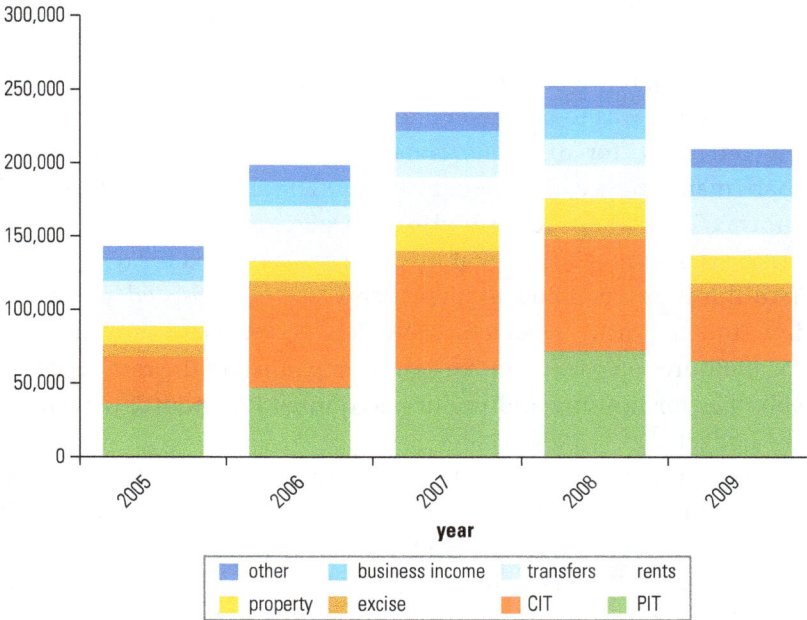

Source: Government of the City of St. Petersburg.
Note: CIT = corporate income tax; PIT = personal income tax.

FIGURE 5.3
Expenditure Composition in St. Petersburg, 2010
percent

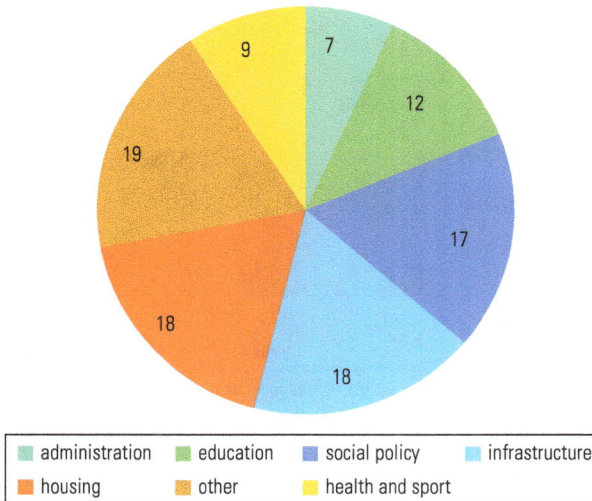

Source: Government of the City of St. Petersburg.

projected to consume 9 percent of total expenditures. Spending on transport (including recurrent subsidies and capital investments) was allocated another 7 percent, while spending on energy (including subsidies to the city's gas company and related investments) also accounted for 7 percent.

According to the 2010 budget, the vast majority of spending on these sectors was to be devoted to capital investment. Most spending on roads, for example, consisted of capital spending rather than maintenance. Recurrent subsidies to the bus, trolley, and subway companies accounted for 24 percent of spending in the transport sector, while capital investment accounted for 65 percent. Two-thirds of spending in the energy sector consisted of capital investments, with recurrent subsidies to the gas company and expenditures on street lighting consuming much of the rest. Targeted subsidies for housing and utilities accounted for about 2 percent of the budget.[17]

Kiev is financed largely from its total share of the personal income and land taxes. Over 2007–09, personal income tax contributed half the city's revenues, with the land tax contributing another 7 percent (figure 5.4). Other taxes, including a tax on small business, contributed 4 percent, with ad hoc subsidies and capital transfers accounting for much of the remainder.

FIGURE 5.4

Revenue Composition in Kiev, 2007–09
thousands of 2009 Hrv

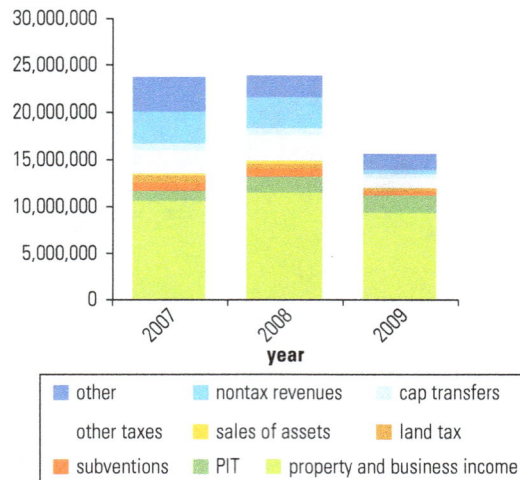

Legend:
- other
- nontax revenues
- cap transfers
- other taxes
- sales of assets
- land tax
- subventions
- PIT
- property and business income

Source: Report on Budget Execution: City of Kiev.
Note: PIT = personal income tax.

Like St. Petersburg, Kiev has a strong local tax base that provides revenues that exceed its expenditures. Under Ukraine's equalization formula, it must contribute part of the difference to the treasury. In 2009, payments from Kiev to the treasury were equal to about 35 percent of the city's revenues. Kiev spends half its budget on social sectors (figure 5.5).[18] It allocates just 16 percent of its regular budget to infrastructure services (housing and communal services and transport). This spending is supplemented by spending that a "special fund" finances, most of which consists of urban infrastructure investments.[19] Kiev owns various enterprises providing communal services and transport. It is a majority shareowner of a water company and a gas distribution company,[20] and it owns two public transport companies (KievPasTransit, which operates buses, trams, trolleys, and the funicular railway, and KievMetroPoliten, which operates the subway), a construction company, and numerous smaller enterprises. Expenditures shown in the budget include subsidies to these enterprises (including spending on capital works relevant to them), but they do not include expenditures financed from tariffs.

FIGURE 5.5

Municipal Expenditure Composition in Kiev, 2009
percent

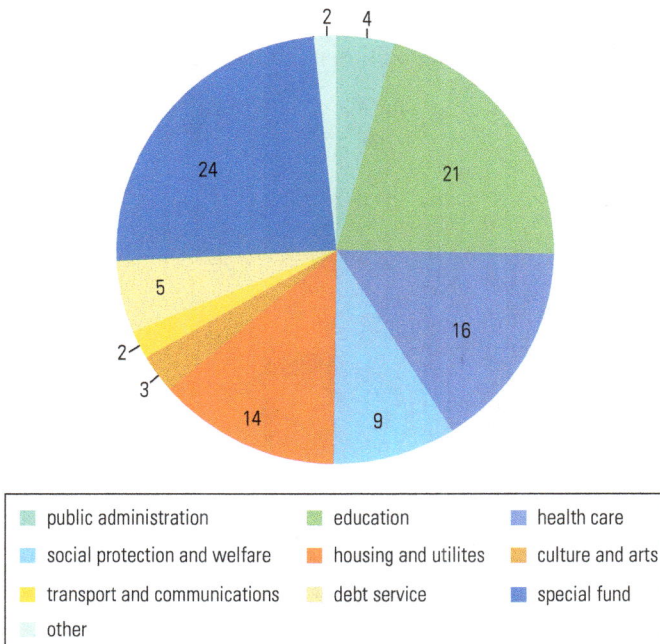

Source: Report on Budget Execution: City of Kiev.

In Tbilisi, most of the budget is allocated to urban infrastructure services rather than social services. Spending on social sectors—which consists largely of preschool and social assistance (education is a central government expense)—consumes only 20 percent of the budget. Transport, housing, communal services, and the environment consume the rest (figure 5.6).

In the smaller Eurasian cities, one would expect somewhat different expenditure patterns, reflecting the narrower scope of their functional responsibilities. Social assistance is the responsibility of oblasts in Russia and rayons in Ukraine. Still, even Cities of Oblast Subordination have to manage education in Russia, Tajikistan, and Ukraine. (In Ukraine, Cities of Rayon Subordination are also responsible for education.) Thus, demands for increased spending on infrastructure services have to compete with demands for more social spending throughout Eurasia.

Options for Increasing Revenues

Revenues of large Eurasian cities could be increased by increasing the aggregate level of central government taxes or by reallocating central government expenditures from other budget users. Neither

FIGURE 5.6

Municipal Expenditure Composition in Tbilisi, 2009
percent

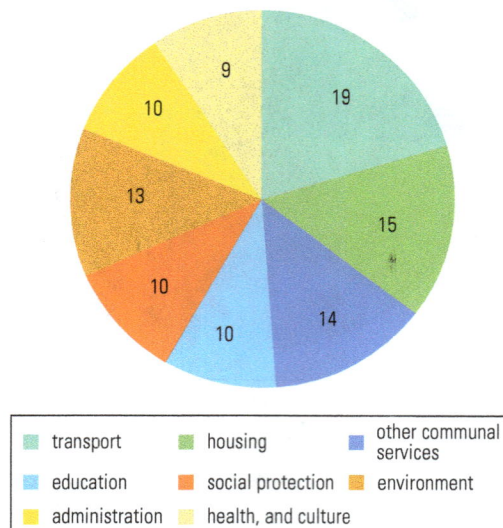

Source: Report on Budget Execution: City of Tbilisi.

option is particularly promising. The aggregate tax burden in most Eurasian countries is already fairly high, except in the oil-producing countries, ranging from 13 percent in Kazakhstan to 25 percent in Belarus (figure 5.7).[21]

It is also not obvious that increased transfers to large cities should be paid for by reducing transfers to smaller and poorer jurisdictions. The large proportion of direct central government taxes collected in large cities and the high level of transfer dependence of smaller and poorer jurisdictions suggest that large cities are, indeed, subsidizing their smaller and poorer counterparts. But this is not necessarily undesirable. Because lower tiers of government provide services with important distributional implications (education, health), a considerable degree of revenue redistribution is worthwhile. The quality of education provided to a Ukrainian child should not depend on the strength of the tax base where the child resides. Taxes generated in large cities should help out.

The alternative route is to increase taxes on taxpayers and fee-payers who live in big cities, since there is a wide dispersion of aggregate tax burdens in Eurasia (see figure 5.7). Doing so would not imply that such revenue sources must be locally administered or that subnational governments must control their rates. It merely requires that the burden of such revenue sources fall on the people who benefit from the services they finance—that is, that they function as benefit taxes.[22]

FIGURE 5.7

Aggregate Tax Burden in the Former Soviet Union, by Country, 2009
tax revenue as percentage of 2009 GDP

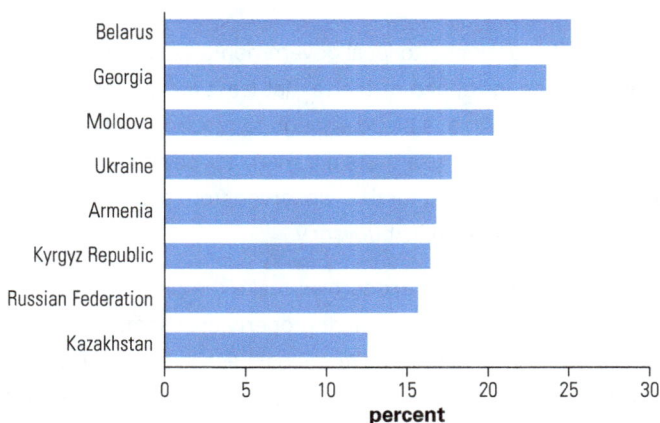

Source: IMF 2010.
Note: GDP = gross domestic product.

Raising Personal Income Taxes

The most promising vehicle for increasing revenues in almost all Eurasian countries is the personal income tax, which is well positioned to serve as a benefit tax (box 5.4). Personal income taxes have a geographically defined incidence. Unlike a corporate income tax or VAT, their incidence is not shifted across jurisdictional boundaries. The personal income tax also has a broad base (unlike excise taxes or taxes on motor vehicle ownership). From a practical standpoint, it can be cheap to administer, at least in countries with mainly formal economies. Although the personal income tax is extremely difficult to impose on the self-employed or people working in the informal sector, it is readily imposed on formal sector employees through payroll deductions.

BOX 5.4

Choosing among Local Benefit Taxes

Local taxes are an appropriate means of financing urban services whose benefits cannot be confined to individual consumers but do not extend beyond the municipal boundaries. Local taxes are the collective analogue of user charges—just as user charges are the way that individuals can express their demand for services whose benefits are largely private, and local taxes are the way that taxpayers within a community can express their demand for services consumed collectively. Benefit taxes also provide a degree of geographical equity to the financing of municipal services, imposing the costs of municipal services on the people who benefit from them.

Property Taxes

The property tax is the most common tax assigned to local governments worldwide. In theory, it performs well as a local benefit tax. The incidence of the tax (at least its residential component) is geographically confined, and its coverage is broad enough to reach most beneficiaries. But the property tax is difficult to administer, because there are many tax-paying units, property values must be imputed (based on assessments) rather than observed from actual transactions, and the base must be revalued annually to maintain its buoyancy.

Conditions in developing countries and transition economies make the property tax particularly difficult to administer, because the basic market data that property assessments are based on are inaccessible or unreliable. In addition, there are political costs associated with the property tax: as a direct tax, its burden is particularly visible, and as a tax on wealth, its burden falls disproportionately on groups with political influence.

continued

BOX 5.4 *continued*

Income and Payroll Taxes

Local income and payroll taxes are an attractive alternative to the property tax. They are used widely in Europe. Personal income taxes have the geographically defined incidence sought in a benefit tax and, where imposed with a national income tax, are inexpensive to administer.

The constraint on income taxes in developing countries is their narrow coverage. The personal income tax is very difficult to impose on the self-employed or people working in the informal sector. Most personal income tax revenues are thus derived through payroll deductions, which fall on only a small share of the population. High personal income taxes can also drive up formal sector labor costs, encouraging firms to remain unregistered. In Western and Central Europe, as well as in the more developed countries of the former Soviet Union, the administrative constraints on the personal income tax are less binding. Fixed shares of the personal income tax are the most important source of local revenues in Eastern Europe. Even so, few national governments are willing to allow the tax to be imposed at high rates.

Utility Taxes

Local taxes are often imposed on utility bills, particularly those for electricity. In principle, such taxes have localized incidence and, given the ubiquity of electric service, broad coverage. Costs of administration are low, as the tax can be tacked on to electricity bills. The extent that an electricity surcharge can be relied on exclusively is limited, however, by the base of assessment. If the tax is imposed ad valorem, it distorts the price of power. If it is imposed as a flat fee, it fails to capture variations in ability to pay and is thus limited by the tax-paying ability of the poorest electricity consumers.

Automobile Taxes

Local automobile taxes—recurrent taxes on automobile ownership and one-time taxes on purchase—are a substantial auxiliary source of revenue. Except in multijurisdictional metropolitan areas, the incidence of such taxes is easy to confine, and such taxes are easier to administer and enforce. However, potential yields are limited.

Source: Authors.

Not surprisingly, the personal income tax is already a large revenue source in most Eurasian countries. To varying degrees, it has the added practical advantage of already being assigned to subnational governments.[23] In Tajikistan, part of revenue from the personal income tax is shared with the subnational jurisdiction where it was collected (the share varies from jurisdiction to jurisdiction and year to year).

Yields of the personal income tax in Eurasian countries are constrained by the modest rates at which the tax is imposed. Most former Soviet Union countries impose the personal income tax at a flat rate, varying from 10 percent in Kazakhstan to 22 percent in Uzbekistan—Azerbaijan is an outlier, with a tax rate of 30 percent (table 5.5). Armenia, the Kyrgyz Republic, and Moldova have graduated tax rates, with a maximum tax bracket of no more than 20 percent.[24]

So, the yield of the personal income tax in Eurasian countries is generally lower than in Western European comparators. Personal income tax revenues range from 1.5 percent of GDP in Armenia to 7.6 percent in Georgia, with most countries falling in the 2–5 percent range (figure 5.8). By contrast, in Western Europe, where the personal income tax is a principal source of central government revenues and is imposed at fairly steep and progressive rates, revenues represent 8–10 percent of GDP. In Eastern Europe, the personal income tax is assigned mainly to subnational governments and imposed at fairly low, flat rates.

Raising the personal income tax to the levels of Western Europe could generate considerably larger subnational revenues in Eurasia. Raising the personal income tax in Russia to German levels

TABLE 5.5

Personal Income Tax Rates in the Former Soviet Union, by Country, 2010

percent

Country	Minimum	Maximum
Armenia	10	20
Azerbaijan	30	30
Belarus	12	12
Georgia	20	20
Kazakhstan	10	10
Kyrgyz Republic	10	20
Moldova	7	18
Russian Federation	13	13
Tajikistan	13	13
Ukraine	15	15
Uzbekistan	22	22

Source: Europe and Central Asia region fiscal database.

FIGURE 5.8

Personal Income Tax as Percentage of GDP in Selected Countries, 2009 or Most Recent Available

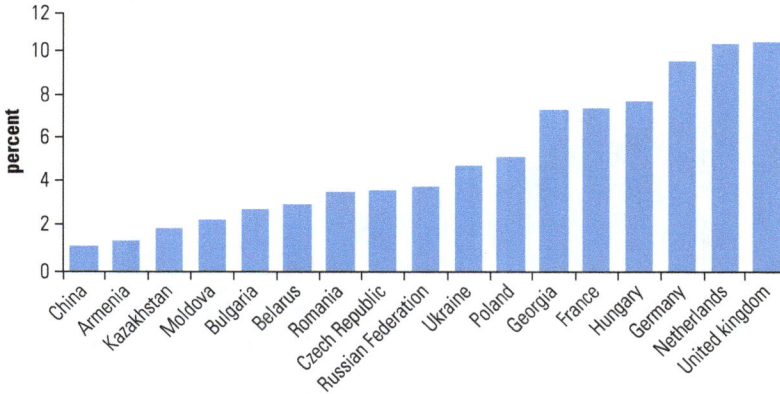

Source: IMF 2010.
Note: GDP = gross domestic product.

(9.9 percent of GDP) and transferring the increase entirely to subnational governments would raise their revenues by roughly two-thirds. But central governments may be reluctant to authorize major increases in the personal income tax, particularly for the benefit of subnational governments, which in some cases may be controlled by opposition interests. Moreover, an increase in the personal income tax would compete with the central government's efforts to increase tax revenues. There may also be legitimate policy reasons for keeping the personal income tax low. By and large, the personal income tax is imposed on the same base (payrolls) as the social contributions that support centrally financed health insurance and pension schemes. Raising the tax could thus increase the tax wedge between net and gross salaries, raising the cost of labor and discouraging employment in the formal sector.

Raising Property Taxes

Local governments across the world impose property taxes (figure 5.9). Except in France and North America, however, property taxes generate very little revenue (0.4 percent of GDP in Germany, 1.1 percent in China, and 1.7 percent in the United Kingdom). In France, they bring in 3.5 percent of GDP, but even this represents less than 10 percent of the aggregate tax burden, including social security taxes (IMF 2010).

FIGURE 5.9

Property Tax as Percentage of GDP in Selected Countries, 2009 or Most Recent Available

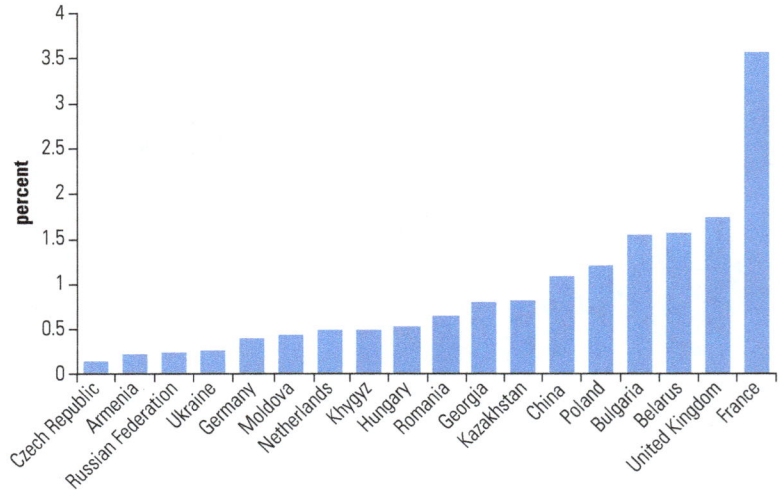

Source: IMF 2010.

Note: Figures for China as well as other countries may be overstated because of the inclusion of taxes on corporate assets and real estate transactions. GDP = gross domestic product.

Property tax revenues are generally inconsequential in Eurasia (0.20 percent of GDP in Russia, 0.25 percent in Ukraine). Yields are low because of a mix of politically motivated administrative failures and deliberate policy decisions.

In strictly mechanical terms, the yield of the property tax is a function of four factors. The first is the completeness and accuracy of data on the physical characteristics of the tax base. Land parcels may be missing from the tax rolls or inaccurately measured. Data on improvements (for example, buildings) may be missing, inaccurate, or out of date.

The second is the unit cost factors used to convert the data on physical characteristics into value estimates. Property valuations are rarely based on market analyses of individual properties. They are derived from a limited number of physical characteristics of each property, which are converted to an estimate of market value based on standard unit costs. (These unit costs are normally set out in a table, which specifies a value per square meter of land and square meter of built-area, varying by the property location and the building characteristics.) Calculating unit costs can be difficult, particularly where underlying market data are unreliable. In countries with substantial inflation, unit costs can quickly become obsolete unless they are indexed.

The third is the tax rate. In countries with low property tax yields, taxes tend to be very low, and exemptions widespread. In Russia, residential buildings are exempt entirely, and the maximum tax on land zoned for agriculture, housing, and dachas is just 0.3 percent.[25] In Ukraine, the maximum tax rate on land is 1 percent—fairly high— but buildings are exempt.[26]

The fourth is the collection rate—the proportion of the billed amount actually collected. Data on collection rates in Eurasia are not available. Experience elsewhere, however, suggests that property taxes can be very difficult to collect. Unlike the personal income tax, which can be imposed through withholding, or the VAT, whose burden can be passed on to consumers through higher prices, the property tax must be collected directly from the taxpayer. Unless the taxpayer faces a credible threat (such as the property seizure), compliance is normally poor.

Efforts to boost property tax yields could focus on all four of these factors. A reinventory of properties (particularly in fast-growing urban areas) could be used to update data on property characteristics. Unit cost factors could be adjusted to reflect market values more accurately. The tax on land could be raised, and the exemption of buildings eliminated. Measures could also be taken to improve collection efficiency, including systematically monitoring overdue accounts, increasing penalties, and auctioning off major delinquent properties (auctions tend to have a particularly salutary demonstration effect on delinquent taxpayers).

But the property tax is a political poison. As a result, what appear to be administrative weaknesses are in fact a reflection of the political sensitivities surrounding the tax. Even countries thought to have mastered subnational finance, such as China, face their own hurdles (box 5.5). In addition, attempts to extend the property tax to residential properties are likely to run afoul of a particular anomaly in the post-Soviet housing market. Because properties were transferred directly to their occupants during privatization, there is little correlation between the value of a housing unit and its owner's ability to pay. A building tax on a residential apartment block might be easily affordable to some of its occupants but beyond the means of others. All of these factors suggest that expectations concerning the potential yield of the property tax should be modest.

BOX 5.5

Subnational Finance in China

China, as a rising economic power, is often looked to as a model for reform in many fields. But China's system of subnational finance is quite similar to those in Russia, Ukraine, and the larger countries of Eastern Europe. Thus, it is a model for reform only in the few Eurasian countries (such as Tajikistan) that still adhere to the former Soviet model.

China's system of subnational finance is the product of a radical centralization of tax authority instituted in 1994 and extended in 2002. Although it stabilized the division of taxing powers between the central and subnational tiers of government, it left subnational governments with almost no control over tax policy and only limited control over tax administration.

China has a four-tier structure of subnational government, consisting of provinces, prefectures, counties, and townships. The relationship between each tier is strictly hierarchical—the central government defines the terms of its relationship with the provinces, the provinces with the prefectures, and so forth. Under the 1994 and 2002 reforms, the central government assigned the provincial governments fixed shares of some central government taxes—namely, 25 percent of the VAT, 40 percent of personal income tax and corporate income tax, and all of some local taxes. Of these, the highest yielding are the gross receipts tax on businesses not covered by the VAT and an income tax on enterprises owned by subnational governments (revenues from the enterprise income tax are retained by the government that owns the enterprise). Local taxes also include a recurrent urban land tax and several taxes on real estate transactions. They do not include recurrent taxes on residential buildings.

These tax revenues are supplemented by intergovernmental transfers, including hold-harmless guarantees arising from the 1994 reform, equalization transfers, and many special grants for capital works and calamities. Each province has the authority to determine how much of its taxes it retains and how much it passes on to subordinate tiers of government. In Gansu Province, for example, the province retains 40 percent of urban land tax, assigning the rest to cities and prefectures.

With few exceptions, the central government sets all taxes. The 1994 law allows subnational government control only over the urban land tax (within a band of rates set by the central government) and whether to introduce such contrasting taxes as one on entertainment and one on the slaughter of livestock. The lack of formal revenue autonomy has led subnational governments to exercise "informal" revenue autonomy, particularly through the imposition of fees well beyond what has been prescribed in the law (World Bank 2002a).

Provincial governments can exercise some control over the administration of taxes. One of the important outcomes of the 1994 reform was a division of China's tax administration system into two separate bodies—a central tax administration to collect central and shared tax revenues, and a local tax administration to collect local taxes. This was a more incentive-compatible

continued

BOX 5.5 *continued*

arrangement than the previous system, in which a single tax administration body collected all types of taxes. Thus, provincial governments have direct control over the administration of the gross receipts tax, the tax on subnational enterprises, and the urban land tax. Indirectly, they have some influence over the administration of shared taxes. Provincial governments commonly provide performance bonuses to central tax administrators working at their level. Subordinate tiers of subnational governments have no such influence. Counties and prefectures thus complain that the tax authorities do not address their interests adequately.

The government is considering granting some degree of subnational control over the rate of local taxes. According to a November 18, 2010, announcement from the Ministry of Finance, the government may allow provincial governments to adjust the rates of local taxes. The government is also considering introducing a recurrent tax on residential buildings.

Source: Authors.

Raising Housing Maintenance Charges

Before the breakup of the Soviet Union, the state was responsible for housing. State enterprises constructed new housing, and state maintenance companies were responsible for maintaining the façades and roofs of the apartment blocks that littered the Soviet landscape. These services were highly subsidized.

After the breakup, individual units in apartment blocks were typically transferred, without cost, to their occupants. Responsibility for maintaining exteriors and common areas fell, however, to local governments (Lipman 2010). Their attempts to charge large amounts for these services met immediate resistance. Many citizens were unaware that their previous rent payments included payments for communal services and maintenance. Efforts to establish homeowner associations—which would assume responsibility for external maintenance and common areas—have been slow (box 5.6).

In the absence of homeowner associations (see chapter 2), Russia's housing policy envisions that municipally owned housing maintenance companies finance themselves largely through fees. The 1992 housing policy law authorized an increase in housing maintenance charges large enough to cover their costs, with subsidies to be limited to low-income households. In 1993, the Council of Ministers authorized local governments to set their own tariffs for housing maintenance. But they were slow to implement full cost-recovery, because continued state support of the housing sector was available

BOX 5.6

Resistance to Homeowner Associations in the Former Soviet Union

Homeowner associations are, in principle, an attractive alternative to municipally owned mainte-nance companies. Paying fees to their homeowner association rather than to the municipality ensures that the residents' money is spent on their building. Homeowner associations also pro-vide a means for residents to control the maintenance and utilities provided to their buildings. Through their homeowner association, residents can decide what repairs are done and when and whether to contract with private companies for managing and maintaining their buildings.

Homeowner associations in Eurasian countries have been slow to form, partly due to public skepticism. According to the (Russian) Institute of Urban Economics, "the public is inclined to believe that encouraging the formation of homeowner associations is just one more attempt by the governmental authorities to shift the burden of housing management and maintenance on to them. Regrettably, very often such suspicions turn out to be true" (Lipman 2010, 18).

The lack of instruments to force would-be free riders to participate has also hindered these associations. The Russian Federation's 1992 law on housing policy stipulates that unit owners in multifamily buildings are to be considered co-owners of the common elements in their buildings and envisions that homeowner associations will maintain these areas, which will contract out these services. But membership in a building's homeowner association is not mandatory in Russia, and some residents refuse to participate. As of 2005, homeowner associations govern only about 8 percent of multifamily buildings.

Ukraine initially required occupants to participate in homeowner associations once their buildings were privatized. But in 1996, the Constitutional Court determined that this require-ment violates constitutional protections against forced participation in economic entities. As a result, homeowner associations govern only 6 percent of multifamily units in 2006.

Source: Lipman 2010.

to cushion shocks imposed by reforms in the rest of the economy—a role that continued through the crisis of 1998 (Institute for Urban Economics 2003). As of 2001, payments from residents covered only about 60 percent of expenditures (including both maintenance charges and utilities), with government subsidies financing the rest. According to the Institute for Urban Economics, housing mainte-nance charges still fall far short of cost-recovery levels.

Raising Utility Tariffs

Urban public utilities inherited deteriorating assets and a consumer base accustomed to high levels of subsidies. Immediate efforts to raise tariffs ran afoul of political constraints. In Russia, tariffs were kept low deliberately during the post-transition slump. As a result, in 1994 household tariffs covered no more than 20 percent of the full cost of service provision, with subsidies from the municipal owners financing the rest.

Attempts have been made to increase tariffs. In 1997, the Russian authorities responded to the low level of cost-recovery by setting national norms for recovery in all communal services. The norm was fixed at 35 percent in the base year and scheduled to increase to 100 percent in 2005 (figure 5.10). After the 1998 financial crisis, however, the real value of communal services tariffs eroded. While consumer prices rose 80 percent, communal services tariffs rose only 15 percent. After the crisis, the government resumed a policy of permitting real increases in tariffs. In real terms, average tariffs doubled between 2000 and 2004. Still, as of 2004 it was estimated that charges to households were still equal to only 50–60 percent of the federally defined "economically justified tariff."[27]

The situation may have improved since then. In 2004, the federal government enacted legislation (Law 210) requiring that municipalities impose tariffs on communal services companies high enough to cover "full operating and capital investment costs." It explicitly permitted municipal governments to impose tariff surcharges and connection fees to recover the costs of capital works. The law was expected to take effect in 2006.[28]

FIGURE 5.10

Household Payments for Communal Services in the Russian Federation, 1994–2005

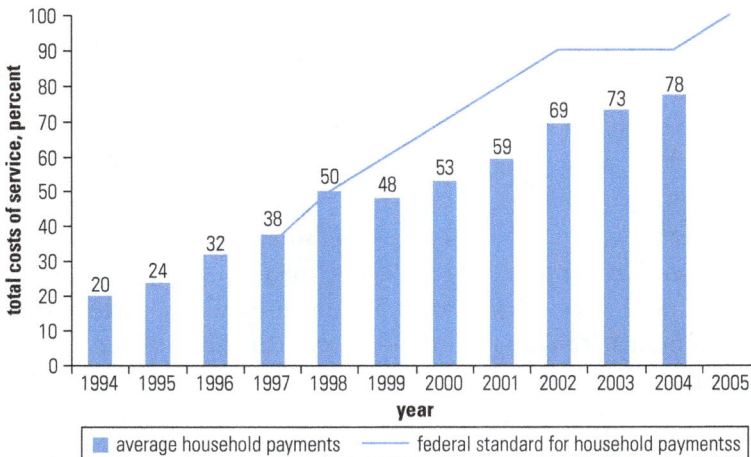

Source: World Bank 2006a.

Even Tajikistan now has a tariff law. A World Bank (2005) project appraisal document states that "in accordance with the provisions of the law on state enterprises, the national communal services company (SUE-KILOMETERSK) as well as its subsidiaries operate on the principle of financial autonomy and are independent of the state budget. KILOMETERSK has the authority to set tariffs (though approval of tariffs is subject to control by the state Anti-Monopoly Agency)." In theory, tariffs set by KILOMETERSK should allow subsidiaries to self-finance both operation and maintenance and a minimum of capital asset replacement. But, in practice, the document admits, the revenues of these enterprises, are in most cases not enough to cover the actual cost of their operations.

Billing and collection has also been a problem in Eurasian countries. As of January 1, 2005, accounts receivable in Ukraine totaled $588 million in the water sector and $723 million in the heating sector. In Georgia, a 1999 survey of 23 water companies found that the collection rate in 2003 was 58 percent (the collection rate for households was only 42 percent; Government of Georgia 2004).

Various reviews of the water and heating sectors in Eurasian countries yield a range of recommendations for improving billing and collection. To address the specific technical problem of measuring consumption and assigning charges to residents of apartment buildings, a report on Ukraine recommends installing bulk meters at the entry point to each apartment building and then allocating costs to units based on indicators, such as square meters and the presence of water-using facilities (World Bank 2006c). Residents would then be forced to join a homeowner association, which would be responsible for collecting tariffs from individual households. In some countries, however, individual metering may not be physically possible (box 5.7).

The Ukraine report also recommends initiating public information campaigns (to convince customers that paying bills is the only way to improve communal services) and installing modern billing and payments monitoring systems capable of sending timely bills for consumption, monitoring overdue accounts, and sending regular reminders of overdue bills. It notes that some companies may need to prepare new inventories of customers (to identify illegal connections and ensure the accuracy of the indicators used to measure residential consumption). They may also need to repair the smashed meters of industrial and commercial consumers.

Tougher penalties for nonpayment may be required. In some cases, the problem is a lack of appropriate legislation. Ukrainian legislation prohibits communal services companies from charging penalties for

BOX 5.7

Technical Constraints on Water Metering

Efforts to improve cost-recovery levels in water and heating have run afoul of technical constraints arising from the layout of interior heating pipes and water cutoff valves in apartment blocks. Soviet apartment buildings were not designed to allow individual household consumption to be measured or service to be shut off. In Russia, residential water users are thus charged based on water-use norms that the central government set. (Note that this information is from 1996 and may be obsolete.) In Tajikistan, residential water consumers (at least those with individual household connections) are charged flat rates, adjusted for factors affecting water consumption, such as the presence of an indoor bathroom.

Without water metering, consumer bills cannot be raised to reflect actual consumption, and households have no incentive to conserve water or heat, driving up operating costs. And without a mechanism for shutting off services to individual housing units, utility companies cannot shut off service to delinquent accounts without cutting off entire buildings. As a result, collection rates suffer.

Source: Pennell 1999.

late payment. Utilities also face legal and technical problems when attempting to disconnect delinquent households. Although Ukrainian legislation allows delinquent customers to be disconnected, the regulations setting out the procedures for doing so have never been issued. Thus, each case must be decided by the courts.

Enforcing penalties already on the books is more important than imposing tougher penalties. A report on water utilities in Georgia, for example, found that the 23 companies it studied did not implement formal collection control procedures (Government of Georgia 2004). Rather, their accounting offices merely issued bills and sent collectors to collect as much as they can.[29] Failure to enforce penalties can also arise from dysfunctional relationships between utilities and their municipal owners.

A report on Russia's water sector cites a lack of cooperation between city governments and Vodokanals (the water company) as the main cause of poor collection rates (Pennell 1999). Although city governments are responsible for billing and collecting water charges, they are indifferent to the financial situation of their water utilities. Indeed, they fail to transfer whatever tariff revenues are received or transfer them through promissory notes, bartered goods, or debt swaps instead of cash.

Raising Public Transport Tariffs

During the Soviet era, municipal urban transport companies carried 80–90 percent of traffic in cities. Services were highly subsidized, with average cost-recovery of 10–25 percent. Some groups (the largest of which were pensioners and schoolchildren) were given additional discounts off already low fares. Others, such as veterans, rode for free. In Russia, 64 categories of people were exempt from paying for public transport, accounting for about 60 percent of travelers (World Bank 2002b). In Tbilisi, about half of all passengers enjoyed extra discounts.

After the breakup of the Soviet Union, central governments reduced or withdrew their financial support to urban transport companies, shifting financial responsibility entirely to municipal governments. Although municipal governments could not afford the requisite subsidies, transport companies did not try to increase fares or even rigorously collect fares at prevailing levels. Passengers, whose real incomes had fallen, resisted efforts to raise fares or remove fare discounts.[30] As a result, municipally owned urban transport services in Russia suffered average losses equivalent to about 30 percent of revenues in 2004. Tariff levels were enough to cover only 45–65 percent of costs in 2003; suburban trains recovered just 20 percent (figure 5.11).[31]

FIGURE 5.11

Cost-Recovery Levels in Public Transit in the Russian Federation, by Mode, 1995–2003

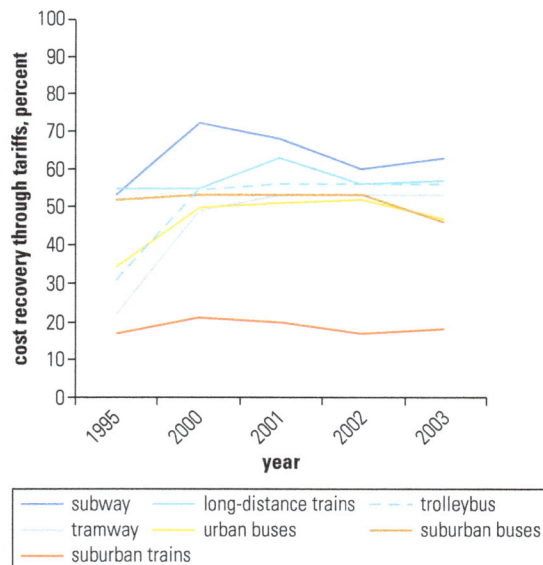

Source: World Bank 2006a.

Some better-off cities (such as Moscow) managed to sustain services, usually with the help of the federal government. But even financial deficits there meant that maintenance and operations were underfunded and fleet replacements deferred. In most cities in Russia and Central Asia, deficits were so large that normal operations became impossible. Only a small fraction of the fleet could be placed in service, and people could not get to work.

Informal private operators rose to meet the demand (World Bank 2002b). Although services are improving in some areas—Tbilisi and Yerevan are investing in new buses, for example—service levels on publicly owned systems are generally declining, and some services, such as tram systems in the Caucasus, are being closed (OECD 2007).

Financial recovery will require reform on both the revenue and expenditure sides. On the revenue side, fares will have to be raised, which may require adopting a more systematic regulatory framework. In most of Russia, for example, city governments set fares for urban transport services, though in some cases they require approval from the oblast level. According to a 2006 infrastructure financing report, city governments adjust fares largely based on political considerations, tempered by some pragmatic concerns to ensure that basic operating costs can be met (World Bank 2006a). No systematic procedures consider the detailed operating and capital costs that transport operators face, and no mechanism routinely reviews and updates fares annually.

At the same time, exemptions will have to be cut. To make transit affordable for some low-income households that may be priced out by the move, higher tiers of government should provide social assistance (World Bank 2002b).

Financial recovery will also require improved efficiency on the expenditure side. Overstaffing is still a problem in some companies, and some countries still operate routes that are uneconomic. These problems can be addressed, to an extent, by reducing the scale of publicly funded services, allowing private operators to pick up the slack. Under the most radical form of this approach, private operators would function alongside the surviving public sector operators with little or no licensing and little or no regulation or monitoring of performance. A less radical alternative would be to introduce competitive bidding for routes or groups of routes. Tenders would be based on performance agreements, detailing the service parameters, quality norms, internal performance indicators, fares, remuneration (subsidies), and performance incentives. Competitive bidding has been instrumental in driving down costs in other European countries—the European Union has reduced costs by 20–40 percent in this way.

Although the initial effects may be partly lost in later rounds of tendering, evidence suggests that allowing market competition produces lasting cost reductions (World Bank 2010c).

This approach has been tested in several World Bank projects in Central Asia. In Kazakhstan, deregulation even allowed operators to set fares.[32] Large state-owned operators were broken into many smaller joint stock companies, creating a pool of competitors (World Bank 2002b). Cities in Uzbekistan and the Kyrgyz Republic (excluding Bishkek) and many secondary cities in Russia have also introduced market competition. Elsewhere public sector companies have retained their dominance of the urban passenger market and succeeded in halting the declines in passengers, restructuring their service networks, maintaining or improving their service quality, increasing cost-efficiency, and improving their financial position by raising fares and receiving regular subsidy payments from the authorities (Podolske 2010).

Conclusion

Most former Soviet Union countries have made remarkable strides in transforming their urban finance systems. They have replaced a system of subnational finance based on intraparty negotiations with a range of systems generally based on stable revenue assignments and fairly transparent and mechanical transfer mechanisms. Big Eurasian cities can now tap their large and growing tax bases. More city revenue could be gained, in principle, by improving the administration of the property tax, but the property tax has political costs disproportionate to its yields. A more promising route could be to raise the personal income tax. These measures should be complemented by higher tariffs for housing maintenance, heating, and water supply and by efforts to improve their administration.

For intercity rail passenger transport, tariffs passengers pay are generally not high enough to pay for the full operating cost, as they are in most countries worldwide. Railways in Eurasia typically compensate for losses on the passenger transport side through cross-subsidies from freight transport revenues. Such a system is unsustainable. Governments should permit tariffs to rise enough to at least cover operating costs. Where doing so is not politically acceptable, governments should compensate railway passenger operators through public service obligation contracts, which are common elsewhere (World Bank 2002b).

The major expenditures required to address the maintenance backlog for highways will have to be financed by taxes. Governments can do so by raising broad-based taxes, such as the VAT, or by increasing road-related taxes, such as excises on fuel.

Annex 5A: Financing Connectivity

During the Soviet era, strategic considerations made railways the backbone of the long-distance transport system (see chapter 3). As such, they were well funded and fairly well managed (World Bank 2006a). But soon after the transition, demand for both passenger and rail services declined, sharply reducing revenue. At the same time, motor vehicle use expanded dramatically, adding pressure to a road network that was not designed to accommodate it. Demand for telecommunications services also increased.

Rail

The Soviet Union was served by a single integrated railway system, Sovetskie Zheleznye Dorogi (SZD), which was financed largely from tariff revenues. As a national monopoly, SZD had substantial scope to use its tariff structure to meet wider social objectives through various cross-subsidies. Freight tariffs were set to equalize the burden of transport costs of different commodities. By ensuring that heavy industries in remote areas were not rendered uncompetitive due to high transport costs, the tariff structure helped spread economic activity across the Soviet Union's vast area. Profits on rail freight services were used to cover the operating losses associated with rail passenger transport and other nontransport social services, such as hospitals and kindergartens for railway workers (World Bank 2006a).

SZD was disbanded in 1992 and succeeded by 19 regionally autonomous railway administrations. All faced changes. The breakup resulted in a drop in freight volumes throughout the former Soviet Union, largely thanks to declines in the heavy industry and manufacturing sectors, the partial severing of trade links among former Soviet republics, and increasing competition from road transport (World Bank 2006b).

Some successor companies were affected more than others. As chapter 3 showed, freight volumes in Belarus, Kazakhstan, and the Russian Federation have returned to their 1992 levels. By contrast, volumes in Azerbaijan and the Kyrgyz Republic are less than half their former levels. Traffic densities in Belarus, Kazakhstan, Russia, and Ukraine are far higher than densities in the Caucasus or the southern central Asian countries.[33] Other things equal, companies with higher densities are likely to be more profitable than countries with lower densities.

The successor companies also vary in operating efficiency and tariff regimes. Companies with high traffic densities tend to score high on other indicators of operational efficiency.[34] They also generally manage to finance their operating costs through tariff revenues. But in recent years, their tariffs have proven vulnerable to political manipulation, favoring some sectors or industries and damaging the financial viability of the railway companies. Moreover, it is not clear that the ambitious expansion plans of some railway companies are financially viable.

Belarus

Belarusian Railways is operationally efficient. Indicators of staff productivity and asset use—such as ton-kilometers per locomotive or traffic units per wagon—compare favorably with those of European Union countries. The company has historically financed itself through tariff revenues. Over 2005–08, tariff revenues were more than enough to cover operating and investment costs. Indeed, the company's working ratio averaged 68 percent and its operating ratio 78 percent during this period—far better than EU25 (European Union-25) averages.[35]

There are, however, important cross-subsidies. Revenues from international freight traffic (largely transit traffic) are subsidizing both domestic freight and passenger services (World Bank 2010a). Passenger service is particularly loss-making, with 2005–08 working ratios of 125–135 percent. The rail system is vulnerable to downturns in international freight traffic and to declining market shares in the freight traffic market thanks to competition from road transport.

Belarusian Railways has an ambitious capital investment program. It believes that to sustain its market share, it needs to achieve full European Union interoperability on its key trans-European rail corridors (Corridors II and IX), which will require considerable upgrading of infrastructure. A World Bank transport sector policy note for Belarus estimates that investment needs of Belarusian Railways could be as much as $690 million a year. Much of this could be financed from internal cash generation (World Bank 2010a). In 2008, the allowance for depreciation plus profits was $424 million. The rest, however, would have to come from government grants or borrowing, which would in turn require tariff levels high enough to cover debt service.

Russia

Russia's new national rail corporation, RZD, has retained a strong, competitive position in freight transport and dominates the national market (World Bank 2006a). The company is operationally efficient (World Bank 2011). Until recently, revenues were more than enough to cover operating and investment costs—partly thanks to reforms adopted in 2001 that improved flexibility in determining operating tariffs and reduced cross-subsidies.[36]

The financial condition of the company has worsened since the global recession. In 2009, the government rejected a proposed 14 percent increase in tariffs, approving instead an 8 percent increase. It provided RZD with a Rub 40.6 billion subsidy to cover the difference. The government has also been forced to provide higher levels of funding to cover RZD's investment expenditures. This support has come through equity injections or grants from special government funds.

The first phase of RZD's transport strategy envisages annual expenditures of more than $38 billion, more than 50 times the company's investment expenditures during 2007–09. The plan expects external sources to finance 90 percent of these expenditures. In addition to state capital injections, grants, and internal cash generation, RZD has a record of financing its investment program through debt. The company has continually received investment-grade ratings by the international credit rating agencies, and the volume of its debt issues has been rising. But the viability of the company's capital investment plan depends on its long-term profitability, which in turn depends on maintaining tariff levels high enough to cover costs. Although the recent Russia *Public Expenditure Review* notes that the company could finance a scaled-back investment program through bond issues, it also recommends a tariff policy for full cost-recovery (World Bank 2011).

Ukraine

The financial condition of Ukraine's railroad depends greatly on freight volumes and government-regulated tariffs (World Bank 2010b). The state railway company, Ukrzaliznitsya, has historically financed operating costs and investments from tariff revenues. Doing so has been particularly difficult since the global economic crisis, which caused freight volume (in ton-kilometers) to fall 24 percent.

Government-imposed tariff reductions for some types of rail freight have also adversely affected Ukrzaliznitsya. Discounts to the coal, steel, chemical, and other industries, as well as mandated loss-making passenger services (not fully compensated by the government), have especially reduced the company's ability to self-finance operations and necessary investments.[37] Thus, profits, which were Hrv 621 million in 2007, fell to zero in 2008. In 2009 the company, failing to make a payment on a syndicated loan, was forced to cut investments in infrastructure and rolling stock by 50 percent. Since then, however, traffic volumes have recovered. The company has restructured the syndicated loan and is now ramping up investments.

Highways

Although rail transport still accounts for most freight traffic in the former Soviet Union, road traffic has been rising rapidly. Because the road network was not designed for the heavy vehicles today, networks in nearly all the republics have deteriorated, heightening the need for funding for road rehabilitation, reconstruction, and maintenance.

In Russia, only a third of almost 50,000 kilometers of federal roads are in good or fair condition. According to the Russia *Public Expenditure Review*, the rehabilitation and reconstruction of the federal highway network over a 6-year period could require a near tripling of expenditures on federal highways (World Bank 2011). Rehabilitating the subnational (regional) highway network could require a doubling of expenditures on subnational highways.

Unlike rail infrastructure (funded mostly by the railways themselves), road infrastructure depends largely on funding from the government budget, as opportunities for toll roads are limited (box 5A.1). How such budgetary support should be provided, particularly for road maintenance, is a subject of long-running controversy. The controversy centers on two issues: first, whether funding for highway maintenance should be earmarked—that is, financed from a fixed share of specified taxes and deposited in a fund to be used only for road maintenance—and second, if so, whether the taxes earmarked for this purpose should be road-related (box 5A.2).

Without a compelling case to the contrary (such as the systematic underfunding of road maintenance over many years), decisions about the level and allocation of road maintenance spending should be made through the overall budgeting process. By the same token, policies on road taxes should be based on the same considerations that apply to any other tax: their implications for the overall tax

BOX 5A.1

Financing Highways with Toll Roads

Toll roads are, in principle, an attractive means of financing highway expenditures that satisfies both the benefit equity and allocative efficiency objectives of road pricing. But opportunities to use them in former Soviet Union countries are limited. In Russia, only a small percentage of the trunk road network has traffic volumes high enough to support toll roads based on full cost-recovery. Tolls could be set up on only about 20 percent of the federal trunk road network.

Even this opportunity has not been fully exploited. Although the legal basis for levying tolls on the road network was established in 1998, efforts have been derisory.[38] Russia has only one toll section in its entire federal road network—a 20-kilometer detour around the village of Khlevnoe in the Lipetsk region.

But policy toward toll roads may be changing. The federal government of Russia recently created a new road agency (AVTODOR) to plan and implement toll roads, and the government of Belarus has decided to introduce tolling for trucks on all major trunk roads.

Source: Authors.

BOX 5A.2

Is Earmarking Road Taxes a Good Idea?

Any tax could be earmarked for road maintenance: a fixed percentage of the value added tax (VAT), for example, or a share of the income tax. There are, however, three good arguments for earmarking taxes on road users.

The first, and main, argument for earmarking funding for road maintenance is that it provides a stable source of revenue, protected from short-term political pressures and the vagaries of the annual budget process. Advocates of such earmarking point to the widespread tendency of governments to underfund road maintenance—a practice that results in the rapid deterioration of roads and the eventual need for far more costly road rehabilitation. Earmarking funding for road maintenance may correct this tendency.

A second argument is based on benefit equity—that people who use a service should be the ones who pay for it.

A third argument is based on the notion that earmarked road taxes can function as prices. By confronting road users with the cost of the roads they "consume," road taxes can ration consumption based on willingness to pay. Road users can opt for better roads at higher prices or

continued

worse roads at lower prices. So, earmarked road taxes can create a market in roads that yields the same allocative efficiencies as markets in more conventional products.

To function in this way, however, a market-clearing mechanism is needed. Decisions concerning the level and allocation of road taxes have to be made by an entity that accurately represents the collective interests of road users. Attempts to establish such entities have been made—particularly in Africa where "second-generation" road funds are popular. Experience suggests, however, that governments rarely allow such entities to set tax rates or spending priorities. Under these conditions, the allocative efficiency argument for earmarking road funds is moot.

Opponents of earmarking argue that road spending is only one of many claims on the government budget. In their view, all sectors should compete for funding on an equal footing, unimpeded by earmarking.

As Gwilliam (2007) points out, views for and against are irreconcilable because they are based on different assumptions about the budget process. Opponents of earmarking assume that the budget process works; advocates of earmarking assume that it does not. Thus, Gwilliam argues that earmarking has to be evaluated case by case, predicated on a review of the ability of the budgetary process to adequately fund road maintenance.

Whatever the merits of either arguments, there may be good political economy reasons for earmarking road taxes: road users may be more willing to pay higher fuel taxes if they know the revenues are earmarked for roads.

Source: Authors.

burden, where their burden will fall (and the resulting impact on the distribution of income), and how they will affect the behavior of taxpayers. Thus, increasing the tax on fuels would be justified to encourage fuel efficiency but not to fund investments in roads or their maintenance.

Earmarked road taxes were common in the Soviet Union, for funding both road investment and maintenance. Before 1999, for example, Russia had several road funds, financed from taxes on the sale of oil and lubricants and the purchase and ownership of motor vehicles. By far, the largest revenue source was the misnamed road-user tax—actually a business turnover tax of 1 percent levied on all firms that produced or traded goods—which generated revenues equivalent to 2.2 percent of GDP. Fiscal reforms over 1999–2001 eliminated the road-user tax and phased out the other earmarked taxes (World Bank 2006a). The result was a sharp drop in road funding, neglect of road upgrading and rehabilitation, and a general deterioration of the road network from poor maintenance.

Even where road funds still exist, they do not always ensure stable financing. Ukraine's Law No. 1562-XII, for example, establishes a fund to finance road construction, rehabilitation, repair, and maintenance. It also designates particular revenues that are to be paid into the fund. State budget legislation has, in practice, suspended various provisions of the law, and the specified funding has not always been forthcoming.[39] By contrast, Moldova recently allocated some taxes to its road maintenance fund to persuade its external partners to provide loans and grants for much needed road rehabilitation.

There may nonetheless be a case for increasing road taxes as a matter of overall tax policy. Fuel taxes in Eurasian countries are low. In 2010, the fuel tax in Russia was about $0.10 a liter, though the government intends to roughly double it by 2013. Ukraine recently raised its fuel tax to $0.17 a liter. These taxes are a fraction of what they are in Germany ($1.62 a liter) or the United Kingdom ($1.87; World Bank 2011).

Equivalent revenues could be raised through modest increases in broader-based taxes. In Russia, revenues from fuel taxes (excluding taxes on petroleum products) generated Rub 147.2 billion in 2009, and another Rub 9.7 billion was generated from taxes on motor vehicles. These taxes raised revenues equivalent to 1.2 percent of consolidated government revenues. The VAT generated Rub 1,177 billion in 2009. The proposed doubling of the excise taxes on fuels would thus raise the same revenue as a 13 percent increase in the VAT.

Telecommunications

Telecommunications services have been transformed since the breakup of the Soviet Union. Cell phone services have filled the gaps left in the old landline-based system, and broadband Internet services have been introduced or expanded. All of these services have been financed by the private sector.

A legacy from the Soviet Union is the large gap between coverage of landlines in Russia and the Central Asian republics. In 2009, Russia had eight times as many fixed-line telephones per capita as Tajikistan (figure 5A.1). Cell phones have taken up much of this gap in telephone services, however. Uzbekistan now has one cell phone for every two people. And Kazakhstan has as many cell phones as people. Combined rates of cell phone and fixed-line coverage in Russia are higher than the average in Organisation for Economic Co-operation and Development countries (World Development Indicators 2011).

FIGURE 5A.1

Number of Telephones per 100 People in Selected Countries, 2009

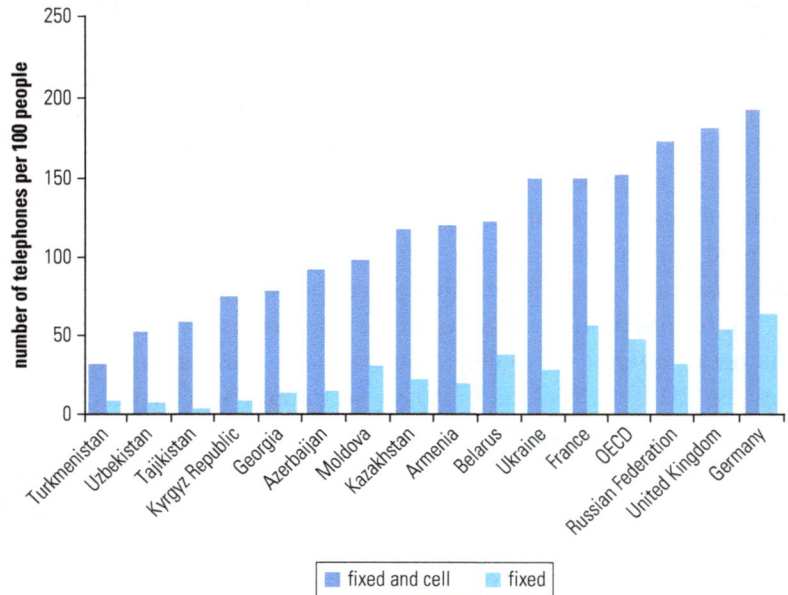

Source: World Development Indicators 2011.
Note: OECD = Organisation for Economic Co-operation and Development.

The private sector will continue to finance the expansion of cell phone services, which are commercially viable except in remote areas (where public financing would be needed). These mobile networks have traditionally been voice-only systems, but they will likely be upgraded to carry data over the next few years. Upgrading will require little additional financing, as most new mobile network equipment is already 3G capable.

Broadband coverage in Eurasian countries remains low (see chapter 3). In most countries, the private sector has financed investment in broadband infrastructure. In less developed countries, such investments have been confined to major urban centers or trunk routes connecting cities and border-crossing points. Investments in core infrastructure will become more commercially viable as the volume of broadband data traffic increases. Extending the networks beyond core routes is likely to require public financing.

Notes

1. This story is drawn from Urban Institute (2010, 35–36).
2. This chapter looks at the financing of urban infrastructure. Annex 5A presents the evolution of the system for financing intercity connectivity: rail, road, and telecommunication services.

3. Under its 1977 constitution, the Russian republic was divided into 91 first-tier units of administration: 48 provinces (oblasts), 16 autonomous regions, 6 territories, 6 Cities of Republican Subordination (jurisdictions directly subordinate to the Republic government, rather than to provincial governments), and 15 autonomous areas within provinces or territories.

4. Before 2005, executives at all three tiers were popularly elected. But in 2005, the government abolished direct elections for executives at the first tier. Executives are now nominated by the president and subject to approval by first-tier parliaments. At subordinate tiers of local government, executives are still chosen through local elections.

5. Although on paper the territorial reform law of 2005 grants local councils greater autonomy than they previously enjoyed, the 2007 Law on the Supervision of Local Government gives the national government responsibility for drafting local budgets and empowers regional governors to overturn decisions enacted by local councils. The results of the 2006 local elections, which left most councils dominated by the president's party, reinforced central control over local government.

6. Despite attempts in Tajikistan to create a third tier of local government with a locally elected executive, the sub-rayonal organizations (*jamoats*) remain administrative appendages of their rayon governments and have few attributes of a separate tier. They do not have their own budgets, but instead depend on line-item budget transfers from their rayons. Until recently, each *jamoat* was headed by a chair, who was nominated by the chair of the rayon. The new law on self-government provides for a locally elected chair, chosen by (elected) councilors from among their members. But beyond this change in electoral arrangements, the law makes few specific changes in the existing role of *jamoats*.

7. In the cultural sphere, responsibility remains to some extent facility-based. For example, if a particular museum is assigned to a third-tier subnational government, responsibility for operating it belongs to that jurisdiction.

8. Although the law guarantees that the amount will equal at least 4 percent of the previous year's gross domestic product (GDP), this stipulation is not reflected in the 2010 budget. The allocation for equalization transfers totals only GEL 522.6 million, or 2.9 percent of Georgia's 2009 GDP. The budget does assign additional special and conditional transfers, mostly for Tbilisi (GEL 196.6 million in 2010) and Batumi (GEL 100.0 million in 2010) along with minor conditional transfers for implementing delegated functions (GEL 10.3 million). Taken together, these transfers represent 4.7 percent of Georgia's 2009 GDP.

9. More precisely, the amount of the transfer is based on each jurisdiction's share of the aggregate expenditure gap of all jurisdictions, multiplied by the total amount allocated to the equalization transfer.

10. The 2005 reform also established the framework for the division of functional responsibilities among tiers of government, outlawed unfunded mandates, imposed a uniform structure of local government (consolidating the various forms of second- and third-tier subnational governments into cities and rayons), and prohibited subnational

governments from owning property "not related to their functions," prompting another round of privatizations.

11. The federal government retains all of the VAT and social insurance taxes and roughly half of tax revenues from alcohol and petroleum.

12. Different norms apply to different grades and different language schools. For Tajik-language schools, the 2005 norms specify 1.06 full-time-teacher equivalents for first grade and 1.81 for eleventh grade (these norms were much lower than the norms for 2004). Norms are slightly higher for Uzbek-language schools and slightly lower for Russian-language schools. Norms for teachers' salaries vary based on seniority and academic qualifications (World Bank 2008).

13. Jurisdictions whose revenues exceeded their expenditure needs were required to transfer part of the surplus to the state budget. The mechanism for doing so was never defined by regulation (Kononets 2002).

14. Shares are based on average actual revenues in 2007, 2008, and 2009 adjusted for inflation.

15. In 2010, one-third of total revenues in this category consisted of federal cofinancing of the western highway project.

16. The figures for infrastructure services represent only subsidies to the enterprises that provide these services. The city owns a range of enterprises, including two housing maintenance companies, a water company (Vodokanal), a heating company (and its subsidiary maintenance company), a natural gas distribution company (which the city has a 51 percent interest in), various bus and tram companies, and the metro (Sankt-Peterburgsky Metropoliten). As corporate entities, these companies do not report their own-source revenues (for example, tariffs) or self-financed expenditures in the city budget. Subsidies to the companies as well as capital expenditures made on the companies' behalf are, however, reported in the budget.

17. These figures exclude spending by district administrations.

18. Expenditure figures are net of Kiev's mandatory contribution to the national equalization mechanism.

19. The special fund is a separate budget account, fed by the proceeds of the motor vehicle tax, revenue from business activity, proceeds from the sale of property, and fees paid by real estate developers earmarked by the city for infrastructure network expansion in these new developments. Expenditures financed by the special fund are combined with those financed from general revenues in figure 5.8.

20. Until 2008, both KievGas and Kievvodokanal were part of a KievEnergo-Holding company. Kiev owned a 61 percent share in the company, with two offshore companies owning the rest. In 2008, the municipality sold 25.4 percent of Kievvodokanal stock and 28.46 percent of KievGas stock, reportedly to a company connected to the mayor's son-in-law, which then resold the shares offshore. The courts have since cancelled the sale.

21. Data for Azerbaijan, Tajikistan, Turkmenistan, and Uzbekistan are not available.

22. Such an approach would increase, in principle, the aggregate tax burden on big city residents in the same way that an increase in central government taxes would. But it can be argued that there is a more compelling case for taking money away from taxpayers who benefit from the

services financed by the taxes than from central government taxpayers as a group.

23. Belarus, Kazakhstan, Moldova, Russia, and Ukraine assign all of the personal income tax to the subnational level. Using a broader definition of the personal income tax, International Monetary Fund Government Finance Statistics (GFS) data for Russia show that only 30 percent is shared with subnational governments. In ruble terms, the data for subnational personal income tax revenues in the GFS are consistent with those reported by the Russian Treasury.

24. These rates apply only to incomes above a minimum threshold level.

25. The government is reportedly contemplating a new property tax that would cover both land and buildings (*Voice of Russia* 2010).

26. This rate applies only to land whose value can be determined. For other land, the rate ranges from Hrv 0.015 (about $0.003) to Hrv 0.21 (about $0.042) per square meter, depending on where the property is. In regional centers (oblast capitals or major regional cities), the tax rate can be increased by a factor of up to three. Even at this rate, however, a 1,000-square-meter lot in the center of Kiev would face a maximum tax burden of $126.

27. As originally specified, the tariff set was based on standardized cost parameters fixed at the federal level. It bore little relation to actual costs and failed to consider capital investment requirements. The proportion of tariff coverage rises to 70–80 percent if government-funded subsidies to eligible households are included.

28. Note that this information is from 2005 and may be obsolete.

29. There are some exceptions. The Poti (Georgia) Water Company sues customers with large outstanding accounts or cuts off their water.

30. In the mid-2000s, the Russian government attempted to delegate responsibility for determining and financing transport subsidies to first-tier subnational governments and to replace fare discounts and free passes with targeted cash payments. These reforms were met by widespread social protest as soon as they were introduced.

31. Performance was much better in cities participating in the Russian urban transport project. According to a 2002 evaluation, the proportion of revenues raised from tariffs on bus and trolleybus companies increased from about 10 percent or less in the early 1990s to an average of 78 percent in 2001, exceeding both formal and informal targets by large margins. Had the problem of exemptions been resolved, through either elimination or fair compensation, most Russian companies would have achieved a break-even position. As of 2002, the Russian government was still resisting all attempts either to give up its power to impose exemptions or to pay fair compensation.

32. In the Kazakhstan project, the aim was not to make formal performance agreements but to improve the traditional budgeting approach, adding productivity targets and explicit subsidy calculations to the existing operating and capital budgets.

33. Densities are based on traffic units per kilometer of track. A traffic unit is equal to one passenger or one ton of freight.

34. Data on the financial condition of railways in the Caucasus and central Asia are not available. The low traffic densities of the rail system in

these countries (except for Kazakhstan) nonetheless suggest that financial viability will be difficult to achieve without higher tariff rates, potentially leading to a vicious circle of declining traffic and declining revenues.

35. The working ratio is defined as total operating expenses, excluding depreciation and debt service, divided by revenues. The operating ratio is defined as total operating expenses divided by revenues.

36. Cross-subsidies to passenger services have yet to be eliminated, however.

37. In addition, in 2009 the government forced the railroad to provide free freight transport to the coal industry. In exchange, the railroad was supposed to receive free electricity from a third party, something that never materialized.

38. These regulations establish the basic rules for toll roads, including the availability of a free parallel route, a preference for converting construction-in-progress or reconstruction projects into toll roads, and the rules for determining toll rates.

39. In 2010–11, excise taxes were raised, leading to large increases in sector financing.

References

Dillinger, W. 2011. Tajikistan Institutional and Governance Review Paper 2 (draft).

Government of Georgia. 2004. *Final Report: Study into Strategy, Regulation and PSP in the Water Sector of Georgia.* Tbilisi: Ministry of Economic Development and Infrastructure.

Government of Russia. 2010. *Report on the Execution of the Consolidated Budget of the Russian Federation and Budgets of the State Extra-Budgetary Funds, as of January 1, 2010.* Moscow: Ministry of Finance.

Gwilliam, Kenneth. 2007. "The Role of Road Funds in Improving Maintenance." In *Transport Infrastructure Charges and Capacity Choice: Self-Financing Road Maintenance and Construction.* European Conference of Ministers of Transport, Transport Research Centre Report 135, April 20. Paris: Organisation for Economic Co-operation and Development.

Hare, Paul, and Alexander Muravyev. 2003. "Privatization in Russia." In *International Handbook on Privatization,* ed. David Parker and David Saal, 347–62. Cheltenham, U.K.: Edward Elgar.

IMF (International Monetary Fund). 2010. *Government Finance Statistics Yearbook 2010.* Washington, DC: IMF.

Institute for Urban Economics. 2003. *Practice of Reforms in the Housing and Communal Service Sector: Analytical Overview.* Moscow: Institute for Urban Economics.

Kononets, Alexey. 2002. "The Reform of Intergovernmental Fiscal Relations in Ukraine: New Approaches and Emerging Problems." In *Fiscal Autonomy and Efficiency: Reforms in the Former Soviet Union,* ed. Kenneth Davey, 347–74. New York: Open Society Institute.

Kudosova, L. 2007. *Current Budget System for Financing SUE Khojagii Manziliu Kommunali and Its Subsidiaries through Service Provision and the System of Financing HMS Enterprises.* Washington, DC: U.S. Agency for International Development.

Lipman, Barbara J. 2010. *Homeowners Associations in Cities in the CIS: Stalled on the Road to Reform.* Washington, DC: World Bank.

OECD (Organisation for Economic Co-operation and Development). 2007. *Policies for a Better Environment: Progress in Eastern Europe, Caucasus, and Central Asia.* Paris: OECD.

Pennell, John A. 1999. *Key Tariff Reform Issues in the Energy and Water Sectors of the ENI Region.* Washington, DC: U.S. Agency for International Development.

Podolske, Richard. n. d. Eurasia Study: Urban Transport Input to Urban Public Service Annex. Background paper for this book.

Reminga, Oksana, Oleksiy Bakun, Olga Mrinska, and Olena Romanyuk. 2003. "Ukraine." In *Sub-national Data Requirements for Fiscal Decentralization,* ed. Serdar Yilmaz, Jozsef Hegedus, and Michael Bell, 133–60. Washington, DC: World Bank.

Saavedra, Pablo. 2008. *Ukraine: Improving Intergovernmental Fiscal Relations and Public Health and Expenditure Policy. Selected Issues.* Report 42450-UA. Washington, DC: World Bank.

Urban Institute. 2007. *Review of the State Unitary Enterprise Khojagii Manziliyu Kommuna.* Washington, DC: Urban Institute.

———. 2010. *From Concept to Reality: Ten Years of Decentralization and Building Local Self-Government in Kyrgyzstan: 1999–2009.* Washington, DC: Urban Institute.

Voice of Russia. 2010. June 30. http://english.ruvr.ru.

World Bank. 2002a. *China: National Development and Sub-national Finance.* Report 22951-CHA. Washington, DC: World Bank, East Asia and Pacific Region, Poverty Reduction and Economic Management Unit.

———. 2002b. *Urban Transport in Europe and Central Asia: World Bank Experience and Strategy.* Report 25188. Washington, DC: World Bank.

———. 2005. *Project Appraisal Document on a Proposed Grant to the Republic of Tajikistan for a Municipal Infrastructure Development Project.* Report 32920. Washington, DC: World Bank.

———. 2006a. *Funding Infrastructure in the Russian Federation: From Resources to Finance.* Washington, DC: World Bank.

———. 2006b. *Infrastructure in the Europe and Central Asia Region: Approaches to Sustainable Services.* Report 37552. Washington, DC: World Bank.

———. 2006c. *Ukraine: Addressing Challenges in the Provision of Heat, Water, and Sanitation.* Report 38598. Washington, DC: World Bank.

———. 2008. *Tajikistan Second Programmatic Public Expenditure Review.* Report 43280. Washington, DC: World Bank.

———. 2010a. *Belarus: Transport Sector Policy Note.* Report 55015. Washington, DC: World Bank.

————. 2010b. *Project Appraisal Document on a Proposed Loan to the Ukrzaliznitsya for a Railway Modernization Project*. Report 52531-UA. Washington, DC: World Bank.

————. 2010c. *Poland: Mazowieckie Public Expenditure Review Local Responses to the Global Economic Crisis*. Report 52037. Washington, DC: World Bank.

————. 2011. *Russia: Public Expenditure Review*. Report 58836-RU. Washington, DC: World Bank.

————. 2011. *World Development Indicators 2011*. Washington, DC: World Bank.

————. 2012. *World Development Indicators 2012*. Washington, DC: World Bank.

www.ingramcontent.com/pod-product-compliance
Lightning Source LLC
Chambersburg PA
CBHW080606270326
41928CB00016B/2944